SONS OF THE WHITE EAGLE

IN THE

AMERICAN CIVIL WAR

SONS OF THE WHITE EAGLE
IN THE
AMERICAN CIVIL WAR

Divided Poles in a Divided Nation

Mark F. Bielski

CASEMATE
Philadelphia & Oxford

Published in the United States of America and Great Britain in 2016 by
CASEMATE PUBLISHERS
1950 Lawrence Road, Havertown, PA 19083, USA
and
10 Hythe Bridge Street, Oxford OX1 2EW, UK

Hardcover Edition: ISBN 978-1-61200-358-0
Digital Edition: ISBN 978-1-61200-359-7

A CIP record for this book is available from the British Library

Printed and bound in the United States of America

For a complete list of Casemate titles, please contact:

CASEMATE PUBLISHERS (US)
Telephone (610) 853-9131
Fax (610) 853-9146
Email: casemate@casematepublishers.com
www.casematepublishers.com

CASEMATE PUBLISHERS (UK)
Telephone (01865) 241249
Fax (01865) 794449
Email: casemate-uk@casematepublishers.co.uk
www.casematepublishers.co.uk

Cover image: Allen Christian Redwood – *Starke's Brigade Fighting with Stones Near the "Deep
Cut."* A.C. Redwood was born in Virginia, studied in Baltimore and New York before the
war, enlisted in the Confederate army, served with the 55th Virginia at Chancellorsville and
was wounded at Gettysburg. In 1864 he joined the 1st Maryland Cavalry and served until his
capture before Appomattox. He contributed numerous illustrations to the *Battles and Leaders of
the Civil War* series.

CONTENTS

For my parents, Joan and Frank Bielski

FOREWORD

America, as we have been told for so many years, is a land of immigrants. Nonetheless, immigration is still one of the most volatile social and political questions in America at the start of the 21st century. But this is certainly not a new phenomenon. From as far back as the start of the 17th century immigration has been a controversial issue. Established in 1607, Jamestown was the first permanent English settlement in the Americas, and although it was founded by Englishmen, the colonists soon had to import various highly skilled craftsmen from other European countries. Thus, there formed a dividing line between the English immigrants, who as subjects of the English king, were full-fledged citizens of the colony, and non-English immigrants, who were not. In 1619 the Polish glassware, pitch, and tar makers of Jamestown staged the first labor strike in American history, and in so doing won for themselves full voting rights in the colony's elections that year.

That was the first immigrant-based friction in America, but hardly the last. The succeeding centuries brought waves of other immigrants to America's shores, including the Irish, Italians, French (by way of Canada), Swedes, and other Western and Eastern Europeans. By the 19th century Chinese, Japanese, and other East Asians started to arrive in the United States, largely in response to severe labor shortages in the far west. To the south, the border with Mexico was always very porous until the middle of the 20th century. Initially there was no distinction between legal immigrants and illegal aliens until well after World War I. Nonetheless, the continuous waves of immigrants all faced immense social, political, and economic challenges during their first generations, especially the language barriers. At various times they were vigorously and sometimes violently opposed by a wide array of nativist movements, including the Native American Party, also known as the "Know Nothings," a major political force between 1845 and 1860. Ironically, true Native Americans, known at the time as Indians, were not welcome in the Native American Party. After more than 400 years, immigration in America remains an evolving story.

Mark Bielski has written a penetrating analysis of one small but significant slice of that story: the Poles who served on both sides of the American Civil War. From the 16th through the end of the 18th centuries Poland was one of the most formidable military powers in Europe. The important role played by Polish soldiers in the War of American Independence is well known. In addition to Generals Tadeusz Kościuszko and Kazimierz Pułaski, hundreds of other Polish volunteers served the American cause. But after the Third Partition of Poland in 1795, the country disappeared from the political map of Europe for the next 123 years, divided among and subjugated by Russia, Prussia, and Austria. With Poland's demise, its vaunted military traditions also withered. In 1855 then-Captain George B. McClellan wrote that the Poles were "… unpleasant, unintelligent, and degenerate, and wondered how such a people had ever achieved any historical prominence."

McClellan wrote those words as a member of the Delafield Commission, which in 1855 and 1856 traveled throughout Europe examining the military systems and innovations of the Continental powers. Their final report was published in 1860 as *The Art of War in Europe*. By 1862, when he was the commanding general of the U.S. Army, McClellan was saying something quite different. According to Colonel Ludwik Żychliński, McClellan, "who, knowing I was a Pole, praised our nation, stating that we Poles are soldiers from childhood and that in our blood lies courage and subordination." McClellan at that point was more than happy to have Poles and anyone else serving in the Union Army.

In these pages Bielski unfolds a fascinating but little known story. By the Civil War there were about 30,000 first and second generation Poles in America. Some 4,000 to 5,000 served in the Union Army, while 1,000 to 1,500 fought for the Confederacy. The Polish Legion was one of the most prominent of the ethnic Union units, and in the South the Louisiana Polish Brigade. Two Poles, Jozef Kargé and Wladimir Krzyżanowski, became Union general officers. Kargé defeated the near-legendary Confederate General Nathan Bedford Forrest in a skirmish at Bolivar, Tennessee in May 1864, and Krzyżanowski is buried in Arlington National Cemetery.

As the book's title implies, the ethnic Poles who served in the American Civil War were anything but a homogenous lot. Some were officers, some were enlisted men. Many were first generation immigrants, but some were second generation. While the majority served the North, some served the South, although most of those were also opponents of slavery. One of the main reasons for this rather odd situation was the fact that Russia was the only major European power to support the North. After the Polish revolt against Russia failed in 1863 and many Poles were scattered throughout Europe as exiles, there was an ultimately unsuccessful effort to bring up to 5,000 of those exiles to the South. It was the old story of "the enemy of my enemy …"

The Poles who served in the American Civil War generally considered themselves sons of a nation that no longer existed, except in their hearts. Even after Poland was reborn at the end of 1918, that long-suffering nation spent much of the next 70 years under first German subjugation, and then under Soviet Communism. Poland today, of course, is a member in good standing of the European Union and the North Atlantic Treaty Organization, where its armed forces are once again considered among the most professional in the world. That is something my own Polish immigrant grandparents never could have conceived of during their lifetimes.

Maj.Gen. David T. Ząbecki, PhD
United States Army, Retired
Freiburg, Germany

INTRODUCTION

There were a number of Poles who fought in and played significant parts in the American Civil War, but their story is largely unknown. They span three generations and are connected by culture, nationality and an adherence to their principles and ideals. They came from a country that had basically disintegrated at the end of the previous century, yet they carried with them to America the concepts of freedom that they inherited from their forefathers. The Poland of their ancestors had been openly democratic and forward thinking, and deemed dangerous to the autocratic imperial neighbors that partitioned it. These men who had lost their country then came to a new one and exercised their "Polishness" as they became embroiled in the great American upheaval, the Civil War.

There are nine men in this book, four of whom have Louisiana affiliations. The first group had fought in the 1830 war for freedom from the Russian Empire. In the Civil War they continued the legacy begun in the American Revolution by their countrymen, Casimir Pulaski and Thaddeus Kościuszko. The next generation was formed in the European revolutionary struggles of the 1840s, and the two of the youngest generation came of age just as the Civil War began. They entered military service as enlisted men and finished as officers. Of the group, four sided with the North and four with the South. The other began the war in the Confederate cavalry and finished fighting for the Union side. They came from different parts of Poland that had been partitioned by the autocratic powers of Prussia, Russia and Austria, but were remarkably similar in many ways. All but one, from a Silesian peasant family in the Prussian sector, came from aristocratic backgrounds.

In a war that has commonly been categorized as a fierce internecine conflict between two American regions, major historical studies have not devoted a great deal of attention to Poles and foreigners in general. These men carried their belief in democratic liberalism with them from Europe into this American war. Whether for the North to keep a Union together or to form a new nation from the Southern states, they held to their ideals and made a significant contribution.

The involvement of Poles in the American Civil War has not received a good deal of historical study. Although their representation was relatively small compared to the Irish and Germans, the connection they made between the revolutionary movements of Europe and that great upheaval in America deserves notice. The number of Poles who came to America in the two and a half decades prior to the Civil War included many from the educated gentry who had fought for independence movements in Europe. The more familiar emigration of peasant and working class Poles would not reach the United States until later in the nineteenth century.

The Poles in this book came from a tradition of freedom and liberalism in their country that had developed over hundreds of years. When scholars consider the American Civil War, the perspective is generally that of a struggle between countrymen of two separate regions with blurred borders: the American "brother against brother" stereotype that has been memorialized. Yet it is important to consider this concept in another light.

This book tells of Poles who shared the same ideals and political philosophies in Europe and carried them into the fight in America—and yet sometimes took up arms against each other. These Poles rebelled against the empires into which their homeland had been absorbed and fought to resurrect their nation. They brought this same democratic liberalism to America and it inspired them to participate in the Civil War. Their contributions, whether they fought for North or South, demonstrated their belief in their adoptive cause. In doing so, they were not unlike the Confederates attempting to break from the United States and form an independent country. In the same way, other Poles who were new to America could identify with the struggle to keep united a fragmenting nation.[1]

EXPLANATORY NOTES

The names and spellings of many of the Polish names used in publications, official records and documents have varied considerably depending on who compiled the materials. In this work, the spellings have been made consistent according to the preferred usage. For the purposes of this work, rather than produce a primer for pronunciation, it is easier to phoneticize the names of the primary characters. Tochman and Kargé are the simplest, with Gurowski, Sulakowski and Jastremski being fairly easy to read syllable by syllable, as is Kiołbassa (somewhat like the sausage, the "ł" is a "w," so it would be Kee-ow-bassa). Szymański, Krzyżanowski and Żychliński are slightly more challenging. The first is roughly *Shi-man-ski*. Krzyżanowski is Kshi-zha-nov-ski, which accounts for why his men referred to him as "Kriz." Similarly, Żychliński transliterates to Zhikh-leen-ski.

Generally, the preferred use is the spelling of the given or Christian names used in military records. For surnames, the preferred usage is the actual Polish spelling. The Anglicized forms of names will make English pronunciation easier, but the true Polish spellings for surnames provides accuracy. For example, "Joseph" appears for the original "Józef" in the military records of General Kargé. However, Włodzimierz is the actual Polish spelling for General Krzyżanowski's first name and is used by his biographer, James S. Pula, while often one may instead see Vladimir or even Waldemir in various texts. Krzyżanowski's service record, however, lists him as "Waldimir." In the *Official Records* he is Wladimir.

The endnotes for each chapter are numbered separately. For ease of reference, I have written a complete endnote the first time the referenced work appears in each chapter. Additionally, I have limited the use of "ibid" for footnotes. For clarity, the *Official Records of the Union and Confederate Armies,* which has numerous citations throughout, is referenced as *Official Records* as opposed to *OR,* which is commonly used in other works.

All translations are mine unless otherwise noted.

CHAPTER 1

BEARING THE STANDARD
IN AMERICA

In 1834 two Austrian ships left the Adriatic port of Trieste and set sail for America with a group of Polish exiles from the failed 1830 revolt against Russia. Some of them were unwittingly destined to be participants in the American Civil War. They were the next wave of fighters from Poland who continued a movement initiated by their countrymen who had arrived in the late eighteenth century and spoke out for self-determination and Polish nationalism to the people of the American republic. They were the successors of craftsmen who had settled in Jamestown, Virginia, and created the first American insurrection in the British colonies. Not subjects of the king of England and not having the same rights and privileges as English citizens, they staged a work stoppage to express their dissatisfaction, gain deserved freedoms, and obtain voting rights. They also carried forth the standard of the Poles who had been part of the American Revolution in the previous century. Later came a 19th century group of Poles whose lives in the years leading up to the war and exploits in support of the Union or Confederacy during the conflict are the focus of this study.[2]

During this age of revolution and change, nationalism was growing in Europe, and a movement away from imperial power that had begun in the previous century was gaining momentum. What had started with the American Revolution, followed by the French one, coincided with the dismemberment of Poland by the three Continental powers of Russia, Prussia and Austria. In the first half of the nineteenth century there arose new insurrections with the resurgence of nationalism. This came about by peoples working to reestablish their sovereignty such as in Poland, to form a new nation as in Italy, or to break away from an empire, such as in Ireland.[3] The Poles were the "ferment" of Europe and the continent's "revolutionary army" ("*ils sont l'armée révolutionnaire du continent*"). They were as brave on the battlefield as they were troublesome politically.[4]

By the time the first southern states seceded in 1860, there had been several decades of revolutionary spirit and activity in Europe and the Americas that provided seeds of inspiration for national self-determination in the American South. This same spirit spurred a determination in those who wanted to save the Union and protect and preserve the revolution that the American founding fathers had started in the previous century. The revolution in Poland in 1830 that rose against imperialism in Europe was analogous to American pro-republican thought that "challenged monarchical legitimacy." The subsequent revolutionary actions of 1848 Europe were influential to both the North and South in the years preceding the Civil War. Southerners demanded their right to break with the Union and establish their own country. The pro-Union northerners held the conflicting view that the southern slaveholding society was akin to the European aristocracy that had repeatedly subjugated "progressive revolutionaries" in the first half of the nineteenth century.[5]

When South Carolina voted to secede from the Union on 20 December 1860, it was the culmination of years of festering regionalism in the relatively new United States of America. The actual act of secession, and the subsequent withdrawal of fellow states of the Deep South—Mississippi, Florida, Alabama, Georgia, Louisiana in January, and Texas in March—provided the springboard for launching the Confederate States of America. Only after the first shots were fired at Fort Sumter on 12 April 1861, which made the imminent war official, did Virginia secede. The states that had wavered politically between remaining in the Union or joining the other southern states followed: Arkansas and North Carolina in May, and finally Tennessee in June. The border states of Maryland, Kentucky and Missouri, where slavery was allowed, never left the United States' fold but were plagued with divided loyalties and suffered the casualties, privations and destruction that the war was to provide.[6]

Whether by means of political machinations, military force or popular sentiment, these Border States remained in the Union. President Abraham Lincoln could not let the pro-secession firebrands in the

Maryland legislature win. He and the Federal government would then be trapped within enemy territory, since Washington, D.C., was situated on the banks of the Potomac River between Virginia and Maryland. He suspended *habeas corpus* and even had state delegates jailed to prevent their votes for secession. Kentucky and Missouri sent delegates to the Confederacy, but their leaders who favored remaining loyal to the Union prevailed. Soon to follow would be Federal troops physically exerting control over territory.[7]

While hostilities were brewing between and within northern and southern states, there were many newcomers to America who would cast their fortunes with one side or the other. As an ethnic group, the Poles numbered about 30,000. This was significantly smaller than the German and Irish immigrant populations, as well as the more entrenched French Americans. However, just as the more numerous ethnic groups, the Poles would make a contribution to both sides. Numerical estimates are about 1,000–1,500 troops for the Confederacy and 4,000–5,000 for the Union.[8]

With an upward estimate of 6,500 combined Poles fighting for both sides, a direct comparison of them as an ethnic presence with the Germans or Irish is hardly valid. There were about 164,000 Irish in the ranks of both armies, roughly 144,000 Union and 20,000 Confederate. Just as the Poles, the Irish exhibited a fierce nationalistic pride, and there were others who were motivated by the desire to gain military experience in the Civil War, then return to fight for a free Ireland. However, in sharp contrast with the Poles counted in the 1860 census, there were nearly seventy times more Irish in the United States. In sheer numbers there were already nearly 2 million that had arrived in America prior to the war.[9] For the Germans or German-Americans, out of a total population of approximately 1.3 million, the estimate ranges between 180,000 and 216,000 on the Union side and as many as 7,000 in Confederate service. The number of other ethnic groups represented (Austrians, Poles, Czechs, Swiss, Hungarians) that may be included because they were in German-affiliated units or spoke German, could skew these numbers downward somewhat. Additionally, it is difficult to give exact numbers because as the war developed "German ranks thinned to include more Americans." A similarity some of the Germans shared with the Poles is the roughly 5,000 who were considered "Forty-eighters." As did their Polish counterparts, they had fought in many of the insurrections in Europe in the 1840's and many had "fought to establish a democratic and unified Germany."[10]

A soldier would be a "German American" if he came from a region in Europe where the prominent language was German and whose primary language spoken in his family and household was German. More Germans migrated into the North and thereby avoided the issue of slavery. If they settled in the Southern states, either they assimilated into society and accepted the existing norms such as the "peculiar institution," or they kept their opinions guarded. In the summer of 1861, Jefferson Davis issued a proclamation that foreigners had to "declare their loyalty to the Confederacy" lest they "be treated as alien enemies." The result was that Germans in the South either supported the Confederacy or remained silent.[11]

Whereas Germans who came to America in the three decades before the Civil War most likely had reasons other than the seeking of religious freedom, it was an issue for many of the Irish immigrants. Anglicanism was official in Britain and Ireland, and Irish Catholics suffered legal discrimination. The resulting poverty after the end of the Napoleonic wars and the famine situation later in Ireland made the potential for earning wages and freedom to practice their religion in America attractive.[12]

The Poles who had come to America were there for many reasons, but their journeys all seem to have been fueled by seeking some new form of freedom. Some were men of means possibly hounded by Czarist agents. They had fought in the 1830–31 war against Imperial Russia with the goal of resurrecting the Polish state. Still others, perhaps having their land and possessions confiscated for participation in the insurrection against Prussia in 1848, sought new freedom in America. There were also those from the peasant or working classes who were more motivated by the possibilities of better lives and opportunities, and simply intended to join relatives already in America.

The émigrés from Poland that settled in America had a belief system rooted in a country that was politically and structurally different than any other in Europe. Indeed, the very qualities that gave these people their notions of freedom could easily be construed as the elements that combined to cause Poland's downhill slide from one of Europe's largest, most powerful nations to its eventual dismantling and physical disappearance from the continent's map.

The difficulties perhaps began with the tradition of an elected monarchy. The *szlachta* (nobles of every rank in wealth and standing) voted for the king and placed him on the throne. At the election, the "*szlachta* could exercise the right to choose who would reign over them—a choice unthinkable in most European countries, and therefore a matter of tremendous pride to the man who could freely exercise it."[13] The king did not necessarily have to be Polish and in many cases was not. The Poles favored this system, a combination of republic and monarchy, although seemingly contradictory, and felt it was "superior to all others." Thus Poland "combined all the beneficent qualities of a monarchy, oligarchy and democracy. The fact that it might combine all their faults as well was not thought relevant."[14]

There was a group of Poles that spanned two generations in the first half of the nineteenth century that forged a link between the European nationalistic revolutions and the American war of rebellion. They or their families originated in different parts of partitioned Poland, but they shared similar ideals that had been born in the tumultuous decades of late eighteenth and early nineteenth century Europe. Ignatius Szymański, Adam Gurowski and Gaspard Tochman had been involved in the 1830–31 war. Wladimir Krzyżanowski, Valery Sulakowski, Joseph Kargé and Ludwik Żychliński were products of the later years of European unrest. There were also a number of Poles who came of age in the tumultuous time just as the war was beginning. Leon Jastremski and Peter Kiołbassa were among them.

Krzyżanowski, Kargé, Szymański and Tochman were such Poles. So too were Sulakowski and Żychliński. They were officers who would rise and attain success in different ways before, during and after the war. Adam Gurowski was not part of the military effort but in politics he comprised a relentless weapon for the Northern cause. Krzyżanowski would raise the "Polish Legion" and Kargé cavalry in the North. Szymański would be instrumental in recruiting the Chalmette Regiment and Tochman the Louisiana Polish Brigade in the South. These were sons of Poland, ardent Polish patriots who had fought for their homeland's freedom. Ideologically, they were of the same or similar backgrounds: educated and from the landowning class. But they were products of a new ideal, the new European democratic liberalism, and had come to America seeking a new form of freedom. Now they were raising troops for opposite sides in their respective adopted countries. Now for all practical purposes they would be enemies.

Sulakowski, Krzyżanowski and their contemporaries could have drawn inspiration from the Polish military legacy in America that began in the Revolution of the previous century. They would have looked upon Thaddeus Kościuszko and Count Casimir Pulaski, who fought for the Continental Army, as honorable heroes—as indeed they were. After his service in the American Revolution, Kościuszko later fought the Russians when he returned to Poland. The revolutionary Poles harbored bitterness toward the partitioners and especially toward any of their countrymen who had been "enablers." They despised anyone whom they felt had treacherously betrayed their country. They especially reviled the *Sejm* (parliament) members who ratified the final partition. The delegates who gathered in Warsaw "were mostly the dregs of society." The invaders would have their way because Poland had a "scoundrel" for a Marshal, a "shabby figure" for a general secretary and the *Sejm* was a "witches Sabbath, an orgy of depravity." Kościuszko, perhaps a harbinger of a budding resistance movement, returned to Poland at this time to observe in shock and amazement "the sinister carnival still in progress."[15]

Other factors fueled the desire for independence in these Polish veterans of the 1830 war who later came to America. Their preceding generation had cast their lot with Napoleon. Because of his military successes in Europe, the establishment of the Duchy of Warsaw and the eventual Congress Kingdom of Poland (1815–31) became possible. The Poles had been inspired by the feats of their legions who fought alongside the French, such as the Chevaux-Legers, and individuals such as Prince Jozef Poniatowski, who became a Marshal of France, and the 98,000 Poles who marched into Russia with the Grande Armée in 1812. These were warriors who made their reputation fearsome throughout Europe after Poland had experienced a decades-long drought of major military success. However, Napoleon's cynical "treatment of Polish aspirations" and his use of Poland to achieve his personal goals, were ultimately "of no benefit whatsoever to the Polish cause."[16] Yet the resurrection of the Polish state, albeit short-lived, kept the independent spirit and revolutionary fires burning.

Men such as Krzyżanowski and Sulakowski who fought on different sides of the Civil War were professional soldiers who would go on to have different military careers. Each man was driven by duty and loyalty to the country for which he fought. Neither chose the extreme route of radicalism as did Gurowski, nor the constitutional rationale for separatism of Tochman. Having comparable backgrounds in education, family, social structure and historical knowledge bred into their souls made officers such as Krzyżanowski and Sulakowski alike. It may seem incongruous, but it also prompted them to fight for freedom and their ideals, on opposite sides, diametrically opposed.

Ludwik Żychliński possessed qualities as a soldier and social observer that at once exhibited his similarities to his Polish contemporaries and occasionally his differences. He was first a fiercely proud Pole and loyal to his people and causes. He showed this in his service on both sides of the Atlantic. He never lost the fire and longing to fight for Polish freedom, and he carried his enmity and distrust for the Russians and their imperial system as a talisman.

The youngest of the Civil War Poles examined in this study are Leon Jastremski and Peter Kiołbassa. They shared proximity in age and other similarities, but in the middle of the war they took divergent paths. Kiołbassa originally came from a peasant family that had settled in Texas after emigrating from Poland. He began the war in the service of the Confederate cavalry, but after he was taken prisoner his captors persuaded him to change allegiances and he willingly switched sides to fight for the Union. Jastremski was of an aristocratic family background but with relatively moderate means in America. He was the epitome of steadfast loyalty who repeatedly returned to his unit in the Confederate army after capture. When he was not in the hands of Northern captors or recuperating from wounds, he fought in most of the major engagements of the Army of Northern Virginia. Both men entered politics after the war: Kiołbassa in Illinois, with whose troops he had served and where he settled at war's end, and Jastremski in his home state of Louisiana.

The second chapter of this book discusses the attitudes and formation of the Polish spirit that were manifest in the characters involved. It shows how these characters applied their notions of freedom and independence to their lives and intellectual reasoning as they were becoming Americans. As the country became increasingly divided, their affiliation with one side or the other emerged as much from their ties to their new homeland, whether North or South, as from their adherence to their beliefs and ideals.

Chapter three discusses the 1830 Generation that departed Europe after the unsuccessful war with Imperial Russia and found they could exercise their rights in a new country. They were able to engage in discourse and promote their ideas: Tochman for Poland's resurgence, Szymański on the ills of Poland under Russia's yoke, and Gurowski on comparing European and American societies. The realities of who these men were became apparent when they took up the banner for either the Union or the Confederacy.

In chapter four, Żychliński and Sulakowski exemplify the Poles who kept an almost visceral connection with their homeland. They had the same ideals but fought on different sides in America. Żychliński intended to hone his skills as a warrior fighting for the Union in the American war. Sulakowski, the Confederate, devised a plan to transplant a small army of soldiers from Poland to aid the Southern fight when it was almost too late. The next chapter catalogues the war experiences of their contemporaries, Kargé and Krzyżanowski, who were from neighboring Northern states and served the Union throughout the war. They successfully led their commands despite adversities that came from beyond the battlefield. They were as steady under fire as they were unswerving under criticism and false charges. While these men were experienced soldiers who entered their armies ranked as officers, the sixth chapter details the youngest two of this group. Jastremski and Kiołbassa started as enlisted men and moved up through the ranks, then carried their fight into the political world after the war.

This book is a study of a particular assemblage of Poles who became entangled in the complexities of the Civil War. It provides an examination of the factors that were involved in the development of their identities, and what would have influenced their thinking: their histories, family background, educational backgrounds and experiences leading up to the war. It will then review their actions and their contributions to the conflict itself. Additionally, it considers the outcome of the war for each of them and questions whether or not they were able to fulfill their ambitions.

CHAPTER 2

ON THE APPROACH TO WAR

As we have seen, the Polish émigrés who fought in the Civil War and are the subject of this study were the products of three separate generations. Tochman, Szymański and Gurowski were of the older generation that had been part of the 1830–31 rebellion against Russia. Kargé, Sulakowski, Żychliński and Krzyżanowski were nationalists and products of the European republican movement of the 1840's and subsequent years. Kiołbassa and Jastremski were the youngest of the group, with the latter the only one not actually born in Poland and would have been intrinsically the most American of them since he came to the United States (from France) as a young boy.

The attitudes that motivated this select group of Poles who took part in and chose opposing sides in the war require an examination on three different levels. The first is the concept of freedom that was inherent in their being as a product of their long beleaguered homeland. This would include the Polish perception of freedom that often differed from their fellow Europeans, and how well this fit with the American concept of freedom that was yet in its infancy. The ways in which these men adapted to their new country and how they envisioned themselves and their respective roles are the second level. That is, whether it was being part of the struggle to break free and form a separate American nation or helping to enforce the preservation of the country as it was founded. Additionally, it is important to see how well their views meshed with the dissimilar thinking that divided north and south in the United States. The third part of the equation is how these Poles decided to exercise their rights and apply themselves to one cause or the other as the American cauldron was coming to a boil on the eve of the Civil War.

Polish Concepts of Freedom

When the American Revolution began and the colonies were in the process of excising themselves from the rule of the British Empire, Poland was undergoing the Partitions. This dissection, over a period of more than two decades, took place just as America was developing its identity and producing its own constitution. When the Revolution occurred, the Americans were a grouping of related colonies, not yet a nation-state such as those in Europe. [1] Whereas the Poles who arrived in America later knew that they no longer had a nation at the time, they were endeavoring to resurrect it. They were working from a vision of Poland that was based on their knowledge of its prior existence in history.

It would have been difficult for these Poles to fight to suppress freedom. They were anti-imperialists—except for the iconoclastic Gurowski who never neatly fits a category. Indeed, Tochman, Szymański and Gurowski all were part of the November 1830 uprising that had as its immediate spark the orders that mandated they accompany the Czar's army on its mission to extinguish the Belgian independence movement and insurrections in France. Those of this group who fought in the 1830 war became known as the "Novembrists," and several hundred later emigrated to the United States. [2]

The attitudes and ideals that motivated these Poles who participated in the American Civil War developed over generations prior to their arrival in the United States. Many brought with them a military tradition, a zest for freedom and a will to defend liberty. The concept of defense would have been inherent in Poles who would take up arms since they had emigrated from a country that in the 18th century had disintegrated and had come to be dominated by external powers. Whether peasant or gentry, they would have seen their liberties eroded as foreign systems of government, and often armies, replaced most opportunities for self-determination. Yet even with the encroachments imposed by the authoritarian regimes of Russia, Prussia and Austria, the fires of freedom burned and military traditions stayed sufficiently alive to foster armed, organized insurrections. There arose in Poland the new concept of freedom and increasingly progressive ideas "fired by the spirit of the European Enlightenment and by the example of the states of North America."[3] The exemplary service of Poles in the American Revolution was partly responsible for fostering this attitude. It developed into the zealous willingness to defend homeland, property, family and friends, a way of life and ideals. It also sprang from the Enlightenment concept of "men enjoying equal rights to form nations which in turn would" lead to "lasting peace, the growth of morality—in other words, the growing liberation of humanity from the rule of backwardness, superstition and despotism."[4]

These were concepts that had an historic germination over the centuries prior to the first Poles arriving in America. As early as 1425, Poland enacted laws that guaranteed due process with *Neminem captivabimus nisi iure victum* ("No one will be held captive without legal decision") and *Nihil Novi nisi commune consensus* ("Nothing new without common consent") in 1505. This gave the *Sejm* (Parliament) and regional assemblies "enormous power ... Although certainly not a modern democracy, this was a unique constitutional evolution of great significance for later history."[5]

Even at its greatest levels of wealth and power in Europe in the 16th and 17th centuries, new ideas with respect to freedom and liberty were fomenting in Poland. Under King Zygmunt III Vasa, the vast kingdom stretched from Poland's modern day western borders on the Baltic Sea near Szczecin, along the coast north to Finland, including the present countries of Lithuania, Latvia and Estonia. East and southeast to the Carpathian Mountains and Hungary, it held the Ukraine, the Steppe to the Black Sea and the cities of Kiev, Pskov, Minsk and even Moscow for a brief few years. Several decades of wars and civil wars followed: the Swedes, the Cossack rebellion, the Russians and Turks, sometimes in succession, followed. The military high water mark may have been in the late 17th century when King Jan Sobieski led an alliance of Poles, Austrians and Germans spearheaded by his *Husaria* of winged heavy cavalry to a decisive and crushing victory over the Ottoman Turks at the battle of Vienna in 1683. As saviors of European Christendom, this army became legendary and the Poles exalted their cavalry and its military exploits for generations thereafter. Count Casimir Pulaski served with the Continental Army in the Revolution and later became revered as the father of American cavalry.[6] Years later in the Civil War, Joseph Kargé recruited and successfully organized and led mounted regiments for the Union Army.[7]

At the peak of prosperity in the 16th century, freedom of thought flourished. Wawrzyniec Goslicki, a professor at the Jagiellonian University in Krakow, as well as the universities in Padua and Bologna, Italy, published his work, *De Optimo Senatore* ("On the perfect senator") in Venice in 1568. He was expounding what would later become very American sounding ideas. He taught about "human rights of citizens under a just and responsible government ... limitation of royal authority, equality of all citizens under law, and equal opportunity for all based purely on merit."[8] He went so far as to suggest that a ruler must abide by the Senate that in turn is empowered by "all the Orders of his Realm." Although he specifically refers to a Polish King, Goslicki uses language that preceded the ideas of the future Enlightenment:

> A *King* of *Poland,* in the Administration of his Government, is obliged to make the Law, the Sole Guide and Rule of his Conduct. He cannot govern according to his own Will and Pleasure, nor make War or Peace, without the Advice and Consent of the *Senate.* He cannot go beyond, or break in upon their Decrees, nor exceed the Bounds, which They and the Laws have set him. What follows from such a Constitution, is plainly this, That a King [is] thus Limited in his Power.[9]

Throughout Europe the books were outlawed, burned and destroyed, but kept reappearing and the work was even "subversively translated as "*The Counselor.*" Queen Elizabeth I banned it in England, but with Goslicki's "appallingly humanistic views" it became a "standard text on democratic government for eighteenth-century social revolutionaries and reformers."[10] In this number was to be Thomas Jefferson, and indeed "many principles found in the Declaration of Independence can be traced to this monumental work."[11]

The progressive ideologies continued to develop, but the prosperity and might of Poland as a unified entity began to wane. The elected monarchy, though a progressive tradition the Poles had fostered, was to cause the greatest difficulty. There was not necessarily the need for wealth and power to be a noble—the *szlachta* ranged from penniless men with education and title to extremely wealthy magnates. These were the delegates who voted for the king, and from whom he drew his authority and power. That "unthinkable choice" of electing a king that empowered the *szlachta* would cause most other European ruling classes to recoil with fright, but it became "a matter of tremendous pride" to the Poles.[12] The elected king often came from elsewhere in Europe, and the electorate favored this system that combined the best features of republic and monarchy in some respects, along with the inherent faults of a fairly weak central government. Nevertheless, the Poles felt their system was "superior to all others."[13]

In the late 18th century, King Stanislaw August moved to regulate the *Sejm* and "limit the principle of unanimity" that had traditionally "clogged all progress."[14] This and other reforms alarmed Poland's authoritarian, imperial neighbors Prussia and Russia, where the ruling regimes discouraged freedom of thought and liberal reforms. Czarist supporters and the absolute monarchs of Prussia and Austria, for example, were not pleased by the carryover of such ideals into their societies. "Constitutions and civil liberties ... were regarded as a dangerous disease ... and the Poles were suspected of being the main carriers of the contagion."[15] Just as the Poles began spreading this "disease," they developed a new strain of it by passing the Constitution of 3 May 1791. The *Sejm* was to have full legislative power by majority—the *liberum veto* (ability of one member to veto legislation favored by the majority) that had so often crippled the government was abolished. The king had to have approval of the Royal Council to make policies, and the council was answerable to the *Sejm*. Catholicism was the country's official religion, but the Constitution guaranteed freedom of religion for everyone. The country had a tradition of religious tolerance, but this codified it into law. Equally disturbing to the autocratic powers were the social and economic reforms. These extended new rights to "property relationships, the protection of labour, investment, the establishment of a national bank and the issue of a paper currency." While acclaimed the world over, the "events in Poland assumed alarming significance in the light of the political situation in Europe."[16] These ideas were considered dangerous by Poland's neighbors. The reaction was to "make sure that Poland had no ability to engage in future experiments in ordered freedom." To do this Russia and Prussia planned the second partition.[17] This would prompt the return to Poland of Thaddeus Kościuszko, the general who had served in the American Revolution.

The Partitions that took place in 1772, 1793 and 1795 would have influenced the thinking of any Pole of the early 19th century. Prussia, Russia and Austria expanded their empires in wealth and population greatly at the expense of Poland in little more than two decades. With the first partition in 1772, the "troubled and dissension-ridden Polish Commonwealth was overthrown in Europe." In the autocrats' view, the country "as an architect of radical social and political thinking, had come to an end."[18]

Even though its borders had changed, Poland lived on as an entity, an ideal and a nation. Two major characters that were to be influential in Polish thought in Europe and the New World surfaced. Count Casimir Pulaski and Kościuszko emerged during the great freedom movement that was to be the American Revolution. In them the Poles who followed in the 19th century had genuine military role models who embodied all the ideals of their Polish homeland.

In assessing two of the most influential Polish figures in early American history, a study of their backgrounds before arriving in the New World provides insight into their motivation. What was their family background? Where were their origins in Poland, what were their military traditions and how did Kościuszko and Pulaski carry on these traditions in order to become heroes of the American Revolution? Kościuszko was also a close friend of American founding father Thomas Jefferson, yet actually pursued and believed in a purer idea of freedom.

There is a necessary comparison and contrast between the philosophical thinking of Jefferson and the thoughts of Kościuszko. Jefferson put forth his ideas of freedom in writing and by means of political channels. He did this amidst the upheaval the colonists were creating in their quest to achieve independence from Britain. Kościuszko was primarily a warrior and freedom fighter—in America and in his native Poland. His thoughts were unwavering on individual rights and he was in adamant opposition to slavery.[19]

As a freedom fighter in Poland and one of the early military patriots in America, Kościuszko left an indelible mark on both sides of the

Atlantic. Polish Americans especially remember and celebrate his valor and service and they also "commemorate him as their homeland's George Washington." He had fought with and led Americans for seven years in the Revolution against Great Britain and was a well-known hero in America. Later, after his return to Poland, "he reached legendary proportions during the Polish rebellion of 1794, which he led against the Russian army." This became known as the Kościuszko Insurrection.[20] Although not as well known as his military exploits, he had meantime developed ideas about the abolition of slavery in America and serfdom in Europe. He urged the Americans after the war to act fully on the first words of their Declaration of Independence and put an end to slavery. In his will, Kosciuszko went so far as to appoint Thomas Jefferson as executor. He directed Jefferson to use "[Kosciuszko's] assets to free and educate black slaves and thus erase the last blot of inhumanity that marred the image of the America he loved."[21]

Abolition of servitude was not the only driving force behind Kosciuszko. He agonized over the travails of his weakening Poland. His experiences at home and in Paris had made him "a dedicated son of the Enlightenment." He had become a firm believer in "national self-government, personal liberty, tolerance of divergent religious and cultural traditions, and a general humanitarianism spanning all classes and varieties of people."[22] These are the same ideals that many of the subsequent generations of Poles adopted. The wealthy *szlachta* magnates (primarily of eastern Poland) that went along with the Russian intervention— but gave up their political freedoms—traded wealth and personal gain for their country's sovereignty. Years later, "it baffled and appalled them when some of their sons and daughters took up arms for Polish independence in the nineteenth-century insurrections, often to end up in a forest grave or a Siberian penal colony."[23]

In America the situation was different in that men such as Pulaski and Kosciuszko were joining idealistic revolutionaries. Not all the colonists were part of this movement. Between 1775 and 1783 there were some 500,000 Americans who remained loyal to England. "Loyalty to the Crown was the normal condition of American colonials before 1775," and nearly twenty percent of the white citizens of the colonies either made the choice to remain loyal, or were unable to "give up the customary allegiance to England."[24] It follows that there were those who remained loyal to the Crown who felt that "the people in the Colonies were more free, unencumbered and happy than any others on earth."[25] They were not, as were the Poles, subjugated by foreign powers.

Pulaski wrote to George Washington with regard to the American independence movement, emphasizing that "wherever men can fight for liberty, that is also our fight and our place."[26] He affirmed his support for the Revolution and continued, "In coming to America, my sole object has been to devote myself entirely to her welfare and glory, in using every exertion in my individual power to secure her freedom."[27] Such sentiments as Pulaski expressed would have been well known to the next generations of Poles who followed him. How they would apply these tenets to their new experience in America would surface on both sides of the conflict to come.

In Poland, Kosciuszko and Pulaski had sided with different factions despite their devotion to the same ideals. Kosciuszko and his family were loyal to King Stanislaw August even as he weakly presided over the disintegrating country. Pulaski allied himself with the Confederation of Bar in an effort to bolster the country, and he made his early reputation fighting Russians. The Confederation had originated as a protector of Roman Catholicism in Poland, and its efforts were "directed against Russia and the pro-Russian policies" of the King. He had been part of the failed plot to kidnap the very same king that Kosciuszko supported. Yet in America, they fought on the same side.[28]

Becoming Americans

Kosciuszko, being a military man, had a tendency toward action rather than political process. This trait also manifested itself in many of his countrymen who later came to America. In the Civil War, there were Poles who were idealistic as well as militaristic. Ludwik Żychliński had fought in Italy before he came to America, and sided with the Union in the Civil War. He favored abolition and was willing to fight for it. He also wanted to further his military experience for use in continuing the struggle for freedom when he returned to his native land.[29] In his memoirs he reflected on the respect that he and other Poles received as soldiers fighting in America. He stated that they are accepted because of the "great feeling of gratitude to Kosciuszko and Pulaski which is deeply rooted in the hearts of the free citizens of the American republic. Poles are considered to be heroes and champions of freedom." It is with this attitude that Żychliński pursued his enlistment and sought a regiment in which to serve in the United States.[30]

Żychliński echoed Kosciuszko when he wrote about his earnest desire to defend liberty and equality by stating that "a Pole is always willing to sacrifice his life on the altar of freedom."[31] Then he contrasted the lack of zeal of his fellow Northerners to the patriotism of the Southern people for the Confederate cause: "The Southern states are fighting for their independence … in order to repel the Northern invasion and defend their land."[32] Men such as Tochman and Żychliński, though of two different generations, had both fought in the insurrections of their homeland and had been part of a Polish political system that had at its core "an unfocused hatred of anything Russian," and were "prepared to use violence to maintain themselves and armed revolution to achieve their ends." In America, "Tochman demonstrated his loathing of Russia twenty years before the outbreak of the Civil War. He gave a series of anti-Russian lectures" to influence public opinion while he traveled around the country.[33] In his memoirs, Żychliński refers to Russia as the "eternal enemy of freedom."[34] Tochman, Żychliński and their comrades rebelled against "the Russian tradition of total, utterly centralized and despotic authority" and worked to further Poland's tradition of free speech and limited central power. They would carry this with them to the fight in America, serving for opposing armies.[35]

In the South the issue was often ambiguous. The abstract idea of fighting for freedom and the more tangible motivation of fighting to protect their home soil and repel invaders (a notion that would come naturally to Poles of that era) was a motivation for some. Southerners feared subjugation by a "despotic North" and were willing to fight for their personal freedom and sectional liberty. Remaining in the Union through Federal force of arms was a direct threat to liberty. The Southern Poles, who saw their European homeland subjugated by foreign powers, could easily identify with this.[36] Others who were of the gentry fell in step with planters and plantation owners who wanted to preserve Southern society and way of life. Some even became anti-abolitionists, such as Tochman, who recruited and organized troops for the Confederacy.[37]

Tochman became a citizen of the United States in 1843, and within a few years became a member of the bar in New York. Ironically, he began to practice law in Washington, D.C., after some relatives of Kosciuszko approached him "to recover the share of the property which Kosciuszko had left in this country [the United States]." They had no representation in America and these Poles were facing legal and political opposition from the Czar's minister to the U.S. The Imperial Russian government also was hoping to "punish Tochman for his political offences against Russia" as well as for his part as an officer "in the Polish army during the Polish insurrection against Russia in 1830."[38]

The Russian government was claiming all of Kosciuszko's property and was maneuvering by means of litigation and diplomatic influence to have the heirs drop the case and Tochman relieved as counsel. "When the Russian Minister was not successful in his move, Tochman was threatened with the loss of his American citizenship, which would result in his disbarment and loss of livelihood."[39]

Tochman won the legal battle, but perhaps this skirmish with the Russian government and their agents who were later in league with the American government influenced his decision to side with the South. Additionally, for the nine years prior to the Civil War, Tochman resided in Virginia. "Jefferson Davis [U.S. Senator from Mississippi, then Secretary of War] and other leaders of the secession movement were his friends. Tochman's influence on Davis appeared in speeches" Davis made that expressed solidarity, "sympathy and admiration for the Polish nation."[40] During his Virginia residency, Tochman was active in political circles and ultimately became a delegate to the Virginia Democratic Convention in 1860. Prior to that year's pivotal election, he felt that the issue of slavery should be negotiated between the North and the South. He avidly supported Stephen A. Douglas as a presidential candidate and also shared the "view that a compromise solution must be sought in the approaching 'inevitable conflict'."[41] Republican Abraham Lincoln won the election, however, and thus began Tochman's metamorphosis from compromiser to firebrand.

Tochman was among the Polish exiles who came to America rather than accept amnesty and live under Russian rule. These were the groups of Poles who sailed as deportees from the port of Trieste on the Adriatic Sea, then part of the Austrian Empire. They pledged to continue the Polish fight for freedom and felt their cause had the general support of the American populace. However, they became "bitterly disappointed that the American government maintained a strict policy through the years between Andrew Jackson and Abraham Lincoln that the Polish question was an internal affair of the Russian Empire."[42] It was just such a policy that would give Poles settling in the southern states added impetus to support the Confederacy. These sentiments would surface later during the Civil War years when the formation of the Confederacy occurred simultaneously with a new series of revolutionary episodes in Poland that would lead to the January 1863 insurrection. The American press varied in attitude from sympathetic to critical of the hopelessness of rebellion against the Russian empire. Some newspapers "made veiled comparisons between the draft in Poland and the conscription introduced in the North," while in the South President Lincoln and the Czar were labeled as tyrants. In similar fashion, "so did the famous cartoon in the British *Punch,* which pictured Lincoln and Alexander shaking hands against the background of gallows and destruction inflicted upon their respective rebels."[43] The Russian Navy even sent its fleet to visit the ports of New York and San Francisco and entertained President Lincoln aboard one of its warships, *Alexander Nevsky.* During this time an incident occurred that would punctuate U.S.–Russian relations and color Southern sentiments. A conscripted Polish sailor in the Russian Navy had jumped ship in New York. The sailor, Aleksander Milewski, had joined the Union army and was serving in active duty. He "was hunted down, discovered in an artillery regiment he joined in Virginia, and returned to the Russians." Milewski received a court-martial and was hanged aboard ship in the New York harbor.[44]

When Gaspard Tochman arrived in America one of his first missions was to champion the cause of Polish freedom. In a series of speeches in which he displayed his legalistic skills, he railed against Russia's illegitimate claims to any Polish territory or people. It was in the mid-1830s and could not have been a conscious effort, but he foreshadowed his future commitment to and justification for Southern states rights and secession. He equated the enemies of Poland to "the enemies of liberty" and declared that it was the Polish peoples' destiny as well as "their privilege" to come to the "defense of the rights of mankind." He made comparisons between Poland and Russia often. The Czar's empire was the "despotic hydra" that used assorted "artful machinations" to maintain control over the people. Among these were travel restrictions within and out of the empire, suppression of information from the outside, surveillance of dissident activity by the secret police and propaganda. Tochman included Prussia and Austria with the imperial powers that would have to "soon yield to this natural course of human affairs" that were coming to fruition in Europe because of Polish "influence on the welfare of mankind, past and future."[45]

In some instances, other Poles who shared the same philosophies and shouldered arms together when they were in Europe became adversaries after settling in America. Kosciuszko and Pulaski had sided with opposing factions in Poland, then came to America and served under one banner in the Continental Army. Just the opposite occurred with Count Adam Gurowski and Gaspard Tochman. These two Poles, though not of the same luminary status as their predecessors in the American Revolution, found themselves ideological opponents in America. Both had served together in Poland in the 1830 war as countrymen opposing Imperial Russia. However, in the Civil War, Gurowski emerged as a pro-Union abolitionist while Tochman became the Confederate who supported slavery.[46]

For playing a minor part in the Union's war machine, Gurowski attracted a good deal of attention. He descended from a long line of nobility that had fought for Poland and in European wars since the ninth century. Gurowski trumpeted his military pedigree and wanted a commission in the Union army. When this did not occur, he went to work in the U.S. State Department. Customarily dismissed as merely a minor influence by many historians, even his biographer LeRoy H. Fischer excoriated Gurowski. Fischer asserts that Lincoln thought of Gurowski as one of the "diabolical elements of the Radical Republican ranks" who was dangerous and even a possible assassin. On the other hand, the Radical Republicans, many of them high-ranking appointed or elected officials, thought of Gurowski as a visionary.[47]

Gurowski's exploits in Europe before coming to the United States provide further insight into the development of his later character. These include studying under Georg Hegel in Berlin, threatening Grand Duke Constantine, the Czar's viceroy in Warsaw, and a death sentence *in absentia* in Russia for his involvement in a plot to kidnap the Czar. He then went through a period in which he promoted Pan-Slavism and became an apologist for Russian ambitions in order to receive a pardon from Czar Nicholas and "an invitation to live in Russia ... as a pan-Slav propaganda adviser." This movement that gained popularity among Russians, Czechs and some other Slavic groups in the nineteenth century promoted the "idea of cultural, and hence possibly political union of all Slavs ... rarely found favor among the Poles."[48] He "devised, developed, and administered measures to Russify Poland," but soon saw this system did not "meet his expectations."[49]

The turnaround in character and transformation of thinking that Gurowski underwent are as remarkable as his intellect and abrasive personality. In 1825, he returned to Poland after completing his studies and administered the affairs of his family's properties in the Kalisz region. He immediately involved himself in revolutionary activities directed against Russia. With his brother, Joseph, he joined the radical Patriotic Society that was organizing an armed insurrection.[50] In order to recruit troops for the military that was re-forming to oppose the Czar, he freed the serfs on his family's estates and gave them land in exchange for their pledge to fight the Russians. In this way, he demonstrated a consistency with the cause of emancipation, but thirty years later was willing to forgive the Czar's prior transgressions, once he finally put an end to serfdom. Gurowski asserted in April 1864 that he had been an abolitionist since he had been a young boy:

> The aspirations of my whole life are finally fulfilled; they have become a fact. The Polish peasantry or agricultural population, than which I have not found a better, worthier, more honest, more intelligent in any country in the world, the peasantry of ancient Poland is finally and emphatically *emancipated*. It is emancipated as man and as laborer; it receives land—that is homesteads, and is only subject to the laws and to the power of the sovereign. This is a progress.[51]

He "blessed" Czar Alexander and went on to say that "in the name of those restored to the fullness of human rights," he forgave all the dynastic Romanoffs for "all the misfortunes and evils [they] heaped" on the Poles.[52]

As a revolutionary, Gurowski proved to be overbearing for even the insurrectionist Polish National Government. Just as he would later in the United States, he aggressively singled out leaders and factions within the group with whom he disagreed. Rather than initiate a compromise of any sort, he charged that the ineptitude of the leadership was "ruining the revolution" because they lacked the focus of a "single purpose" that was necessary for victory over Russia.[53] In joining the revolutionary army, he proved his willingness to fight, and later referred to his time serving in the field in his diaries. He juxtaposed his hardships with that of Union soldiers quartered outdoors when there was plenty of space: "so many empty large [government] buildings," McClellan with a train of wagons just for his coterie of staff officers, and even "the empty (intellectually and materially empty) White House could have given the soldiers comfortable night quarters." In a comparison of American and European officers, he said that "in European armies aristocratic officers would not dare to treat soldiers in this way." He had joined the Polish army in February 1831 and later related from his personal experiences soldiering in Poland without giving a specific location and time:

> More than once in my life, after heavy fighting, I laid down the knapsack for a cushion, snow for a mattrass [sic] and for a blanket; but by the side of the soldiers, the generals, the staffs, and the officers shared similar bedsteads.[54]

Despite such fervor and dedication, he determined at one point that the struggle was futile and even deserted briefly. He reemerged in Warsaw once more the radical political rabble-rouser who often found himself at odds with and alienating many of the leaders of the movement. When Warsaw fell in September 1831, he went to Paris and became involved with the Central Franco-Polish Committee and worked with the Marquis de Lafayette, one of the committee's sponsors.

During his sojourn in Paris, Gurowski wrote attacks on Adam Mickiewicz, the Polish poet and literary voice of Poland's "nationalistic spirit," for representing himself as a prophet for his country's hopes. Such behavior merely rallied other Poles behind Mickiewicz and further pushed Gurowski away from the mainstream. In his involvement with other radicals, he even consorted with Louis Napoleon "in planning revolts." Later to become emperor of France, Louis Napoleon was then a republican with decidedly anti-imperialist views and apparently never fully accepted Gurowski's radical doctrines.[55]

Gurowski's change of heart toward Russia would earn him the ever-lasting disdain of his fellow Poles. Embracing Pan-Slavism with Russia, not Poland, as the leading power and aligning himself with the court of Czar Nicholas made him virtually an ostracized "man without a country." He blamed the Poles for the disintegration of their country and accrued complete and utter scorn when he suggested that Russian replace the Polish language in schools. Gurowski went further and began to promote ideas that were absolutely heretical in light of Polish patriotic thinking at the time. He even implied that Russian would eclipse Polish as a language, and the Polish language would become an "insignificant dialect" for the common people. In essence, in the eyes of the Poles with whom he had once waged war against Russia, he had completed his transformation as a collaborator with the oppressor and a traitor to the ideals of his fatherland. He eventually became disenchanted with his erstwhile, lukewarm patron Russia, whose power-wielders, from the Czar down, never fully trusted him, and made his way through Europe to America.[56]

Gurowski was one of many observers in the early nineteenth century to address and embrace American exceptionalism. He pointed out that there were "two hearth-stones" on which the American nationality was centered: "democracy and self-government." He followed by citing that every other nation, "past or present," had different origins "from that of the American commonwealth."[57] Being of aristocratic background himself, he facilely pointed out that "privileged aristocratic superiority" is not what determined leadership, but that Americans had been brought together by "identical convictions, aims and principles" as well as ability and "mental superiority." He said this was especially evident in the New England states. In this way, he eschewed the idea of "gentry idleness" which he equated with the wealthy landowners in the South. He was of the republican view, popular in the decades following the Revolution, in which Americans appreciated the "dignity of labor, which aristocrats traditionally had held in contempt."[58]

There is evidence of Gurowski's sincerity with regard to his anti-slavery beliefs. He was not an abolitionist merely for political expediency, nor did he consider putting an end to slavery as just one part of the

North's war effort. In 1860 he published his analytical treatise on the subject. In it he disagreed with the concept that there were any socially constructive elements in the institution of human bondage. He termed slavery "the most corroding social disease" that was most fatal to "the slaveholding element in a community." He wrote that just as an individual's normal condition was "purity and virtue," it followed that it was normal for members of society to seek freedom over a life of oppression. This was "the normal condition of the individual" in a free society.[59] Gurowski addressed the question of slavery in his work *America and Europe,* and also loosed a diatribe against the culture of the American South. He did this to the extent that his publisher marketed the work only in the Northern states, declining to distribute it in the South so as not to hurt other sales.[60]

In *Slavery in History*, Gurowski did not concentrate on the institution in the American South but expounded on the subject by epoch and major world powers spanning the centuries. He did not equivocate in his critiques of those who were apologists for slavery. They were frequently "florid, sentimental, and idyllic in their praises and glorification of slavery," according to Gurowski. He also resorted to his usual bombastic vitriol when he charged that pro-slavery speakers produced nothing "but gaseous speeches" that were clearly not emanations "from vigorous or healthy minds." The "gas" that they produced was the result of "substances in process of decomposition." He theorized that future generations would only honor those leaders who spoke in favor of "a sacred cause or a grand idea" and carried out deeds of generosity. Such honor would go to those who acted as defenders of "human rights and liberties, and who brand with infamy every kind of oppression."[61]

He alluded to a Europe that was becoming a society with progressively more freedom while America was held back by its adherence to a system of legal bondage:

> Every day freedom gets a firmer and more enduring foothold in Europe. Every nation of the old continent enjoys greater liberty today than it did on the birthday of the American Republic ...
>
> But what civilization and humanity assert to be their greatest afflictions are upheld as blessings in this New World by the Young Republic. Sadness and even despair fill the mind when witnessing the loftiest and best social structure ever erected by man sapped to its foundations by the sacrilegious champions of bondage![62]

Gurowski had difficulty reconciling the concepts of liberty and freedom in America with the institution of slavery. In his view, the Southern planter class had adopted the attitudes of classic republicanism that the ancient Romans practiced where slave labor enabled the many freedoms of the ruling classes. Gurowski despised the slaveholding "aristocracy" of the South, yet he had had no trouble accepting the omnipotent Czar and the practices of the Russian Empire that made all its citizens subservient.[63]

The generation of Poles that succeeded men such as Gurowski, Tochman and Szymański took the mantle and resumed their nationalism and anti-imperial agitation. Contemporaries of Ludwik Żychliński, who took part in the European insurrections of the 1840s and also fought on the North's side in the Civil War, were Kargé and Wladimir Krzyżanowski. The beginning of Kargé's military career was in Prussia, and his first action was as an officer in the Royal Horse Guards during the "Springtime of Nations" unrest in Europe. In this anti-Imperial movement of the mid-nineteenth century in which proponents felt that "true nationalities had rights to autonomous self-expression," the Poles needed no encouragement.[64] The French rose against Louis-Philippe's regime, mobs took over parts of Berlin and Vienna, and Polish revolutionary committees moved to emancipate the peasantry and demand autonomy in Austrian-dominated areas. Even "the first German Parliament assembled in a mood of pan-European liberalism."[65] Kargé simultaneously belonged to a secret organization planning the resurgence of an independent Poland. Stationed in Berlin, he became part of a Prussian military force ordered to quell the uprising in the streets. When he was forced into action during the 1848 People's Revolt, he abandoned the attack on the people and took their side on the barricades. While the guards drew their weapons on the insurgents, Kargé "flung down his helmet and sword and lifting up his hands, he shouted at the top of his voice: 'Hoch lebe das Volk![66] Hoch lebe das Volk!'" With this proclamation of "Long live the people!" he challenged the authority of the army of which he was part. He even fired back on the soldiers, because "the chance to fight for liberty had propelled him into headlong action. The young revolutionary had dared and won."[67]

Despite his courage the victory was short-lived. Kargé returned home to Poznan but was later arrested and jailed. As a royal guard, he received lenient treatment, and after a short confinement he was paroled. As part of his clandestine activities for a resurgent Poland, Kargé had organized an elite Polish cavalry battalion, deserted the Prussian ranks and returned to Poznan to resume leading his horsemen under orders from the Polish Revolutionary Committee. "The Prussians now determined to break up the Polish military camps by force" and dispatched troops to quell the insurgent Poles. In a "savage encounter … with a Prussian cavalry force, Kargé's impetuous life almost ended." He received a pistol shot in the hand and a "second bullet shattered his knee, then an enemy lancer pierced his ribs."[68] Kargé was arrested and jailed as a traitor to the King of Prussia "and condemned to death by the Prussian authorities."[69] At the age of twenty-four, Kargé was awaiting a death sentence: conspiracy, desertion, treason, but while other conspirators were shot on the spot, a technicality saved him. As an officer, his sentence was awaiting "approval by the Secretary of War and countersigning by the King."

Kargé was again to receive a parole due to a technicality, but he was still in jail.[70] He was subsequently able to escape his imprisonment with the help of his family. Smuggled silk rope, bribery of the guards, and "fresh horses every fifteen miles around the route of escape" got him to the seaport of Szczecin. He made his way by boat to London, and eventually to America.[71] As an "enthusiastic republican," Kargé actively had engaged himself in the movement for Polish independence. For his participation in the 1848 insurrection, he "was compelled to leave his native country, and … finally landed in New York in 1851."[72] His escape had been a bold and daring one, but the events caused him to measure his fortunes and begin the practice of carefully weighing his options before making further decisions.

Krzyżanowski came from the same region as Kargé, and the two shared somewhat similar backgrounds. A brief examination into his pedigree yields evidence of his development as a soldier. He was born in the Grand Duchy of Poznan, the son of a land-owning nobleman and into a family that had "long been prominent in Polish political and historical records." He was a cousin of world-renowned composer Frederic Chopin and had three uncles who had thrown in their lot with Napoleon Bonaparte to fight with the French, hoping to further the cause for Polish independence.[73] When he was a student at the university, he was part of the intellectual faction of "Polish students who dreamed, talked and fought for Polish independence." He left his student life to take part in the short-lived 1846 Mieroslawski insurrection against Prussia. "As one of its participants, he was obliged to flee from Poland and sail for New York" where he became a civil engineer.[74]

He was perplexed by the injustices and class differences in an America that was based on freedom and equality. After the Civil War he bristled at the moderation of Lincoln's successor, President Andrew Johnson, who Krzyżanowski felt was allowing the Southerners who had just attempted (and failed at) "disunion by force" to return to power in Washington. He staunchly supported the election of Ulysses S. Grant, and on 29 May 1869 took the position of Supervisor of Internal Revenue for the District of Georgia and Florida, overseeing Treasury Department operations. It was during this assignment that he confronted the attitudes of diehard secessionism and bigotry in Georgia that also still existed in other parts of the South. Being of noble birth, Krzyżanowski was perplexed that certain whites looked upon themselves as aristocrats, while in their eyes Northerners were the descendants of "the scum of the European continent" who came to America to avoid imprisonment.[75] He thought this attitude strange since Georgia was founded as a colony in which imprisoned debtors from England could seek refuge and new lives. None of his rational arguments would sway the diehards and politicians, many of whom were tied to the new extremist, and often violent, Ku Klux Klan.

Ignatius Szymański did not have the antebellum career as a prolific writer of polemics as did Gurowski, or the legal and political work of Tochman, but just as they did, he had fought for Poland before coming to America. He did contribute a significant written work on Poland's situation, however. In 1832 while residing in Boston, the Polish exile became involved in helping the Committee of Aid that had been organized to assist newly arrived Poles.[76] In doing so, he consorted with influential people in literary and social circles. He later wrote the introductory address, "To the American Reader," for Harro Harring's 1834 work, *Poland Under the Dominion of Russia*. In it he used his voice as the instrument of a Polish warrior without a country and set the tone for himself and many of his countrymen who had been forced to leave their homeland because of their struggles against European empires. Szymański wrote in the third person as a witness to what took place:

> [A]n exile of Poland who presents to you this work. The storm which swept over his native land, has involved him [Szymański] in the general ruin, torn him from home, and friends, and country, and cast him a wanderer on a foreign shore. Bred in the Polish military school, it has been his fortune, before he had arrived at manhood, to turn against his enemies the weapons they taught him to use—to join with the enthusiasm in the general struggle for his country's rights—to see her for a moment free—to witness the blasting of her hopes—the slaughter of her sons—and then to be driven out to wander on through various parts of Europe, till he found a refuge in a land, which he had only dreamed of as a new and distant world.[77]

Szymański also declared that he was writing now as an American and that the author of the treatise, Harring, had been a German in the service of Russia. Still living in Boston, Szymański foreshadowed his own "rebel" character by declaring himself an American "who has been an eye-witness to the wrongs and the sufferings of the Poles." Because of his personal experiences, he could justify fighting "against enormous odds."[78] Once he had achieved a comfortable life in Louisiana, he did not express his reasons for espousing the Confederate cause. Whether it was to preserve that way of life, or defend his country—or just because it was his rebellious nature—Szymański did not record.

A decade later, Tochman lectured and published a work in a similar vein. He discussed the decline of Poland, attributed it to its progressive system and laws, and at the same time praised the brilliance of Polish concepts of freedom. He cited the *"Neminem captivabimus"* laws that ensured that a citizen could not be arrested without proof or evidence "until legally indicted for a crime." He added the foresight of such thinking and related it to the American system. Tochman also argued that the Poles had fostered such progressive thinking and liberalism while the rest of the European countries languished in feudalism. Hence it was little wonder why Poland produced people such as Pulaski and Kosciuszko, but did not have a Cromwell as did England, nor a character such as France's Robespierre. To emphasize his point, Tochman added a reference to the connection between America and Poland:

There has always been something in the very nature of her [Poland's] institutions, which must have influenced the social and political condition of all the European family and its offspring, these United States.[79]

Attitudes on the Eve of War

In America, Gurowski became an abolitionist and he displayed these sentiments in his writings for the *New York Tribune* when he worked as a journalist under Horace Greeley. As mentioned, he had freed the serfs on his lands in Poland long before serfdom ended in the Russian empire. Despite his noble heritage, he had contempt for and wanted to punish the self-anointed, aristocratic "southern *Chivalrous*" slave owners, and advocated the recruitment of blacks for colored regiments in the Union army. Gurowski even presented himself with a "willingness to take command of a negro regiment." The *Cleveland Morning Leader* added that there was "a movement on foot to have him commissioned for such a purpose."[80]

With regard to Southern success at thwarting the Union's military efforts, Gurowski marveled that "twenty millions of people, brave, highly intelligent, and mastering all the wealth of modern civilization, were, if not virtually overpowered, at least so long kept at bay by about five millions of rebels."[81] He lost his post at the State Department for publishing his *Diary* in which he criticized many Republicans, including President Lincoln and Secretary of State William H. Seward. Seward, he felt, was too conciliatory toward the South and put ambition above country. Ironically, Seward had been a colleague and associate of Tochman's in Washington before the war. Gurowski compared Lincoln to France's King Louis XVI—both had good intentions but neither had the intellect to deal with the huge cataclysmic events occurring while they were in power. His detractors felt that Gurowski was in a position in which he did not have full knowledge of the situation and "did not quite know what was going on."[82] Indeed he was one of the Radical Republicans of the period. He and they wanted to move on Richmond immediately and pre-emptively and felt that the Washington politicians who were in disagreement were "wiseacres." They were completely oblivious to the will of the populace: "not one understands the superiority of the people."[83]

The Radical Republicans considered him "one of the greatest thinkers of his age ... most would agree that Count Adam Gurowski was highly influential in both European and American politics." To others he was just another bothersome radical.[84]

Tochman had developed into an advocate for states' rights and felt the southern states had the right to self-determination. In his legalistic mind he supported "the assertion that each state was sovereign and had the right to secede whenever it wished, for the individual states were older than the union which they" had originally formed.[85] He wrote to President Jefferson Davis in Montgomery, Alabama, on 1 May 1861 and offered his services to the Confederacy. Yet there was more depth to his reasoning. Although he had always opposed serfdom in Europe and lauded the framers of the U.S. Constitution, he supported slavery in America. "After reviewing the history of slavery in the United States, he warned against the infusion of the white race with the colored on the grounds that the law of nature would eventually destroy the supremacy of the whites and create a degenerate race through biological process."[86] Jefferson Davis, in a message delivered that same year about the "Right of Secession," gave a similar justification for slavery:

> In moral and social condition they [the slaves] had been elevated from brutal savages into docile, intelligent, and civilized agricultural laborers, and supplied not only with bodily comforts, but with careful religious instruction. Under the supervision of a superior race, their labor had been so directed as not only to allow a gradual and marked amelioration of their own condition, but to convert hundreds of thousands of pure square miles of wilderness into cultivated lands, covered with a prosperous people; towns and cities had sprung into existence, and had rapidly increased in wealth and population under the social system of the South.[87]

Virginia, Tochman's state of residence, seceded from the Union on 17 April 1861. South Carolina had seceded 20 December 1860 (immediately after Lincoln's electoral victory) and the early Confederacy began with Montgomery, Alabama as its capital.[88] Davis accepted the Pole's May 1st offer, and Tochman went to New Orleans to begin recruiting troops for the Southern cause. One of New Orleans' prominent newspapers, the *Daily Crescent,* published the news: "A Polish Legion composed of our citizens of Polish birth, is about being organized. A meeting for this purpose was held on Saturday Evening, May 4, 1861."[89] Further news of his efforts appeared in another newspaper, the *Daily Picayune*: "Major G. Tochman, the well known Polish political exile, has tendered his services to the Confederate States, and has been authorized by the President to raise ... a brigade." It continued that Tochman was very influential "among his countrymen" and would be successful in his military efforts. The article made a special mention that Tochman "acquired quite an extensive notoriety in the country a number of years ago by his efforts to procure aid for his native Poland in her struggle for independence. He is now heartily with the South, and in all his exertions in behalf of the independence of the Confederate States, we wish him the greatest success."[90]

Not all Poles who emigrated to the U.S. were from the nobility. Though the main wave of Polish immigrants came to the Chicago area after 1865, "a scattering of Polish exiles from the Polish Insurrection of 1831 had filtered into Illinois in search of the land grants Congress had voted them." At the outset of the Civil War there were only about 500 in Chicago and around 800 more in the state of Illinois.[91] Just as Żychliński and Tochman, many of these arrivals had gained combat experience in Europe's wars and uprisings.[92] There was also the curious case of Captain Peter Kiołbassa, who started out in the Confederate service in a company of Poles from Panna Maria, Texas. Kiołbassa switched sides after capture, swore allegiance to the United States and then served with the 18th Illinois *Union* cavalry. Kiołbassa was "one of the most colorful Poles to become identified with Illinois." He grew up in the first Polish colony in the United States (Karnes County, Texas) and began his wartime service with the 24th Cavalry Regiment, Texas Mounted Volunteers. On an official muster roll for the 24th Texas Cavalry, he is listed as a "Bugler" with Capt. B.F. Fly's Company of Carter's Brigade of Texas Mounted Volunteers (see Appendix A). Kiołbassa's name disappears from the Confederate rolls after his capture at the start of 1863. According to the muster rolls, "part of this regiment was captured at Arkansas Post, Arkansas, January 11, 1863 and exchanged east of the Mississippi River in April and May 1863."[93]

Once a captive in Union hands, Kiołbassa had a choice to make on the spot: either remain in a Union prisoner of war camp in the

North or join the U.S. Army. Had he heard of comrades who, when captured, were sent to spend the winter in an open prison camp near Lake Michigan in Illinois or on Lake Erie in Ohio, it is likely that such a prospect would have facilitated his choice. He chose to join the U.S. Army, and after his assignment with the 18th Illinois Cavalry, ultimately rose to the rank of captain in the 6th U.S. Colored Cavalry in which capacity he served until the end of the war (see Appendix B).[94] This certainly would have afforded a different military perspective than that which he would have acquired in his service in the Texas Confederate cavalry.

In general, the Poles who settled in Karnes County, Texas, were not wholeheartedly in support of Secession. When Texas seceded from the Union and joined the Confederacy in March 1861, the entire process and upcoming tumult of the Civil War was new to the Poles. As recent arrivals, they "had not been in the United States long enough to participate in that election." The issue of slavery, threat of conscription and general difficult living conditions during the Civil War did not necessarily endear many of them to the Confederate cause.[95] These factors conflicted with their ideas of freedom and defense of liberty. The bleak picture of internment in a Yankee prison, and an uncertain future and assured privations would surely have influenced Kiołbassa's decision—as well as certain others in the same position—to avoid prison-of-war camps and go over to the Union side with some conviction.

In the South "peasant immigrants ... were concentrated mainly in two states, Texas and Louisiana, while the political emigrés were to be found mainly in Virginia and some of the bigger towns such as New Orleans and Richmond." By peasant standards, they were well off, skilled and could afford to buy land and establish farms. However, "the outbreak of the Civil War did not generate much enthusiasm among this group which considered the King Cotton ideology of the cotton-plantation owners something alien."[96] The Texas Poles were primarily grain and livestock farmers, and not in the planter class such as the large landholders of the eastern part of the state. According to the 1860 census, none of the Karnes County Poles grew any cotton. The typical farm had horses, dairy cows, oxen and other cattle, and "the average farm size was sixty-eight acres, thirty in improved land and the remainder in unimproved land."[97] In the Texas settlements of Silesian Poles "their life's profession is cultivating the land—farming."[98] "Only after compulsory military service was introduced in April 1862 did the Polish immigrants begin to don the gray uniforms of the Confederate Army."[99]

Just as they were throughout the South, the war years were difficult times for the Silesians of Karnes County. "Many of the things needed in daily living were simply not available or were too expensive for the peasants to afford." Additionally, their aversion to conscription by a foreign army (Prussian) had been among the reasons for emigrating to Texas from Europe. "The strong Unionist sentiment at Panna Maria after the war suggests that the settlement was opposed to the conflict from the outset."[100] This is evidenced in the 1866 recollections of Father Adolf Bakanowski who wrote about the post-war years in his memoirs:

> This [unsettled time in Texas after the end of hostilities] was shortly after the Civil War, which the Southerners lost. There was still no organized government, on the contrary, the Texans were even more lawless ... We still had to suffer much before the Northern states brought permanent order by means of military force. Texans, with few exceptions, are a purely wild nation ... The upper class is accustomed to being served by Negroes whom they treat according to whims with a totally unchristian tyranny ... In a word, we fell on bad times.[101]

Father Bakanowski was a Resurrectionist priest who served as one of three who ministered to the Polish Silesians in that part of Texas. The Resurrectionists were a distinctly Polish order established in Rome in 1842. Their formation as a ministry that would serve expatriate Poles primarily was a response to the Polish Insurrection of 1830. They "flourished in the Polish émigré community in western Europe. The principal centers of the congregation were its motherhouse in Rome and its mission to the Poles in Paris."[102] In this excerpt, Father Bakanowski gives a decidedly non-Southern view of post-war conditions. Although many of the Silesians served in the Confederate Army, the pro-Union sentiments of the community were to prove troublesome in the unsettled years after the war.

Grzeloński draws a distinction between the political émigrés who came to America and those of the peasant class that came for a "better life." He suggests that in comparing the two, it seemed that the Polish economic immigrants who became volunteer enlistees in "the Confederate Army had more often done so due to poverty or political disorientation rather than a belief in the justness of the southern cause. The same cannot be said, however, of the volunteers recruited from amongst the Polish political emigrés, for their choice was conscious and their commitment genuine." In this group he would include Tochman and his fellow gentry. These "Polish 'southerners' espoused the theory" that secession was a right provided for in the Constitution. It appears that with regard to support of slavery, southern Poles had less favorable opinions: "On the other hand, the system of slavery was supported by only a very few of them … And only a handful of them actually owned plantations and slaves themselves."[103]

Ludwik Żychliński addressed the slavery issue on moral grounds when he encountered some captured Poles from the Confederate army. He wrote that they had enlisted in the Southern army because of "poverty" but were willing to join the Union and pledge loyalty:

> In the Southern army there were quite a significant number of Poles. It seemed to me that fighting in a certain battle … we took prisoner quite a few Poles serving in the cavalry who were much amazed when I spoke Polish to them and upbraided them on how they could serve a cause so debased and in defense of slavery. They explained that the war found them in the Southern states and being poor they had to enlist in the army. But they would willingly enter into the ranks of the United States, and they gave a promise that they would not again fight against the army of the Northern states. I helped them gain their freedom and they were sent to General Krzyżanowski, who at the time led a division. What happened to them I did not find out because on April 20, 1863, I left the ranks of the United States in order to take part in the uprising and in this way to pay my debt to the Fatherland.[104]

Żychliński never refrained from criticizing American ways if he felt they went contrary to his ideals. Monetary reward had not been in the equation that had provided his incentives to fight for a cause. He was dismayed by the practice in which certain citizens could avoid induction into the army by paying to have another enlist in his place. The substitute would then serve and fulfill the sponsor's military service obligations.

Żychliński's countryman, Valery Sulakowski, also clung to the ideals of revolutionary thought fostered by the Springtime of Nations that had motivated him in Europe. Sulakowski recoiled with shame at what he characterized as Americans conducting their lives as if gaining wealth was their loftiest goal. He expressed hope that after fighting and suffering in Europe, he was coming to an America still burning with the spirit of George Washington and the country's founders. He would have rejected the notion that the equality envisioned by the revolutionary thinkers had devolved into a system that allowed money to become more important than rights.[105]

Adam Gurowski was always prepared to weigh in with his opinion on the best ways to conduct international affairs but did not exhibit the idealism of Sulakowski and Żychliński. In the early days of the conflict, he spoke out on the involvement of European powers and advised the U.S. government on how best to cultivate alliances. England could not be trusted and might go so far as to take the opportunity "to avenge many humiliations" and side with the Rebels. He recommended nurturing favorable diplomatic relations with France and his former republican colleague, Louis Napoleon. This would put a "wedge" between the French and the British who were in an alliance. Less doctrinaire than pragmatic, the Count suggested that the "cold, taciturn Louis Napoleon is full of broad and clear conceptions," and that the North could rely "almost explicitly, on France and him." He ignored the fact that the latest Napoleon had joined the exclusive, anti-republican European imperial club and had other interests that would keep France non-committal in the American war.[106]

Żychliński's European training and attitude toward military service were evident in his conduct in the Union army. He downplayed the hardships of soldiering while complaining about camp life, but relished the idea of fighting for something in which he believed. Żychliński differed from other officers in that he was not seeking political advancement or pursuing a military career. However, as an observer and critic, he was always willing to express his sentiments. In his memoirs, he easily admired the dedication of his enemies, the Confederate soldiers, and praised the virtues of the Southern people and their ability to put their cause above their hardship. On the other hand, though he shouldered arms to protect America, he was not afraid to be opinionated about the lack of patriotic zeal he perceived in Federal recruits and the existing system in the army that enabled privileged citizens to avoid service.

Throughout his memoirs, he drew comparisons frequently but overall Żychliński loved America and he loved his native Poland. Ultimately he proved he was willing to fight for both.

Żychliński did not shy away from expressing his frank opinions of the Union army, its officers and men. He offered his assessment of the morale, motivation and sincerity of the soldiers. "Despite his obvious support for the Union cause," wrote one historian, "Żychliński is not uncritical of various aspects of American life; he is scathing about military corruption and war profiteering and condemns the treatment of the Indians."[107] He also discusses military efficiency and organization, sometimes during specific actions. Żychliński also told of being able to see President Lincoln "up close" and "note his attendants and behavior" when visiting the army. This may have been a reference to a visit made in early May on the Peninsula when the President reviewed General George B. McClellan's troops.[108] Lincoln's next official visit was in July when he "was received with great enthusiasm ... dined with General Burnside on board the *Alice Price*" and departed after an hour and a half.[109] At this time, however, Żychliński would have been recuperating from wounds and not present. Significant and illuminating are his comparisons of American and European military ceremony. He described a review of troops by President Lincoln, as leader of a nation of 40 million people and a million-man volunteer army, and contrasts it to how it would unfold if the situation occurred in Europe:

> In America the spirit of freedom and equality was everywhere serious and powerful, whereas in Europe, with the pomp of a feudal atmosphere, reviews and parades in the armies were conducted with a certain stiffness and slave-like submissiveness, fraught with fright and a disheartening of the spirit that was always visible on the faces of the generals, officers and soldiers. In Europe, each soldier shook from fear during a parade. ... raised their hearts in joy that this torment had finished [when the parade and review had ended].[110]

Żychliński attributed McClellan's difficulties with Washington to his affiliation with the Democratic Party and the enmity of the Lincoln Republicans, and to a greater degree the radical or "Black Republicans," one of whom was Secretary of War Edwin Stanton. Another was Żychliński's fellow countryman, Count Adam Gurowski, a friend of Stanton's. This element of Lincoln's own party believed in the total abolition of slavery, the granting of legal equality to blacks, and was willing to "dismember the Union to accomplish their goals." They (Gurowski among them) also charged their opponents with supporting a "slavocracy," which was a "slaveholding aristocracy" for the elite few who would "destroy the country by its promulgation of slave dependency."[111] McClellan did not improve his standing by writing a letter to Stanton in which he accused the government of not "sustaining" the army. He also stated that he owed "no thanks to you or to any other persons in Washington. You have done your best to sacrifice this army." It hastened the general's removal from command, as Stanton had wanted for some time.[112]

Count Gurowski, always trivialized by his contemporary critics as well as later historians because he held only a minor position in the government, wrote disparagingly with regard to Northern military preparations. He predicted seriously heavy losses of men and materiel if the faulty preparations were not remedied. A cabinet member and some-time Lincoln detractor, Secretary of State William Henry Seward, agreed with this view. But the Count often was considered a "caustic and intransigent émigré."[113] As a character he was "saturnine" and "doctrinaire," a "self-deceived observer," and despite being a friend and associate, he criticized Seward for wanting to compromise and negotiate with the South. This occurred when Gurowski took up residence in Washington during the build-up to war in the spring of 1861. He worked behind the scenes of the Peace Convention and met with delegates to further his anti-secession views. He also revealed plots that he and his fellow radicals insisted were brewing. One of these plots was the planned armed take-over of the Federal government by a mobilized Southern faction in conjunction with President Lincoln's inauguration on 4 March 1861. Gurowski also expressed his willingness to take up arms and defend the capital, despite his age (56 years), if there was an assault on Washington.[114]

Gurowski had led a full life and developed his portfolio as a revolutionary in Europe before coming to the United States. In America, Gurowski became an abolitionist and he displayed these sentiments in his writings for the *New York Tribune* when he worked as a journalist. While in that position, he also expounded on other ideas, including the then current affair of the Italian Federation and the discord between the various autonomous and feuding states in Italy. It seemed a metaphor for the American situation. At one point he affirmed that "traditions, love of localities, or nationalities ... are inherent in human nature, and must be respected." He went on to write, "Italy cannot be divided into two units—a Northern and a Southern. Between them a counterpoise is necessary." If not an overt, it is an implied comparison to the growing tension between the northern and southern states in America.[115]

In his book *America and Europe,* published in 1857, Gurowski described America and its people and compared them with Europe in several areas, including the character of the citizenry and slavery. He asserted that the "ancient hereditary alienations" that different nationalities may have had toward each other ancestrally in Europe "melt and evaporate" in the United States. Independence was sacred and patriotism was "not an effort, but a natural lineament of character, a simple but inherent element of national life."[116] With regard to slavery, he advocated a gradual emancipation of the slaves who had been in a systematically degraded condition that barely recognized "in them any human and social qualities." He summarized his convictions on the issue:

> Slavery ... has eaten itself, not only into the political and municipal institutions, but into social, domestic and family life, into the mind, the conscience, the judgment, the reasonings, the religion, the human and animal feelings, the comprehension of the rights, obligations, and duties of a man, of a citizen, of a member of society, as it has permeated those devoted to its growth and preservation.[117]

Gurowski proves to be the most curious study among this group of Poles. In another comparison with his fellow Pole who fought in the Civil War, it is important to note that he and Ignatius Szymański were both members and soldiers of the Polish Patriotic Society to which they had pledged fealty. The group opposed every facet of Russian authority and Czar Nicholas ordered its dismemberment. The oath of initiation to the Society, sworn before God and country with all sincerity included:

> I pledge my sacred honor, that I will exert all my powers for the reestablishment of my beloved native land; and that, if necessary, I will sacrifice for her independence, my fortune and my life. Reckless of personal consequences, I will spare not the blood either of a traitor, or of any one who shall be in action against the good of my country. If I violate these engagements, may the death of a dog and a traitor be my lot! may my name pass accursed, from mouth to mouth, till the latest posterity, and may my body be abandoned to the beasts of the forest!—I call on God to witness my sincerity.[118]

This was before Gurowski adopted his Pan-Slavic views and went to Russia. It also preceded his residency in the United States and his promotion of an alliance with Poland's enemy. Szymański, on the other hand, obeyed his forsworn promises and even bore his attitudes with him to America.

There is no simple method with which to categorize the Poles who came to America and became embroiled in the Civil War. Whatever extent their involvement, whatever their positions politically, ideologically or culturally, they represent a microcosmic glimpse of the complexities of the war. To juxtapose Poles who fought in the 1830 war as compatriots with their identical nationalistic notions and the same political goals is to find them in lock-step ideologically. However, if examined some thirty years later when they were in America, they have dichotomous views. Tochman and Gurowski exemplify this. Gurowski's mid-life embrace of the Russian version of Pan-Slavism and his virulent support of abolition would have been anathema to Tochman. As a Union soldier, Ludwik Żychliński was on another level. He chastised captured Poles in Confederate uniforms for fighting for an unjust cause, yet would have bristled at Gurowski's extremism and furthermore despised anything Russian. He, like Tochman, would have rejected the Pan-Slavist movement and characterized it as Russia's justification for its imperial expansionism.

The Poles on either Union or Confederate side who came from the peasant or working classes would not necessarily have the depth of philosophical knowledge or ideals embraced by their counterparts of the educated gentry. The Polish Texans or Chicago Poles may not have been familiar with the philosophical writings of Goslicki; however, concepts such as liberty and self-determination, for example, would still have been part of their composition. This would come about by means of a "trickle down" effect through social and cultural channels. They would have been aware of the struggles and achievements of their predecessors (Kościuszko, for example) as well as the ideals that inspired them.

The Poles who took up arms for the Union and were supportive of preserving the unity of the United States did not arrive on American shores envisioning themselves as crusaders. Though sharing similar political reasons among themselves for departing Europe and settling in America, they frequently had divergent goals and used different methods to achieve them. Some of them may have agreed politically and philosophically on most issues with many of their Polish counterparts on the Confederate side, with the exception of their allegiances to the new country. However, once they were in America and the fever of war had taken hold of the populace, they set about their martial work with the zeal of crusaders. These supporters of the Union who had had military experience in Europe were willing to put it to use and embrace the movement to preserve the United States. Besides their Polish origins and unwavering support for Polish independence, the common threads that ran through their lives were intangibles: sense of duty coupled with rigid principles, republican ideology and anti-slavery sentiment.

CHAPTER 3

ALLIES TO ADVERSARIES

The first major rebellion against Russian rule in Poland after Kościuszko's Insurrection produced the future Civil War participants Gaspard Tochman, Adam Gurowski and Ignatius Szymański. The three went in different directions afterward: Gurowski adopting pro-Russian Pan-Slavist views and becoming a Northern abolitionist and radical, Tochman and Szymański siding with the South. In their pre-war careers in America, they each successfully bridged the chasm between the already boiling revolutionary insurgencies in Europe and the simmering turmoil in the United States. In Poland, they had been actively involved in the armed insurrections, whereas in their new country they strove to create an impact with the written and spoken word. In their separate ways, each of these men produced seminal work that in some cases would inspire and have an immediate impact on others, and have a lasting effect on those they touched. Gurowski expounded on his views of Europe and America in his personal writings and those as a journalist. Tochman wrote, addressed the public, and was active in the legal system, sometimes at the highest levels. Szymański, though less prolific, produced a striking essay on Poland's plight from an ex-revolutionary warrior's perspective.

As the country edged closer to armed conflict, they too sidled from the ideologue's lectern toward the militant's camp. Gurowski, in his late 50s, did not take to the battlefield in the war, even though he was willing, but he held significant sway with the Radical Republicans. Tochman produced effective orations and writings before the war and then organized troops in the young Confederacy. Szymański played a part in the failed defense of New Orleans and then had a more effective role as a negotiator for prisoner exchanges between the Union and Confederate armies later in the conflict.

Gaspard Tochman

Gaspard Tochman was originally from the Rzeszów region in the Austrian section of tripartite Poland. He studied law in Warsaw and served as an officer under his uncle, General Jan Skrzynecki, in the Polish army in the war against Russia in 1830–31. After the failure of the insurrection, he went into exile rather than accept the amnesty offered him by the Russian government. The fact that he had refused the Czar's pardon four times suggested that he was unwilling to bend in spirit to his enemy. He fought with distinction at the battle of Białołęka in February 1831 for which he was awarded the highest military honors. After spurning the proposed amnesty, Tochman began his exile abroad in France, first settling in Avignon and later in Paris. He worked for the military-aristocratic group of the Polish National Committee there until he departed for America in 1837.[1] Once there, he became a successful lawyer and campaigned for Polish independence while touring the country. Using his legalistic analysis of the U.S. Constitution, he justified siding with the Confederacy and raised troops for the war effort.[2]

When Gaspard Tochman brought his campaign for Polish independence from Russia to America, he was unaware of the sectional strife that existed in his new country of residence. He entered the legal profession and began his mission to raise awareness for Poland's situation and influence the opinions of the people he met. In doing so, he always kept his eye on events in Europe with a goal of restoring Poland to its pre-partition independence. Like Żychliński who arrived later, he recognized and appreciated the liberties enjoyed by citizens in the United States that did not exist in a Europe dominated by imperial powers. In America he could travel freely, address groups in planned assemblies, and he could do so without interference from the authorities. In this aspect, it hearkened back to a Poland known by his ancestors, the Commonwealth that enjoyed an earlier antecedent version of such freedom.[3]

Gaspard Tochman

Gaspard Tochman was resolute in carrying the Polish war against occupation by the Russian empire to the United States. In doing so, he laid the groundwork for the identification of the future Southern cause for secession and independence with that of Poland's struggle for freedom. In an address given to members of state legislatures from seven states at the New Jersey state convention, he addressed the "social, political and literary condition of Poland." In his speech, he paid special attention to relations with Russia with regard to its disposition toward the United States. He connected aspects of the history of Poland with that of the development of the United States. Tochman pointed out that during the "age of universal intolerance" in Europe that was beset by the Thirty Years War and religious persecutions, "there always was in Poland more freedom in the spiritual power, and more independence in the secular than [in] any other" of the countries of the Christian world.[4]

Tochman invoked the spirits of Pulaski and Kościuszko when he said that the "muskets of the heroes of Lexington, Concord and Bunker Hill echoed in Europe" for liberty, while Poland was suffering from the oppression of despotic foreign governments during the partitions. Poland, he said, never produced an intolerant leader such as an Oliver Cromwell, and "the welfare of all mankind has always been closely identified with the very existence of Poland, [a country which has] always been the champion of Christendom, the patron of civilization."[5] With that statement, Tochman presaged Jefferson Davis' speeches of later years that expressed umbrage at the general intolerance that Northerners had toward the Southern way of life.

At the end of his lecture, the bodies unanimously passed resolutions in support of Poland and Tochman's proposals. Attendees included the legislatures of two states, Virginia and Massachusetts, one slave and one free, that had led the colonies in the Revolution against Britain. In fewer than fifteen years they would be opposing each other in the Civil War.

Tochman would have been comfortable addressing these legislative bodies. He had been a successful lawyer in Warsaw, where he had attended university and law school before the November Insurrection of 1830–31. In the fighting against the Russians, he held the rank of Major and received the "cross of the Polish Legion of Honor," the *Virtuti Militari* medal for his gallant services.[6] He lived in Paris for a time after the failure of the insurrection, then came to the United States after 1837. He became a naturalized U.S. citizen in 1840 and began to study law in New York. He passed the bar, "opened an office in Wall Street" and later obtained a license to practice before the Supreme Court.[7] He became popular among intellectual and literary circles with his extensive lecture tour in which he worked to promote Poland's independence. Tochman determined that in the press there was an increase in favorable commentary on Czarist Russia that was not in Poland's best interests. He declared that he lectured "the American public on behalf of" Poland in "defense of the same cause whose failure" brought him to America, not to provoke a war by the Americans "on Poland's hangmen, but in order to win over public opinion."[8] He also conducted publicized debates, especially in print, with pro-Russian writers. The *National Intelligencer* was one such publication and Tochman was particularly incensed by the assertion that the "resurrection of Poland" seemed as likely as that of the Roman Empire. This was one of several articles written on issues in northern Europe by a "Professor Darby" [sic] who used the pen name of "Tacitus" and challenged Tochman to a debate on the question of Poland, especially with regard to Russia. Darby withdrew the challenge when Tochman accepted, but he did agree to attend a lecture on the subject that the Polish officer was giving in Georgetown and, as Tochman wrote, "the controversy came to an end."[9]

The next stage of Tochman's endeavors in his American experience came with what to him would have been the unthinkable: Russian imperial attempts to confiscate the fortunes and property of Thaddeus Kościuszko in the United States. The Russian ambassador Alexander Bodisco had put forth demands against Kościuszko's heirs in America for the rights to the Polish patriot and American general's property in the United States. Because Tochman served as legal counsel for the heirs, the ambassador went beyond the standard protocols of diplomatic maneuvering in pursuing action against Tochman personally and professionally. He attempted to have him removed from representation in the case, citing that Tochman had fought in the rebellion against the Czar in the 1830–31 Insurrection.[10] This became another facet in his enmity toward Russia and possibly may have furthered his feeling of dissociation from the U.S. government when he initially perceived, then realized, that the State Department was siding with Bodisco and the Russians. Since Tochman had become popular as a public speaker, was an attorney and involved in political circles, he was able to attract an audience and had influential friends. As such, he could present his case to the lawmakers of the country themselves. He summarized his struggle in this case to the United States Congress:

For the last twenty-two months, I have been the object of a most wanton and unwarrantable persecution of a foreign policy: or of an attempt to visit upon me, in this land of liberty, the penal laws of a despotic power, for alleged political offences against that power, to wit: for the part which I took in defending the liberties and independence of Poland, against the encroachments and rapacity of Russia … I am a native of Poland; that I took an active part against Russia as a major in the army, during the war for independence of Poland, in 1830; that for having done so, I was exiled from Poland, in 1831, and had my property confiscated by that ever grasping sovereign—the autocrat, in 1835.[11]

Tochman thought it unconscionable that the autocratic empire against which he had fought was now attempting to seize assets of a hero to America and Poland on the very soil for which Kościuszko had fought to make free. The Czar's Imperial Russia, still a stronghold of serfdom, was seeking gains from a patriot who had spoken against slavery in America. In fact, he had conditioned in his will that the slaves given to him as part compensation for his military services be freed. Further galling Tochman, the Russian ambassador was attempting to make "the penal laws of Russia for political offences against that country" applicable to him in America.[12] Certain aspects of the legal wrangling also disturbed American friends of Tochman who were concerned about the possibilities of a foreign delegation exerting influence in U.S. courts. Through a series of petitions, Tochman's supporters and those of Kościuszko's heirs asserted that it was the "duty of every American citizen not to permit the interference of a foreign minister near this Government, with rights, privileges, and professional pursuits of a naturalized citizen of this country, to attain the end of a foreign policy."[13]

The next step was to make public the workings of the Russian diplomatic delegation and the American legal team in its employ. Tochman did that with an exposé about the lead attorney opposing him, Joseph H. Bradley, whom he said had attacked him personally and professionally throughout the legal proceedings. In a series of letters, he demanded satisfaction to the point of even suggesting a more serious confrontation of the sort "recognized by gentlemen in the settlement of personal matters."[14] Tochman's attorney interceded and wrote to Bradley that he easily could make baseless accusations and commit slander but was unable to substantiate anything, and Bradley backed away from the confrontation.[15]

Alexander de Bodisco was the Czar's ambassador to the United States whom Tochman battled while representing the Kościuszko heirs against Russian claims against their property.

During this period, Tochman was largely the driving force behind the formation of the Polish Slavonian Literary Association in New York. Members of the group included its President, John McPherson Berrien, U.S. Senator from Georgia, and its Second Vice President, Benjamin F. Butler, later to be known as "Beast Butler" when he was military governor of New Orleans. With his talents as a "dynamic public speaker," Tochman spearheaded the association's activities and worked to further Polish causes. Ultimately a lack of funding limited their activities.[16]

There proved to be three occurrences that proved more instrumental in gaining influence for Tochman's cause: his public speaking, a move to the South, and the broadening of his sphere of personal contacts. Tochman embarked on a lecture tour to promote the Polish freedom movement in the United States. He made his permanent residence in Virginia, not far from the seat of government in Washington. With this proximity to the capital, he was able to increase his circle of influential friends. In his series of lectures given around the country, he presented an argument against Russia's tyrannical and unjust occupation of Poland. He was successful in winning public opinion and gathered the resolutions of several state legislatures in support of the Polish cause. He argued that free people and supporters of liberty should side with Poland (especially against Russia) and be concerned with her fate.[17] From autumn 1840 well into 1841, he delivered more than thirty-five lectures in states including Ohio, Virginia, Kentucky and Pennsylvania. The following year he organized rallies for Poland called "Polish Nights" that were public gatherings in different cities and towns. He continued with his lecture program and delivered the final address of the tour on 23 May 1844 in New Jersey.[18] During that period he addressed well over a quarter million people in more than a hundred lectures, in venues that ranged from town meetings to state legislatures.[19] His lectures often invoked the spirit of Kościuszko, and despite being foreign-born and speaking with an accent, he delivered them with "thrilling bursts of eloquence."

In these speeches, Tochman formulated a nineteenth century argument for the concept of a worldwide community. He told his audiences that because of travel and international commerce, events and "developments on one side of the Atlantic" were "vitally important to communities on the other" side.[20] He shared similar views with his countryman, Ludwik Żychliński, with regard to the concepts of modern progress: "Steam power and the pursuits of commerce, have brought you so near to Europe: that you are no longer inhabitants of a new world."[21] Tochman argued that Americans had two choices: they could either be proactive now or deal with the despotism of Europe's anti-democratic powers later. He especially pointed to the Poles "struggling for their liberties" to resurrect their country.[22]

In finding common ground with those who attended his lectures, Tochman would draw parallels between Poland's situation and the American quest for freedom. He warned that Russia was not an ally of the United States but instead an opportunistic "foe," and his stirring rhetoric imbued the audience with the spirit that "it was the cause of the United States to espouse that of Poland."[23] Citizens' groups would often endorse Tochman's cause by passing resolutions that condemned Poland's partition and called for the country's resurrection following his talks, as exemplified by the Gettysburg, Pennsylvania gathering in June 1843. That same day the Gettysburg *Adams Sentinel* reported that the admission of Texas to the Union would lead to the dissolution of the country over the issue of slavery: by the northern states if Texas were admitted as a slave state; by the southern states, if admitted with slavery abolished.[24]

Tochman moved his family to permanent residence in Virginia in 1852, settling into "an elegant life" on a "beautiful farm near Washington."[25] He immediately involved himself in political activities, and by 1860 was a Virginia delegate to the state's Democratic convention where he was an avid supporter of Stephen A. Douglas. The delegates announced their intentions to promote political moderation, what was best for the country as a whole, and perhaps above all, the "preservation of the Union." Douglas, they felt, was the best candidate for unity going forward. The adoptive Virginian from Poland addressed the convention with enough effect that the Convention ordered immediately the printing and publication of "50,000 copies of Maj. Tochman's speech."[26]

The series of events beginning with Lincoln's election, the secession of South Carolina and states of the deep South, then Virginia's departure on 17 April 1861 led to Tochman's decision to "throw in his lot with the South."[27] When news of his siding with the Confederacy became well known throughout Polonia—in America as well as in Europe—there was an outcry from some circles. Some of Tochman's countrymen roundly criticized him for what they felt was abandoning the principles of freedom. Others could sympathize with his anti-Russian stance and agreed with his position in opposing the Czar's alliance with the U.S. As he was considered a leader among the community of Polish émigrés, his moves created quite an impression in America and Europe.[28] He put forth a rebuttal to his critics in a letter written the day after Christmas 1861. Writing from Nashville, Tennessee, he laid out the rationale for his motives and actions as a "citizen of the Confederate States" who had been "*formerly,* a naturalized citizen of the United States [Tochman's italics]." Tochman's legal mind was evident in his argument when he asserted that the very tenets of the U.S. Constitution guided his decision to side with the Confederacy. The states individually had the right to change their government when it did not meet their needs as provided for in the original Constitution:

> It is submitted, that the Declaration of Independence asserts the people's right to self government, and also their right to change their governments and create new, whenever the old cease to answer the ends for which they had been established; and, the Act of Confederation (the first fundamental law of the new-born federal Republic,) consonant with *that* assertion in the Declaration of Independence, *expressly* reserves to each State its "sovereignty, freedom and independence."[29]

He reasoned that the Constitution and the United States was not the product of ratification by the people "acting in the *aggregate capacity,*" rather by each state "acting in its sovereign capacity." Tochman also weighed in with a justification for slavery and used racial theories common at the time as part of his logic. Slaves were "'persons held to labour' *instead* of slaves," and had the voting representation of "three fifths of their number" which was:

> A wise and humane elevation of a race of men,—which by a logical consequence makes their labour the property of its owner, secures and protects *it* Constitutionally as such, and yet acknowledges *them* to be men of inferior race— consistently with the dictates of the law of their nature—whereby it pleased Providence to segregate them from the homogeneous society of the Caucasian race by the inborn differences in their organism and its properties which no human law can alter.[30]

By making such deductions, Tochman adopted the same rationale used by many southern supporters of slavery as well as northerners who condoned the institution. Here he was lodging a superior versus inferior racial argument similar to the tack that Jefferson Davis used in suggesting that whites were benignly "elevating" blacks to a better position through the institution of slavery. At least southern blacks had partial representation in the system. His logic proved more convincing when he based his argument on interpretation of the Constitution, the subversion of which culminated with Abraham Lincoln's election to the presidency:

> This unconstitutional struggle finally terminated, last year, in the inauguration of the President of the United States elected by the sectional vote of the consolidated Northern Free States *exclusively,* with their sectional majority in both branches of Congress. Their triumph has virtually, though not ostensibly, subverted the Constitution and transformed the United States into a consolidated *empire* under that name merely.[31]

His very use of the term "empire" suggested a comparison of the United States to Czarist Russia and would have made him and like thinkers bristle.

Tochman declared that even if he had been a resident of the northern states, he would have sided with the South for constitutional reasons. While living in Virginia and conducting business and legal affairs in Washington, he became acquainted with and befriended Jefferson Davis. Davis had been U.S. Senator from Mississippi and Secretary of War prior to taking the reigns as president of the Confederacy in 1861. They shared many views on the issues of slavery as well as the Constitution. When Tochman, in a letter of 1 May 1861 addressed to "His Excellency, Jeff. Davis, President of the C.S." offered his services "in any capacity," Davis acknowledged it in his diary notes, referring to Tochman as a "native of Poland who left there in 1831 now a naturalized citizen and Washington lawyer, [who] claims that the North has subverted the Constitution, and that secession 'is only a defensive measure.'"[32]

Tochman's case was unique in that he had lived in both the North and the South, but his real roots were European. Additionally, he formulated for himself and others a legal argument based primarily on the Constitution. He differed from the most famous person who exemplified the agonizing choice between North or South, Robert E. Lee, who decisively placed his primary loyalty in his home state of Virginia. As an adoptive Virginian, Tochman may have held a view similar to many of his contemporaries who were without a personal stake in the institution of slavery: an attitude of benign acceptance. "In general, Confederate officers from Virginia owned very few slaves," and in this way were similar to other Southerners who supported the Confederacy. Many Southern officers and men, and by extrapolation "the great majority of Virginians who fought for the Confederacy had no direct economic stake in slavery."[33] A more precise statistic would be that "9.4% of the men in the Army of Northern Virginia or their immediate families owned 1 or 2 slaves," whereas "6.9% owned 20 or more slaves and qualified for the planter class."[34]

After offering his services to his new country, the Confederate States of America, Tochman began his mission to raise troops for the Southern army. He first journeyed to Montgomery, Alabama, the Confederacy's new capital. While he was away, authorities in Washington arrested Mrs. Tochman on 3 September 1861 and incarcerated her in the Federal jail there. She was among the "suspected and disloyal persons" and listed as "Madam Tochman" in the "persons received at the Old Capitol Prison other than prisoners of war." She reported her release later that month and told the *Daily Republican* that she had received good treatment at the hands of the government officials.[35]

Meanwhile, in Montgomery, Tochman began his services in the new capital. On 20 May 1861 he was armed with official authority from the Secretary of War, Leroy P. Walker, to raise troops.[36] The most fertile recruiting soil for him proved to be Louisiana, and in one and a half months' time Tochman had raised 1,700 men, of which just over 1,400 were foreigners. A small percentage of the men were of Polish origin and the others were Irish, French, German and native-born Americans. One of his aides in the early forming of the brigade was Major Frank Schaller. Schaller, often grouped with the Poles because of his birth, spoke German as his first language. He married into the Sosnowski family of South Carolina and later fought with Mississippi troops. Tochman took him under his wing to assist in organizing Camp Pulaski in Louisiana and drilling a company in the brigade in the summer of 1861. Schaller later served under and had a somewhat stormy relationship with Sulakowski.[37]

Tochman expected a general's commission as fitting a commander of a brigade, and his supporters already had nominally referred to him as having that rank. The *Richmond Dispatch* reported that Tochman's recruitment efforts were successful. In Louisiana in "some six weeks" he raised two infantry regiments that composed a brigade of men who were predominately "foreign-born." These new soldiers for the Confederacy brought military experience, including "many who have fought in the battles of Europe" before coming to America. Tochman's Polish Brigade had an artillery battery in its possession for which the people of New Orleans had raised funds and donated to complement the newly formed martial assemblage. Additionally, the brigade's cadre of officers "unanimously" supported his organizational efforts and popularity when they proclaimed themselves "The Polish Brigade." Here Tochman encountered his initial obstacle in obtaining his sought-after field command, politics, as stated in the *Dispatch*:

> When Tochman's first regiment was completed he repaired to Richmond to obtain arms for the brigade, and take the preliminary steps for getting his command into the field, when the Government, probably giving way to the demands of influential Louisiana politicians, refused to commission him as a brigadier, merely offering him a regiment.[38]

Some of the "politicians" felt that the troops "belonged to the State of Louisiana" because Tochman raised them there. Davis himself noted on 16 September 1861 that Tochman "was insulted by offer of colonelcy" and that the dissolution of his brigade was due to the political machinations of "wire pullers."[39]

There also developed some confusion as to the breadth of Tochman's authority to raise troops. The Confederate authorities willingly accepted the two regiments, but certain detractors cast doubt as to his original mission. The *New Orleans Delta* reported (possibly politically motivated) that Tochman originally was to have raised troops from "Polish and German citizens in the Northern States," but because of the Union army's presence, he proceeded south to recruit his brigade in Louisiana. This made little sense—raising troops for the Confederacy in the North—and furthermore was inaccurate. Tochman provided the actual authorization from Secretary of War Walker and thereby settled the matter of his official responsibility. Only the official confirmation of his rank as general remained at issue.[40]

The *Richmond Dispatch* opined unreservedly in Tochman's favor. The newspaper seemingly took note of Tochman's message delivered numerous times over the years and invoked the Polish ideal of a freedom fighter and the memory of Thaddeus Kościuszko. The *Dispatch* questioned the wisdom of the Confederate government's denial "to the old Polish veteran the command he has so justly earned," then cited that his friends were "legion" and hoped that such a "misunderstanding" would "yet be cleared up" for the benefit of the country.[41] Tochman was the proper choice for promotion. Jefferson Davis may have been misled or misinformed, according to the *Dispatch*, but Walker, the former Secretary of War, was completely misguided:

> General Tochman ... is guided by the most honorable motives, the President, no doubt, has been but imperfectly made acquainted with the facts of the case. Nor seems the late Secretary to have been most friendly [towards Tochman]. Tochman's resignation has not yet been accepted, and we most earnestly request the Administration not to accept it; for in Tochman we would lose a great military leader, a firm hand and a clear head. Every Pole who offers his arm to our cause has a peculiar claim upon our esteem and generosity, we would be ill-requite the memory of the great Kosciusko [sic] did we act otherwise.[42]

Tochman did tender his resignation over what he deemed a snub from the political hierarchy. As he had been in Poland, he had hoped to be a leader in the military effort to establish a new nation, in this instance the Confederate States of America. The rejection, however, did not mark the end of his support for the cause. During the first two years of the war, he was vigorous in his efforts to have his general's rank recognized. He had many supporters and always "retained his belief in the international significance of the Confederacy's fight for independence."[43] In 1863 people still referred to him as "Gen. Tochman" regarding news of "The Polish Brigade" as in the New Orleans *Daily Picayune* report of the dispute over his commission and recompense. He had the authority to raise troops, which "after spending much time and money, he did raise the brigade," but the President "only tendered him the commission of Colonel," which Tochman declined. He wanted the "Brigadiership" and reimbursement for expenses incurred.[44]

In a letter to the Confederate Secretary of State, Judah P. Benjamin, Tochman reaffirmed his support for the Southern cause but expressed his disappointment at not receiving his due rank. He wrote on 6 November 1863 that he was faithful to the cause but that "passing events in Poland … and the attitude which the rest of Europe is assuming in relation to the Polish question," required his services in the rebellion against Russia. He planned a return to Poland to fight, but would continue to "defend the principles" that initially led him to "take part in this war" and even raise "a brigade of troops for the Confederate States."[45] Having spent a considerable sum of his personal funds for recruitment and establishing the brigade, Tochman wrote directly to President Jefferson Davis and sought "the recovery of" his "pecuniary claim" before his departure.[46] Davis acknowledged his request and noted that the "commander of Polish Brigade seeks $5,925 in gold and $1,600 in CSA currency, compensation for expenses in mustering his command; he wants to return to Poland, which has called for his services." The Confederate President still referred to Tochman and the "Polish Brigade," even though the units had been incorporated into the 14th and 15th Louisiana Infantry regiments.[47]

Southern sentiment was with the Poles in their 1863 struggle against the Russian occupation, and Tochman undoubtedly was incensed by the news he received from Europe. Virginia newspapers such as the *Staunton Spectator* published accounts of "atrocities committed by the Russians in Poland," and since "no hopes can be entertained of any benefit arising from diplomacy," France and other European countries "should intervene actively for the re-establishment of an independent Poland."[48]

Ultimately Tochman did not return to Poland to fight in the rebellion, but he did continue his efforts in support of the Confederacy. After the rebellion against Czarist Russia sputtered, there were thousands of Poles, perhaps 15,000, who were seasoned warriors that had exiled themselves to sympathetic countries such as England and France that would harbor them elsewhere in Europe. He wanted to prevent these men from recruitment by Northern agents and direct all who were willing to the Confederate ranks. He worked in league with his countryman, Colonel Valery Sulakowski, who had succeeded him as commander of the Polish Brigade and the Louisiana regiments formed in 1861. Tochman presented a somewhat nebulous plan that faded away from realization due to bureaucratic indecision and indifference on the part of the Confederate cabinet and Congress.[49]

Tochman did not command troops in the field during the war but had made an impression nonetheless. His lecture tours and speaking engagements preceding the war in small towns and cities in several states brought Poland's plight, under partition by the Russian, Prussian and Austrian empires, to thousands of people who generally had been isolated from events taking place around the world. Their news sources, local newspapers and journals, could portray major happenings, but analysis and explanation of the underlying history, power struggles and the effects they had on a nation were more complicated. Tochman's legal mind and logical presentation enabled him to persuasively deliver his message. He personally created an awareness campaign that not only cogently argued for the resurrection of a free and independent Poland but also convincingly put forth the idea that imperialism was a threat to freedom everywhere.

After the end of hostilities, he returned to his farm in Spotsylvania County, Virginia, where he served as an immigration agent for the state by

Tochman's historical highway marker near Locust Grove, Spotsylvania County, Virginia.

appointment of the governor. In this capacity he founded a community he called *Nowa Polska* (New Poland) near Fredericksburg for Poles who would settle in Virginia. He had procured 2,500 acres for the settlement, which did not flourish, but he remained a popular figure in Virginia until he died in 1880 on his farm.[50] An obituary noted that he had been "exiled from Poland for participation in the revolution of 1830, and [a] Brigadier General in the Confederate service" and passed away "in his 85th year."[51]

Adam Gurowski

From a family of longstanding noble lineage, Count Adam Gurowski was born in the Prussian dominated sector of Poland near Kalisz in 1805. His family's estates came under the authority of Russia after the Treaty of Vienna in 1815, and afterwards he developed his early animosity toward the Czar and his empire. His sense of nationalism intensified while his advanced education in universities helped develop his ideological philosophy. When he returned to Poland as a young man, he soon became involved in revolutionary activities that eventually led to his participation in the 1830 insurrection and war with Russia.[52] Later in America, Gurowski was comparable to Tochman in employing rhetoric to advance his positions. He was extreme in his political positions and in his dealings with partisan allies as well as with his doctrinal foes.

Gurowski did not hold a military rank in the Civil War, did not lead troops in the American conflict, nor did he hold a lofty official position of power. He did, however, influence the opinions of many in Washington and was either reviled or respected, depending on the political views of the critic. Gurowski also was the one person in Washington whom Abraham Lincoln considered an actual physical threat. Lincoln stated that "Gurowski is the only man who has given me a serious thought of a personal nature … he is dangerous wherever he may be. I have sometimes thought that he might try to take my life."[53] He was a man who "by temperament as well as by political affiliation exemplified the most diabolical elements of the Radical Republican ranks."[54] He immediately began activity with the Radical Republicans when he moved to Washington in 1861, shortly after South Carolina's secession and the growing movement toward secession among the other states of the Deep South.

Adam Gurowski

The Count's family could trace its martial ancestry back to the Crusades. His father had fought under Thaddeus Kościuszko's banner against the Russians and later under Marshal Josef Poniatowski in Napoleon's army. Adam Gurowski felt that he had a sufficient military pedigree and ample experience, and wanted a commission in the Union army. When an appointment was not forthcoming, he went to work in the U.S. State Department. There he worked as a translator and analyst of European

Edwin M. Stanton, Lincoln's Secretary of War, was a friend to Adam Gurowski and fellow Radical Republican.

foreign affairs, and unofficially as Lincoln's nemesis and spokesman for the Radical Republicans.

Some historians have written that Gurowski was in a position in which he did not have full knowledge of the situation and "did not quite know what was going on."[55] Yet he traveled in high circles and had the ear of many influential politicians. Gurowski indeed was one of the most outspoken Radical Republicans of the period. They were opposed to Lincoln and his moderates "whose purpose was to make the restoration of the Union the one war objective, to be achieved at all costs, but if possible without destroying slavery."[56] Stephen Ambrose is among the historians who dismiss Gurowski as the "self-appointed spokesman for the Radical Republicans" who were critical of Lincoln and the moderates. For one, Gurowski bristled that Henry Halleck, President Lincoln's chief of staff, would not appoint any of his fellow radicals to key commands or General rank. Gurowski wrote frequently to the White House offering advice on decisions of national importance. Given Lincoln's opinion of Gurowski and the Radical Republicans, it is entirely possible that these communiqués, especially considering their source, would give the President cause to decide the other way. He specifically cites a letter urging that Lincoln dismiss Henry Halleck as chief of staff because he had enough power to "ruin" the country. However, Lincoln also considered Halleck a good "buffer" against criticism. Because everyone was dissatisfied with him, Halleck succeeded in uniting all the fractious elements in the North: the Radical Republicans and Lincoln Republicans as well as the Democrats and conservatives, and even McClellan supporters were against him. In the meantime, Halleck's deeds came by means of Lincoln's orders and the President considered him a valuable asset. Ambrose asserts that Gurowski's letter probably assured the President of the wisdom of his use of Halleck.[57]

Gurowski and his fellow Radical Republicans wanted to move on Richmond immediately and pre-emptively, and felt that the Washington politicians who were in disagreement were misinformed and completely oblivious to the will of the populace: "not one understands the superiority of the people."[58] In his position at the State Department on Seward's staff, his duties included reading "foreign newspapers for items of interest" and providing Secretary Seward "with translations or memoranda." Gurowski himself considered one of his duties to protect Seward, but he was constantly opposed to department policies and the attitude of conciliation that Seward favored toward the Southerners. The Count was basically a "Radical agent" in the administration and was able to attract a good deal of attention despite being a minor official.[59]

He lost his post at the State Department for publishing his diary in which he criticized many Republicans including President Lincoln and Secretary Seward.[60] A department bookbinder discovered manuscript pages with derogatory entries about Seward, the cabinet and the administration. Gurowski was dismissed in September 1862, despite having pledged his loyalty and support to the Secretary of State.[61] Seward, he felt, was too conciliatory toward the South and put personal ambition above country. On the other hand, Lincoln was intellectually incapable of achieving the Union's goals and did not have the necessary strength of a wartime leader. He wrote in his diary that the President was "too tender of men's feelings" and "events are too fast for Lincoln."[62] He criticized the leadership of the army, specifically the Army of the Potomac, but not the fighting men. Early in the war, he believed the North could defeat the Confederates in Virginia by "boldness and manoeuvre" if they would become aggressive, but lamented that "there seems to be an utter absence of executive energy." These attributes, "boldness and manoeuvre," were qualities that were the "supreme inspiration of the consummate" leader but were nowhere to be found "in the bemuddled brains of the West-Pointers, who are a dead weight and drag-chain on the victimised and humiliated Army of the Potomac."[63]

Count Gurowski at times could be prophetic when he wrote his acerbic criticisms in his diaries. He envisioned the upcoming disaster at Fredericksburg when he wrote on 7 December 1862 with misgivings about the leadership and lack of preparedness of General Ambrose Burnside. He first lambasted Halleck and his general staff as "lazy or incompetent or traitorous" for not lending proper support from Washington. Then he added that "Burnside and his staff have as much wit as an average twelve year old school boy" because they attributed their inactivity to lack of pontoons and bridges. He also added that the troops were unfortunate to be under "unintelligent" and "thoroughly unblessed leaders."[64]

Days later, after the Confederates achieved a major victory at Fredericksburg, he wrote:

> Dec. 15.— Slaughter and infamy! Slaughter of our troops who fought like Titans, though handled in a style to reflect nothing but infamy upon their commanders. When the rebel works had become impregnable, then, but not until then, our troops were hurled against them! The flower of the army has thus been butchered by the surpassing stupidity of its commanders. The details of that slaughter, and of the imbecility displayed by our officers in high command,—those details when published will be horrible. The Lincoln-Seward-Halleck influence gave Burnside the command because he was to take care of the army. And how Burnside has fulfilled their expectations! It seems that the best way to take care of an army is to make it victorious.[65]

Prior to coming to Washington before the start of the war, Gurowski had lived and worked in New York City on the staff of the *New York Tribune*. This was a time (as was most of the 19th century) when Poles sought support for their efforts to free their country from the tri-partite powers. His editor, Horace Greeley, was a staunch supporter of Polish freedom movements, and assisted in the newspaper as well as with donations. He was actually a member of the Polish American Committee and printed their materials gratis. However, this "generosity was neutralized by the panslavic policy of pro-Russian Adam Gurowski who worked on the editorial staff of the *Tribune*."[66] Later in the capital, he initiated a prolific letter-writing campaign to President Lincoln. "Epistles to Lincoln from the Count came at intervals frequent enough to be annoying, particularly at the beginning of the war" with advice, criticism and admonitions.[67] The letters were handwritten and marked *"Strictly Confidential"* to be delivered directly to the President.

Horace Greeley, Editor of the New York Tribune, employed Gurowski for a time. Greeley was a supporter of the Polish freedom movements.

Gurowski's radical views even prompted him to criticize the Emancipation Proclamation (freeing slaves in the eleven Confederate states) that Lincoln issued on 1 January 1863. The "irascible Polish count, Adam Gurowski, disliking the incomplete nature of the document, denounced it scathingly."[68] He acknowledged its issue, but basically declared that it was merely "words," more symbol than substance:

> The emancipation proclamation is out. Very well. But until yet not the slightest signs of any measures to execute the proclamation, at once, and in its broadest sense … Had Lincoln his heart in the proclamation, on January 2d he would begin to work out its expansion, realization, execution … But it is impossible. Surrounded as he is, and led in the strings by Seward, Blair, Halleck and by border-state politicians, the best that can be expected are belated half measures.[69]

Gurowski's radicalism was such that he spared no one who disagreed with him on the issues of the day. He "denounced with vehemence … slavery and its Northern supporters," and there was no one who could suppress his criticism. In an article reprinted in the Philadelphia *Evening Telegraph* from the *Atlantic Monthly,* a colleague who had admired his intellect and abilities lamented his ultimate lack of effectiveness politically. The article was published after his death and was entitled, "An Admirable Biography," and written by his friend Robert Carter:

> It was really painful to see how utterly his vast knowledge and his great powers of mind were rendered worthless by a childishness of temper and a habit of contradiction which made it almost impossible for him to speak of anybody with moderation and justice.[70]

When he died at age sixty-one of typhoid fever in 1866, the *New York Times* obituary also was complimentary in a guarded way. During his early years in Poland he "imbibed the revolutionary spirit" and "carried his patriotism to such an extent as to render himself obnoxious to the ruling powers." His knowledge of 14 languages made him a valuable asset to the State Department, yet his criticism of ranking politicians and generals for incompetency and softness was "piquant" with "no small amount of wit." Gurowski exhibited "brusque and somewhat eccentric manners" that never made him generally accepted. However, "his patriotic zeal and other noble qualities" afforded him a circle of friends who admired him.[71]

Gurowski lost his job at the State Department for criticizing Secretary of State William H. Seward, pictured here.

It is difficult to measure how much influence Gurowski exerted on the leaders of the country during the Civil War. "So far as is known, no statesman or government official changed a course of action or a policy" as a result of his advice. "To some he was a crank, a splenetic eccentric ... To a few Radicals his words were those of a sage."[72] The Radical Republicans considered him "one of the greatest thinkers of his age ... most would agree that Count Adam Gurowski was highly influential in both European and American politics."[73] To others he was just an eccentric "gadfly."[73]

Generally dismissed or, at best, considered a minor voice by many of his contemporaries and most modern historians, he nonetheless was accurate in some of his political and military analyses of the time. Gurowski prefaces his second diary, "Of all the peoples known in history, the American people most readily forgets YESTERDAY; I publish this DIARY in order to recall YESTERDAY to the memory of my countrymen. Washington, October, 1863."[74]

Gurowski undeniably could have been more effective politically had he been willing to compromise. Even his fellow Radical Republicans were willing to work with the Lincoln Administration toward the common goals of preserving the Union and abolishing slavery. Gurowski never flinched, however, and refused to make any concessions on the principles he espoused. His friends and colleagues considered him brilliant, but whenever they disagreed with him, he dismissed them and even personally rebuked them in public pronouncements. Influential patrons such as Horace Greeley, who hired Gurowski at the *Tribune,* and William Seward, who employed him at the State Department, eventually faded to his list of those he discredited. Greeley was in the "half and half" category that included those persons who still had some redeeming qualities. Seward sunk from favor all the way to the "blame" list (in the company of McClellan and Halleck) of those who had failed to carry out Radical Republican policies. Alienating the powerful in Washington relegated Gurowski to the political and governmental sidelines when it came to exerting meaningful influence.

Ignatius Szymański

Just as Tochman and Gurowski, Ignatius (Ignacy) Szymański fought the Russians as a cavalryman in Poland in the 1830 war. He also was of noble heritage and settled in Louisiana as a businessman and planter after first living in Boston and New York. In America, he made his first mark in promoting the resurgence of Polish freedom by writing as an exiled warrior in Boston. He later commanded a regiment for the Confederacy in the defense of the city of New Orleans and functioned as an official agent for prisoner exchanges with the Union army. He also was instrumental in the surrender negotiations of the last remnants of the Southern army in 1865.

Szymański was a wealthy Pole who fit well into the Southern planter class. He took the oath of United States' citizenship on 14 January 1850 in New Orleans, and his papers state that he came to America in October

1832 from Poland. He was listed as "a free white person" who arrived in the U.S. as a minor under the age of eighteen. Yet other sources give his birth date as 1806, which would have made him eight years older when he reached American shores.[75]

From the generation that fought the Russians in the 1830–31 war, Szymański, like Tochman, came from a noble family in Poland. He also fought in that rebellion and rode with the mounted Uhlans under Prince Adam Woroniecki. In doing so, Ignatius Szymański was taking the figurative saber from his father, who had fought against the Russians as part of Napoleon's army a generation earlier. He then carried on somewhat in this regard when he came to America. His skill as a swordsman and soldier earned him a position as professor of arms at West Point when he first came to the United States. He later resettled in Louisiana where he "started into the cotton press business," the *Szymański Cotton Press* in New Orleans. Here "he soon accumulated a handsome addition to his fortune."[76] He also took up the life of a planter, acquiring a sugar plantation that employed thirty slaves in St. Bernard Parish.[77] He named his enterprise *Sebastopol* in honor of the Russian defeat in the Crimean War in 1854–55. The plantation itself was situated on both sides of Bayou aux Boeufs two miles from the Mississippi River. The thirty slaves did the work on the productive sugar operation that measured "ten arpents front … by a depth of forty arpents on both sides of the bayou." It included a mill, sugar house, equipment and livestock.[78] Easily adapting to the lifestyle of the planter class, he became well known socially in New Orleans, owned a stable of race horses, and even had a pleasure yacht. Szymański was a "genial, cultivated and liberal sporting man. He became a rebel on general principles. His father was a rebel, and he was brought up as a rebel." He was a tall, well-built, athletic sort who had "abundant energy."[79]

Comfortably settled into his life as a planter and businessman, he did not become a political philosopher as did Tochman. Neither did he express his reasons for offering his services and becoming a defender of his country. He merely jumped into duty when his new home region was threatened.

Szymański had two periods of service that qualify as his most notable acts in participating in the Confederate war effort. His command of the

Chalmette Regiment was at the beginning of the conflict, when he took part in the defense of the South's largest city and port, New Orleans. The city had a population of 170,000 and was "the largest *exporting* city in the world." Its defense was vital, yet was inadequately prepared and mismanaged. Later he served as an adjutant and inspector, then, more importantly, became an exchange officer negotiating for the release of prisoners between the warring armies. Szymański began the war as colonel of the Chalmette Regiment, an amalgam of Louisianans from St. Bernard Parish just downriver from New Orleans. Among its companies were French Acadians such as Company H, *Frappe d'Abord,* and the *Clouet Guards* of Company K, as well as the A Company, *Scandinavian Guards.* The regiment came into the Confederate service on 1 March 1862 in response to an imminent threat to the port city. Major General Mansfield Lovell, in command there with seemingly little support from Richmond, faced serious difficulties with regard to lack of soldiers and materiel.[80]

Major General Mansfield Lovell commanded Confederate forces in New Orleans before the city's capture.

The largest American fleet the American Navy ever deployed had sailed up the Mississippi to begin its bombardment of Forts St. Philip and Jackson roughly seventy miles downriver from New Orleans. Under the command of Flag Officer David G. Farragut, the flotilla had the port city as its objective. The populace of the city felt well defended no matter how unfounded the feeling of security may have been. Despite troubles with the logistics of managing the defenses for New Orleans and the surrounding country, Lovell did have the advantage of recently completed telegraph lines. He at least could communicate with his officers at department headquarters and with Forts Jackson and St. Philip downriver. The foundry in the city had forged some new artillery pieces and he also had some heavy guns sent from Pensacola, Florida to the forts. By the late winter in the early months of 1862, he had guns but did not have sufficient ammunition and was faced with bad morale and even an attempted mutiny. Lovell was hesitant to supply arms to some units because of hints of insubordination. It was a deteriorating situation for the defenses, but in mid-April he sent Szymański and the Chalmette Regiment to Quarantine, Louisiana, six miles upriver from the forts. Their mission was to intercept any potential ground assault by Union troops coming upriver after the Union flotilla passed the two forts.[81]

The Federal naval force had 46 ships with 348 guns and 21 mortars arrayed against the two Confederate forts with 147 artillery pieces and twelve lesser gunboats. The garrisons in the forts also were thought to be unreliable and the shelling had depleted morale to a dangerous level. Szymański's regiment waited while the river battle raged with confusion on both sides. Still, the Union ships withstood the barrage and eventually sailed past the forts. When the gunboat *Cayuga* came upon the regiment at Quarantine, it moored ashore. Its captain demanded that the men surrender, since they were practically in an indefensible position and stranded on the bank by rising river water. The Chalmette Regiment gave up five hundred men on 24 April. Farragut subsequently had them paroled.[82]

On 25 April Farragut's fleet steamed upriver and only encountered resistance fire from some defense batteries at Chalmette. By that time, they simply had to navigate the short distance around English Turn, then Algiers Point to come within sight of the city and its focal point, St. Louis Cathedral. From the city's piers, boats loaded with cotton stores, some not-yet-completed gunboats and other vessels had been put to the torch. They were then set adrift and floated downriver to deter and "terrify" the oncoming Union flotilla. General Lovell evacuated his troops to prevent the city from becoming a military target.[83] Some citizens had accused Lovell of reducing troop strength and sending away arms to leave the city defenseless in the face of the enemy. In fact, orders from the authorities in Richmond had drained Lovell's armament and troop strength as well as that of the strength of New Orleans. He had had to ship artillery, twenty-two heavy guns, to Tennessee and South Carolina. Eight of fourteen gunboats that had been reconditioned and equipped were also sent upriver to aid in defense of Fort Pillow and the city of Memphis. He had received orders to send all the boats, but Lovell had insisted (as did Beauregard before him) that the true threat to the city and control of the Mississippi was to come from the south at the mouth of the river. He was able to keep but six in New Orleans.[84] After the evacuation of the army, the city was under civil authority. Lovell had left the mayor and his officials with "full discretion to represent the citizens in the crisis."[85] The high water levels of the Mississippi had Federal gunboats at barrel level with the city. Farragut, "instead of opening fire on the rebellious city, then entered into" negotiations with the "civil authorities" to arranged its surrender.[86]

Some accounts of the events leading to the fall of New Orleans treat the actions at Forts St. Philip and Jackson, the Chalmette Regiment on land defense and the surrender of the city as farcical or a comedy of errors. In certain cases, the views are valid. In the case of the fight at the Quarantine battery on 24 April 1862, "the Chalmettes made a spirited but unsuccessful defense against numbers and trained gunners." They withstood an attack by Farragut's fleet while deployed on flooded riverbanks.[87] As Colonel Szymański stated in later testimony before a military court of inquiry, they were in a position in which a barrage from a gunboat could have devastated his men closest to the bank. With men stationed on the river's edge on water saturated ground on a makeshift levee, he attested that, "a single shell could have cut the light embankment," their only earthen protection.[88]

It was a fact that most of the soldier-aged, eligible men of southeast Louisiana were away at points north fighting in the regular army.

This was especially true that March and early April when the Confederates were amassing the considerable force that would fight the Battle of Shiloh. That left General Lovell and Colonel Szymański the task of raising volunteer units and resorting to their own clever devices to defend the South's largest city.[89] The local press dismissed the militiamen as ineffective, untrained and unpatriotic. Furthermore, the idea that the "Chalmette Regiment surrendered to the USS *Cayuga* without firing a shot," is inaccurate in light of the official accounts.[90] Union Captain Theodorus Bailey's official report attested to the firefight at Quarantine after he had been engaged in a surface battle with Confederate gunboats:

> In the grey of the morning discovered a camp with rebel flag flying, and opened with canister [we opened with canister at 4:00 p.m.]* At 5:00 a.m. received the sword and flag of Colonel Szymański, and his command of five companies, arms and equipage.[91]

Szymański himself later gave sworn testimony at a Court of Inquiry hearing that verified the exchange of fire between the two sides and his position struck by canister:

> When the forts were passed, just about break of day, the fleet came upon my small camp and opened fire. After losing some 30 men killed and wounded, without a possibility of escape or rescue—perfectly at the mercy of the enemy, he being able to cut the levee and drown me out—I thought it my duty to surrender.[92]

After the surrender, Bailey left the prisoners under guard to wait for the approaching boats under his superior, Rear Admiral Farragut. The Admiral was less concerned with capturing prisoners than he was with capturing his objective, New Orleans. So, "pressed for time," he "paroled the officers and over three hundred men."[93]

The Pierson account describes that a New York *Herald* "reporter remembered seeing rebel soldiers lining the shore 'waving white flags' before men from the *Cayuga* landed and took about five hundred men prisoner." This is interpreted as "a notable example of just how little resistance most Confederate troops would offer in the coming week."[94] The *New York Times* had a somewhat different report in that "many of the *houses* displayed white flags ... and some of the *inhabitants* waved their handkerchiefs at us."[95] Szymański had recruited the Chalmette Regiment from the area downriver from New Orleans, and it was very possible

Captain Theodorus Bailey engaged and caused the surrender of Szymański's Chalmette Regiment at Quarantine, Louisiana on 26 April 1862.

that the local residents had family, friends or acquaintances among the volunteers. It is highly doubtful that these same people would cast aside their loyalties to salute the Northern boats. The high water conditions of the Mississippi also would have left the local inhabitants exposed and defenseless (as were the soldiers of the regiment) against the Union gunboats. Such circumstances could have precipitated their display of white flags.

Later in the war, Szymański served as an assistant adjutant general and then agent of exchange who negotiated prisoner exchanges between the armies in Louisiana, Mississippi and Texas.[96] He also played a part in obtaining the release of "political prisoners" that the Federal army had confined. This always was a delicate issue since the Northern authorities considered anyone who was not sympathetic to the Union war effort a potential enemy and could make an arrest on the grounds of disloyalty. The Southerners, of course, considered these same people loyal citizens. Union Major General Nathaniel P. Banks, in command of New Orleans and the Department of the Gulf, had his subordinates cooperate with Szymański in prisoner exchanges of soldiers. The political prisoner exchanges sometimes required more cleverness and diplomacy. In April 1863, Szymański pled the case for non-military individuals who were unaccounted for:

> Many citizens are also confined in different forts and other places as political prisoners whose names it is difficult to ascertain in full, and it is merely by chance we learn of their fate as for instance in the case of James P. Shortridge who has been arrested by order of General Butler and is still in custody. Mr. Walden … taken prisoner while defending his home at Pontchatoula, La., during the raid of Federal troops … and not returned with others who were delivered to us at Port Hudson on the 8th of this month.[97]

Later that year, the authorities in Richmond decided that there was not sufficient control or knowledge of "matters connected with the parole and exchange of prisoners beyond the Mississippi." Upon request, the Secretary of War, James A. Seddon, charged Szymański with specific duties to clear up matters. He was to update and correct the records of Federal prisoners and provide accurate accounting of "the number and locality of prisoners both in camp and on parole, Federal and Confederate." He also was to advise commanders as to proper methods for the parole and retention of prisoners. In discharging his orders, Szymański was allowed free license to perform his duties.[98] He also received word that because of the current state of affairs (Vicksburg and its large garrison had surrendered 4 July 1863), it was better to keep prisoners than parole them wherever and whenever it was possible. In all these matters, he was under orders to use his best judgment.[99]

As the Confederacy's prospects for winning the war began to dim, the handling of affairs regarding prisoners of war took on grave importance. No senior officers wished to be accused of ill treatment of prisoners, or even worse, war crimes. There had been a cartel established in which Union and Confederate prisoners were exchanged on an officer for officer basis and "the excess, on either side, be paroled until regularly exchanged." This system worked for the most part, but after the surrender of Vicksburg and Port Hudson the balance of prisoners was in the North's "favor by nearly thirty thousand." The Federal authorities were hesitant to parole such a number, having "no confidence of the good faith of the Confederate government." At the same time, the Northern army "could raise an indefinite number of men" and strove to use the situation to its advantage. The circumstances were such that the relations between the Union and Confederacy on this increasingly inflammatory issue "assumed a character disgraceful to both Governments." It tested Szymański's skills as a diplomat and negotiator when carrying out instructions from Richmond and maintaining his good relations with his Northern counterparts with regard to prisoner exchanges.[100]

It became increasingly difficult to maintain the delicate balance between the advantageous management of prisoners by having them interred, negotiating exchanges or entrusting them to parole. In the Red River campaign in the spring of 1864, General Kirby Smith defeated General Banks in his quest to gain final control over Louisiana. After the series of victories, there was concern that the exchange of enemy prisoners would enable the Union army to place formerly captured men right back into the ranks. Szymański received instructions from Richmond that "the only way to prevent such a wrong is either to hold on to all" or to conduct a man-for-man simultaneous exchange. There was a definite diminishing of trust between the two opposing sides. Additionally, there was frustration on the Confederate side that the Federals were becoming less cooperative in compliance with exchange agreements. The Commissioner of Exchange in Richmond, Robert Ould, wrote Szymański that if the South ever gets the upper hand we "will give them successive doses of their own physic."[101] Ould also declared further mistrust in August 1864, encouraging only "equivalent" exchanges with the enemy army. He stated that "if this not rigidly observed the Yankees will cheat all of us."[102]

During this period, Major General Benjamin Butler accused the Confederates of using prisoners as "labor in making army material for" Southern forces. Butler demanded that the practice cease or he would "be compelled to employ an equal or greater number of" captured Confederates "in the manner judged by me most advantageous to my army." Butler subsequently said he had proof that the practice was so and that he was ordering "a like number of officers and soldiers captured" to be put into hard labor.[103] He cited information from "two Richmond journals" from around September 1864. The Confederate authorities responded that there was no favoritism in treatment of prisoners, and that "efforts ... have been directed to the release of all our prisoners, without any discrimination in favor of particular persons."[104]

The issue reached the highest levels in both armies. Generals Lee and Grant exchanged correspondence on the matter. Lee asserted that any U.S. Colored Troops captured received the same treatment as other prisoners and were "proper subjects of exchange." He did add, though, that if they had been slaves and whether "through compulsion, persuasion, or of their own accord" joined the Union army, they would still "owe service." He continued that the legal conditions were the same at that time as they were when the Confederate states "were members of the Federal Union."[105] Grant made an interesting reply that reflected his view from a soldierly, not an ethical position. He said that he understood that the prisoners in question had been "withdrawn" from labor and that he would order the same for the Confederate prisoners who had been put into hard labor. He expressed regret that his army had acted in a retaliatory fashion. Grant also maintained a strictly military position. He affirmed that he had "nothing to do with the discussion of the slavery question," and declined to answer "the arguments adduced to show the right to return to former owners such negroes as are captured from" the Union army.[106]

Regarding the same situation in the Trans-Mississippi, Rear Admiral Farragut later wrote that he could not understand how "the commanding general in Texas or Major Szymański can undertake to dictate terms ... for the exchange of prisoners." He said that they had not the right to make demands because of "the inhuman treatment" to which captured Northern soldiers were subjected in Texas.[107]

It is worth noting that it was General Butler who came up with the legalistic solution of how the army was to deal with slaves that came to them seeking freedom. He originated the concept when he was commanding in Maryland in 1861, that "fugitive slaves escaping" to the Union Army were "contraband of war." This made the escaped slaves "a species of property not before recognized in international law." As "contraband," slaves were then spoils of war, or property taken from the enemy.[108]

A notable event in which Szymański played a key part came at the end of the war in 1865. He had dual roles in the closing affairs in Louisiana. One was in shielding the last ditch efforts by the Confederates to make a break through the Union blockade by a gunboat. The second was in conducting the surrender negotiation teams in what was the last major remnant of the Confederate government. After the surrenders in the east of Generals Robert E. Lee's army in Virginia and Joseph E. Johnston's army in North Carolina, the fates of the Confederate troops west of the Mississippi was unsettled. There were from 50,000 to 100,000 soldiers in the Trans-Mississippi Department in various states of organization and nominally under the command of General Smith. The area included most of Louisiana west of the Mississippi and while the Union gunboats controlled the waterways, dominion over parts of the state was questionable at best. Lieutenant J.M. Bundy, U.S. Army, expressed it best from the soldiers' viewpoint. The Federal "hold" on the area "was merely nominal, that is, we held the spots which our troops actually occupied—no more." He stated that it was foolhardy for a Union man to "venture … out of the immediate protection of a military post or without a sufficient escort of troops." Such an excursion would have rendered one's life worthless.[109]

The Federal authorities in Washington were concerned about the ungoverned and non-capitulated area of the Trans-Mississippi. Additionally from General Grant down, Union commanders were worried about the possibilities of guerilla warfare and general lawlessness. In an effort to remediate the situation, Grant authorized that Kirby Smith be offered the "conditional" terms of surrender that General Lee had accepted in Virginia. Two staff officers, Lieutenant Colonel John T. Sprague and his aide, Lieutenant Bundy, led the mission to carry the terms to Smith. They arrived on the Mississippi at the mouth of the Red River at the end of April. Their first task was to meet with Confederate officers "on their flag of truce boat," *General Hodges*. The officer in charge on this "boat was Colonel Skymanski [sic], the agent of exchange for the Trans-Mississippi Department." The Union negotiators soon grew to respect and admire him and Bundy wrote:

> His courtesy, tact, knowledge of the world, and social qualities eminently fitted him for the diplomatic duties assigned him. Whatever he did was done thoroughly, systematically, and well. His word was always faithfully kept, and I have reason to believe that he used all of his influence to prevent the ill treatment of Union prisoners.[110]

Szymański set the tone for negotiations in the first meeting with the Union officers. He was politic in his phrasings but insisted that they not venture up the Red River in their gunboat, the *Lexington*.[111] He suggested that his fellow Confederates might interpret their presence as a hostile gesture and that the river might still be mined with torpedoes. It was more likely that he was protecting a last maneuver by the Confederate ramboat *Webb* to penetrate the Federals' fleet and escape downriver to carry out further action in the Gulf of Mexico. The *Webb* was a reconditioned steamer that ultimately intended to move on to Cuba to sell its cargo of cotton. The mission did not succeed as Union gunboats ran the *Webb* ashore twenty miles south of New Orleans and burned the vessel.[112] When this news reached Szymański, "he had nothing further to detain him." Szymański himself proposed that "he would go up the river and make arrangements with Kirby Smith" for a meeting and would return within five days. He actually returned a day earlier than promised with several other officers. He suggested a plan in which they would accompany the Union negotiators up river on the Confederate truce boat four hundred and fifty miles to Shreveport. There they would meet and arrange the surrender with General Smith and his staff.[113]

The journey to Shreveport included the Union and Confederate officers, exchanged prisoners and parolees, as well as civilians both male and female. The relations between the Colonel, his fellow officers and the Federal contingent were cordial, whereas the civilians were suspicious and looked upon the Northerners as enemies. The Colonel was "supreme and omnipresent" and made sure that discussions remained civil and that everyone was courteous to his two "guests." He also provided for some merriment on the trip. He had his personal brass band and a string ensemble aboard to entertain the travelers, and he was always "the devoted cavalier of the ladies … and the social inspiration of the mixed circle of Confederates and Unionists on board his steamer."[114]

The curious imprint that Colonel Szymański's escorted voyage up the Red River left on the Union officers came from the greetings they received from the Louisiana riverine people. Bundy was amazed and delighted at the sight of the inhabitants welcoming the Colonel's expedition upriver:

> The approach of "Colonel Sky's" [Szymański's] boat was watched from afar and welcomed by ecstatic waving of white handkerchiefs, while white and black, of all ages, would congregate near the bank, and active youngsters would be sent to the boat, hastily laden with butter, milk, vegetables, and other free-will offerings. No man so popular as "old Sky," knew how to win all the women's hearts.[115]

The journey of the "truce boat" to Shreveport was through desolate countryside, much of it laid to waste by the war. Lieutenant Bundy discovered that one of the "suspicious passengers" was a cotton thief and reported him to Szymański's officers. The Union and Confederate officers agreed that men of his ilk should be "lynched" on the spot. But the Colonel would not permit any illegalities on board under his command. Shreveport, in the post-war twilight, was a city that "seemed inhabited solely by soldiers, gamblers, loafers, desperadoes, and the ugliest of 'bushwackers.'" There they encountered a "ragged, dirty, more desperate, villainous-looking crowd" that was "congregated on the levee."[116]

Twenty miles downriver from Shreveport, they met with General Kirby Smith's steamer that was moored at the bank. Szymański took the Union officers to deliver the terms of capitulation to "the chief of what was left of the Confederacy." Smith soon "entered into lively and pleasant talk with Colonel Szymański … and the business of the evening was deferred until the ice had thus been thoroughly thawed." The Polish planter and New Orleans businessman had used his skills as a diplomat to make the uncomfortable situation of surrender more agreeable for all involved.[117]

Colonel Szymański seemed to make the best of the situation. He strove to make everyone comfortable at the end of the terrible conflict and endeavored to achieve the best possible surrender conditions for

Louisiana and the men who served the Confederacy. On 20 June 1865, the operations involving the exchange of prisoners at the end of the war came to a close in New Orleans with the final recording of prisoners released on both sides in the Trans-Mississippi Department.[118]

With the war over, Szymański returned to New Orleans and resurrected his cotton press business in September 1865.[119] He also resumed operations at his plantation in St. Bernard Parish. Having settled back into the comfortable life of a Southern gentleman, he again became active in raising horses. He grew prominent in organizing horse racing in the region and was well "recognized among turfmen as a connoisseur of horses." As a member of the Metairie Jockey Club, he had many entries in the major racing meets as evidenced in the fall events of 1868.[120] An additional title that Szymański attained was president of the Louisiana Oil Company. He held the position for several years toward the end of his life and still was owner and active with the Szymański Cotton Press business. On the social and cultural side of his life, he was a board member and elected president of the New Orleans French Opera Association. Since he had been well acquainted "with the high class of lyric and dramatic entertainments … of European society," the Colonel was the perfect "fit and proper person" for the position. When he died on 11 August 1874, the newspaper report of his passing stated that his wife, Charlotte Hortense Lacoste, had passed away two years prior and that he had "left no children."[121]

Szymański, however, did have three children in another relationship. He had a *plaçage* arrangement with a Creole free woman of color, Eliza Romain. She was most likely a quadroon or octaroon. His first child was a son, Jean-Guillaume Szymański Romain and the colonel's will left the *Sebastopol* estate to him and his mother Eliza. Jean eventually migrated to Tampico, Mexico, where he worked, married and raised five children. Later generations of the family in Mexico have carried on the name of their Confederate ancestor with either the surname, or Ignacio, as part of their familial designation.[122]

An augmentation of his gentleman's lifestyle was Ignatius Szymański's membership in the exclusive men's Boston Club in New Orleans. He had joined the club before the war and continued his participation afterward. Most of its members also had "joined the Confederate Army, took part in war activities, or belonged to the Home Guards." The membership was comprised of prominent businessmen and well-to-do community leaders. Szymański fit in well due to his military experience and as part of the business community.[123] When Russian Grand Duke Alexis made his visit to New Orleans, many Boston Club members refused to attend a luncheon in his honor. Szymański most likely was one of those members. He also was part of a group of influential members who banded together to "protest against political conditions in the city and State" in February 1872. Their goal was to put an end to Reconstruction in Louisiana.[124]

In drawing a comparison between Szymański and the other Confederate officers rooted in Poland and examined in this text, their shared qualities are juxtaposed with disparate characteristics. He was not the legalistic orator that Tochman was in his pre-war campaign for the Polish nation and against the "autocracy of the Russian Czar." Yet the two did hold the same views on the subject, as did Valery Sulakowski.[125] He used his considerable talent and wealth to raise and lead the Chalmette Regiment early in the war, but he was not the respected, feared and accomplished officer in the mold of Sulakowski. Few of their contemporaries could post a record as colorful as the young Jastremski, rising from private to captain, twice wounded, captured three times, in a Northern prison camp, escaping and making his way back to join the army.[126] Szymański put his skills to use in the way to best serve his adopted nation. He had the polish and aptitude of an Old World diplomat and used those abilities to serve as a successful exchange agent in negotiating for the release of prisoners.

CHAPTER 4

ADVENTURERS AND PATRIOTS

During the tumultuous two decades preceding the American Civil War, there were Poles who fought the imperial powers that had a stranglehold on their homeland, and there were others who went elsewhere to fight in other European independence movements. The latter also maintained a strong military connection with Poland. Two such soldiers of the next generation of Poles to fight in the Civil War were Ludwik Żychliński and Valery Sulakowski. They were ten years apart in age and grew up in different parts of Poland. However, they were from families that emphasized the preservation of Polish culture and both were exposed to underground intrigues and schemes designed to bring renewed independence to their country. Sulakowski, the elder of the two, attended military school in Vienna and received his training with the Austrian army, whereas Żychliński had his first wartime experience in Italy. He was too young to participate in the insurrections but was a youthful witness to the unsettled times of the late 1840s.

Sulakowski was born in 1827 into a family of longstanding wealth and nobility in the Austrian section of partitioned Poland. He studied at the military school in Vienna and spent six years in the Austrian army, serving ably as an officer until he participated in the Hungarian revolt of 1848 under the banner and on the staff of Louis Kossuth. When the Austrians quelled this insurrection he departed for America.[1]

Ludwik Żychliński exhibited qualities as a soldier and social observer that at once reveal his similarity to his Polish contemporaries and occasionally how he differs. He was first a fiercely proud Pole and loyal to his people and their causes. He showed this in his service on both sides of the Atlantic. He never lost the fire and longing to fight for Polish freedom, and he carried his enmity and distrust for the Russians and their imperial system as a talisman.

Ludwik Żychliński

Żychliński was a warrior who had fought in Europe before coming to America. Born in 1837 into a family of Polish gentry in the Duchy of Poznan, he was "ingrained with a love for freedom and the ideals of patriotic revolution."[2] In Europe he had fought in Italy under the Papal banner, then with Giuseppe Garibaldi in Sicily in 1860. When the Italian campaign failed, he made his way to the United States in April of 1862. Żychliński, like Joseph Kargé, came from the Prussian-occupied part of Poland. Even after his military exploits in Europe, his goal was to "widen still further his military experience which could be useful later in the struggle for Polish independence."[3] As a soldier in the Union army and subsequently a diarist, Żychliński played the role of patriot, social critic and analytic witness. He left the army in the middle of the war to return to Poland but left behind valuable observations in his *Memoirs.*

Ludwik Żychliński's memoirs and reminiscences, and his references to others who served under arms with him, provide insightful interpretation and analysis from individuals who endured the war in the field or on the home front. Żychliński wrote his memoirs in two different time frames: the first was his diary compiled during the war years and the second consisted of a series of reflections twenty years later. Primary source references specific to this Polish-American soldier are not readily available in the newspapers and journals of that time. However, the actions of his units are fairly well documented and other written accounts substantiate the events he described in his memoirs. His writing offers multi-faceted insights into his service in the Union army, his observations of people both North and South, and his experience in America in general.[4]

Żychliński had always intended to return to Poland to rejoin the cause for independence, but while he was in America he committed himself to the Union cause. He immediately began to seek a military

Ludwik Żychliński

commission and enlisted in the Union Army in April 1862, just a month after he had arrived in New York on 10 March. Żychliński presented his papers and accepted the rank of a non-commissioned officer in the volunteer regiment *Les Enfans* [sic] *Perdu* when told there were no officer positions available.[5] Also known as *Enfants Perdus, Lost Children* or even the German Legion, the infantry regiment consisted of six companies of mixed nationalities organized in New York City under Lieutenant Colonel Felix Confort.[6] The regimental colors bore the inscription *"Independent Battalion Enfants Perdus, N.Y.S.V."* for the New York State Volunteers as they assembled and marched with their own drum and bugle corps, equipped with most of what they needed for departure to Virginia, except that they were without weaponry.[7] Their namesake, the original *Enfants Perdus,* had been a French regiment with a distinguished record of service in the Crimean War. They had performed "hazardous duties" as "skirmishers, pickets and advance guards … and were broken up into small detachments" with varied assignments and acquired the name translated as "Lost Children." Colonel Confort, a French count, had been a captain in the French army and had served 14 years in Algeria.[8] He also had served in the Crimea against the Russians and took the name from that well-known regiment and hoped to capitalize on it with further success with his newly recruited troops in America. Żychliński would have been comfortable associating himself with a unit that took its name from a regiment that fought the Russians.

Initially Żychliński felt that Confort, the new commander, received him "quite coldly." However, his introduction to service proceeded, and as he recounted, "I willingly agreed to his offer and that same day I swore allegiance to the United States of America." Within three days he was with his regiment and on his way to assignment in Yorktown, Virginia.[9] The regiment had an uneasy start once deployed in the South. Before *Les Enfans Perdu* had their first engagement, army authorities detained Colonel Confort at Fort Monroe, Virginia, for questioning regarding payroll irregularities.[10]

Żychliński saw his first action under General George B. McClellan in the Peninsula Campaign. He referred to McClellan as "undeniably one of the most capable generals in the Northern Army" and was perplexed by the "intrigue" created by those in the military and government who opposed him.[11] Although McClellan always seemed to have the support of his subalterns and troops, and Żychliński was in this group, military, public and political opinions differed. After the Union suffered its defeat at Second Manassas, in which McClellan was accused of undermining John Pope's generalship, Lincoln's cabinet not only virulently opposed, but expressed disgust at his reappointment to lead the army. Secretary of the Treasury Salmon P. Chase even predicted that McClellan's assumption of command "could only result in national calamity."[12] Ironically, McClellan had written negatively about the Poles when he traveled in Europe before the war. In his writings he "found them unpleasant, unintelligent, and degenerate, and wondered how such people had ever achieved any historical prominence."[13]

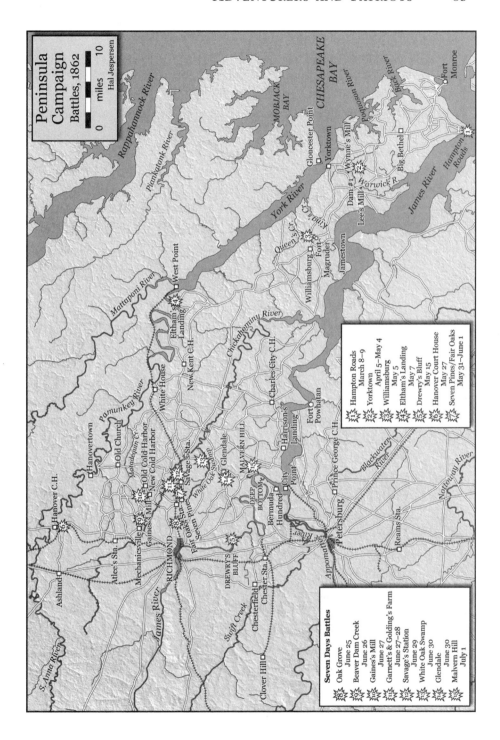

Peninsula
Campaign
Battles, 1862

0   miles   10
Hal Jespersen

CHESAPEAKE BAY

MOBJACK BAY

Rappahannock River

Piankatank River

Gloucester Point

Wynne's Mill

Yorktown

Dam #1

Warwick R.

Lee's Mill

Big Bethel

Fort Monroe

Hampton Roads

James River

Queen's Cr.

C's Dam

Jamestown

Fort Magruder

Williamsburg

York River

West Point

Mattaponi River

Eltham's Landing

New Kent C.H.

Chickahominy River

Charles City C.H.

White House

Pamunkey River

Old Church

Matadequin Cr.

Old Cold Harbor

New Cold Harbor

Gaines's Mill

Hanovertown

Glendale

MALVERN HILL

Savage's Sta.

White Oak Swamp

Harrison's Landing

Fort Powhatan

Prince George C.H.

Blackwater River

Nottoway River

Hanover C.H.

Ashland

S. Anna River

James River

Allee's Sta.

Mechanicsville

Gaines's Mill

RICHMOND

Fair Oaks Sta.

Seven Pines

City Point

Bermuda Hundred

DEEP BOTTOM

James River

DREWRY'S BLUFF

Chester Sta.

Chesterfield

Swift Creek

Clover Hill

Appomattox R.

Petersburg

Reams Sta.

Hampton Roads	March 8–9
Yorktown	April 5–May 4
Williamsburg	May 5
Eltham's Landing	May 7
Drewry's Bluff	May 15
Hanover Court House	May 27
Seven Pines/Fair Oaks	May 31–June 1

Seven Days Battles
Oak Grove	June 25
Beaver Dam Creek	June 26
Gaines's Mill	June 27
Garnett's & Golding's Farm	June 27–28
Savage's Station	June 29
White Oak Swamp	June 30
Glendale	June 30
Malvern Hill	July 1

Żychliński also met General Joseph Hooker while serving in the Peninsula Campaign. Hooker, as commander of the Army of the Potomac in 1863, was soundly defeated at Chancellorsville by Robert E. Lee and Stonewall Jackson's brilliant flanking attack. Żychliński mentioned Hooker and McClellan when he wrote his first memoirs in 1862, and they are accurate according to records and papers that still exist, the editor asserts. However, his memoirs from 20 years later exhibit some conflicting evidence with regard to dates and geographical locations.[14] For example, if he served with General Hooker up until Chancellorsville (early May 1863) but left for Poland in April or May 1863 to fight in the Polish insurrection against Russia, the logistics of obtaining a release from the military in wartime and securing passage for his voyage would have been difficult within such a short time frame. He mentioned a major battle and his involvement before he left for Europe "aboard the steamship *Saxony* in May, 1863." His "second enlistment in the winter and spring of 1863" corresponded to "when Hooker was planning the campaign." This would have made the time sequence very tight regarding his return to Poland. It is possible, however, that Żychliński did receive a release *after* the battle. He "found out about the outbreak of the uprising fourteen days later after a bloody battle in which I took part."[15] After he learned this, he requested a dismissal or leave from the U.S. Army from Hooker. When he did not receive this, Żychliński asked that he be sent on a courier mission to Washington where "he desired to pursue his case at the War Department, or with the President." He stated to his commander (possibly Hooker) that his "primary obligation was to the Fatherland, and ... conscience ordered me to shed my blood in Poland."[16]

Żychliński offered the interesting viewpoints of a Pole who experienced war on both sides of the Atlantic. As a Union soldier with "boots on the ground" in the Civil War, he could be analytical and critical but did so without the zeal or fanaticism of some of his contemporaries (see Count Adam Gurowski). He had great respect for McClellan (as did Robert E. Lee), a key player who had his share of detractors at the time of the Civil War as well as among historians in later years.

Some of Żychliński's most valuable observations came forth when he observed the army, the war and events with his soldier's viewpoint and analysis. He provided an analysis of the organization of the army and a step-by-step assessment of the formation of regiments. He considered the authority of a state's governor to grant "permission to any lawyer or businessman to form a regiment and nominate a colonel," who in turn appointed captains who recruited 75 men or provided financial support as an invitation to failure. He condemned such recruiting methods and did not hide his resentment at not receiving a commission. He reasoned that, "First, the officers themselves are people without military knowledge ... any shoemaker, merchant or tailor is an officer, while in the ranks may be found educated young men or foreigners who arrived in the country with military knowledge."[17] He concluded, perhaps too generally, that "the war is thus fought for pay, not for patriotism, nor for the abolition of slavery." He also added that the military "organization and administration" were inefficient and "terrible" because they were not run by "people with a heart full of love for the fatherland."[18]

A nineteenth century European such as Żychliński would have had two perspectives of military service: a soldier could be a patriot with fervent support for cause and country and the willingness to die for one's beliefs, or one could be conscripted into the ranks and therefore compelled to fight. He marveled at the openness of the American army and that on a visit to the troops, Lincoln "walked freely" among these men and "conversed with the common soldiers." The thought that "no one was prevented free access to the person of the President" contrasted sharply with his view of the downtrodden feudal soldier who would have had little or no access to senior officers.[19]

Żychliński recoiled from the idea that native-born Americans in the North hated the war and had no "military courage" since one could pay a stand-in $100 to enlist in one's place voluntarily. He felt that this was shirking the obligation and duty to protect and preserve the Union and the Constitution. He overstated his portrayal of the army being made up of "mostly foreigners; mainly Irishmen, Germans, and various other nationalities." He also stated that "the highest offices are reserved for Americans, but the lower officers and soldiers are generally foreigners." Żychliński was not being purely ethnocentric, and even envisioned the coming friction between European immigrants and native-born Americans over war issues. He would have disapproved of the draft riots that occurred (after his return to Poland) when conscription was introduced.[20] The unrest caused by the draft was primarily in New York City where protests against forced conscription into the Union army turned violent. Initially, the protesters were a mix of immigrants as well as native-born Americans. There were workers from all the trades as well as laborers from around the city. They were out to paralyze the workings of New York City and demonstrate against the inequities of the draft.[21]

As the protests grew, predominately immigrant crowds took out their anger not only on government institutions, but frequently on civilians, such as free blacks who happened to be in their way. New York's *The Sun* related events of a crowd greeting Federal troops assigned to quell disturbances with curses and hurled stones, then gathering in front of a tenement house, "breaking into the building, capturing a negro" and beating him to death. The troops fixed bayonets, fired grapeshot from a field cannon, then discharged their muskets into the mob. The volleys cut a swath through the crowd:

> instantly killing four or five and wounding as many more. After this the military fired their muskets into the crowd several times, killing four or five more, and severely wounding a large number.[22]

In another incident on the New York borough of Staten Island, a mob of "demons" destroyed the railroad depot and the Lyceum before turning on another innocent victim:

> An unfortunate negro, who happened to be present this morning at the time the assault on the lyceum was made, was set upon by the mob, who, after dragging him to a place known as Rocky Hollow, hung him to the limb of a tree.[23]

In contrast, Żychliński wrote that the Southerners were only too willing to fight for their independence and possessions. All men in the South, no matter their social standing, were willing to take up arms "to repel the Northern invasion and defend their land."[24]

In March of 1862, Żychliński and his brigade were part of General McClellan's massive amphibious operation to start the Peninsula Campaign. The troop movement began on the 17th and was probably the largest in history to that date. From Alexandria, Virginia, across the Potomac River from Washington, he was moving his army down the Virginia coast of the Chesapeake Bay to Yorktown by water. McClellan employed "113 steamers, 188 schooners, and 88 barges" over a three-week period to move in echelons of 10,000 men. The expedition also included all the "equipment and supplies ... horse and wagons" and everything else needed for "146,000 men."[25] At the time, Confederate troops on the lower Virginia Peninsula amounted to 12,000 men who had formed a line of defense consisting of earthworks and artillery.[26]

On 30 March according to his memoirs, Żychliński's unit landed three miles from Yorktown. They were well within earshot of the thunderous Union and Confederate artillery and immediately moved to the front lines "where they spent an entire sleepless night by the light of the bursting bombs and shells." He made specific reference to the explosions of 300-pound mortar shells that shook the very earth.[27] At the outset of the campaign, he highlighted three aspects that would affect the army and its efficacy: the wet and muddy conditions of the countryside, the lack of training and experience of the officers and men, and relative to that, the questions of fear and performance under fire, and communication difficulties. Visiting congressmen and government officials from Washington also reported that:

> The condition of the roads between the fortress and Yorktown was almost indescribable. Thousands of men were to their knees in mud. Of course, under the circumstances, an immediate advance is out of the question. Soldiers in the van are occasionally picked off by the rebel riflemen.[28]

In these conditions the men were under constant fire. Żychliński wondered just how they would respond to actual fighting because of their general lack of training and preparedness. He felt obligated to point out that "as with all other regiments here, our regiment was not trained and the soldiers ... only have a superficial knowledge of the basic movements and manoeuvres." He remarked that the men were "proud but frightened soldiers" who "did not know how to use a bayonet" and could not understand their colonel (Confort), who "could not converse with the Germans and Irishmen who made up half of our regiment."[29] The language barrier was an issue that both sides experienced with foreign-born and ethnically diverse units during the Civil War. Żychliński noted it, and General McClellan himself wrote about it in recounting his stories from the war. He referenced Ludwig Blenker's division and said that they "were from all known and unknown lands, from all possible and impossible armies." McClellan surmised that there had never before been such a polyglot of troops serving under one flag with officers from all over the world. He was fluent in several languages, but once encountered camp sentries with whom he could not communicate in English or any other tongue in which he was conversant. After attempting to reply to them in "French, Spanish, Italian, German, Indian, a little Russian and Turkish" with no result, he concluded that they "were perhaps gipsies or Esquimaux or Chinese."[30]

McClellan had been an official observer in the Crimean War where he had met Felix Confort. He later helped Confort secure his appointment as colonel and Żychliński observed them visiting and conferring several times in camp. At one point, he commanded an honor guard for the general staff and "even had the pleasure of being introduced to the general himself, who, knowing I was a Pole, praised our nation, stating that we Poles are soldiers from childhood and that in our blood lies courage and subordination."[31] McClellan's praise for his Polish subaltern was a changed opinion from what he had expressed in his 1855 travels through Poland and Russia. At that time, he had said that it was "difficult to imagine how they [the Poles] ever fought as they had done in the past."[32]

In the beginning of May, Żychliński's battalion transferred to General James H. Van Alen's brigade. He witnessed the Confederate withdrawal from Yorktown to a defensive position at Williamsburg twenty miles to the west toward Richmond. McClellan's forces advanced up the Peninsula as the Southerners withdrew, and Williamsburg became one of the first significant battles of the campaign. Van Alen had been an attorney in New York prior to the war, was from a wealthy family and had raised and equipped the 3rd New York Cavalry at his personal expense. According to Żychliński the new general had neither the military experience nor tactical training to lead the brigade in an attack.[33] The brigade was on the army's right wing and harassed the rear guard of the retreating Confederates as they moved toward Williamsburg. The battle account in the *Richmond Dispatch* confirms this:

> Our forces commenced the evacuation of the Yorktown line the night of Thursday May 1 ... On Sunday morning the 4th the "grand army" of McClellan entered the abandoned "rebel" fortifications and their advance guard rapidly followed, and constantly harassed our rear on the entire march for Yorktown to Williamsburg.[34]

The battle took place on 4–5 May between McClellan's advancing troops and the 32,000 Confederates moving away from Yorktown. Eventually 42,000 Federal troops would join the action, losing 2,239 compared to 1,603 casualties for the South. McClellan, as was his habit, reported in his nighttime dispatch of 5 May that he was greatly outnumbered, but would hold the enemy "in check" and follow his original plan. The *National Republican* reported that evidently the "original plan" did not involve pushing the Confederate army further back and incorrectly attributed Union success to the engagement:

> When General McClellan waked up on the morning of May 6, he found that the enemy had been altogether worse beaten on the previous day than he had supposed, and were in full retreat. He doubtless changed his opinion as to their superiority in numbers which were never really more than half his own.[35]

Therefore, from the Northern perspective, they had gained the upper hand by making the Confederates withdraw from the field. The Southerners had inflicted greater casualties on the Federal army and had checked their advance. Meantime, the soldiers on both sides had gained confidence. The *New York Times* mentioned the "gallantry" of Union division commanders, the regimental pride of the men and a "successful close" of the day.[36] Żychliński credited the generalship of the Confederates for their ability to keep the Union army at bay, but gave McClellan credit for boosting the men's morale and having them "advance." However, he described the battle itself as anything but an orderly progression of tactical movements:

> The enemy ... began to scorch us with grape shot, shells, and shrapnel. I thought that this was "The Day of Reckoning" since not only did bullets fall like hail, but trees and branches broken by shots, bomb fragments, and shells fell on my head and wounded our frightened soldiers.[37]

Then later, the entire brigade "shortly packed up and began to withdraw in complete disarray" and when attacked, "such anarchy arose on our battle line" that men and officers alike scattered in every direction. He ascribed "the miracle" that delivered himself and his regiment from "such a burning hell" to "Providence and the grace of God."[38]

There is some discrepancy in the reporting of the positions and actions between the *Memoirs,* Frederick Phisterer's *New York In The War Of The Rebellion* and Dyer's *Compendium.* The latter two works list Żychliński's battalion as being on garrison duty at Yorktown and not actively engaged. However, McClellan's constant appeals for reinforcements may have resulted in the *Enfans Perdu* being called into action and moved to the front lines at Williamsburg. His accounts of McClellan's arrival on the field as well as other occurrences suggest that Żychliński's unit did participate in the battle.[39]

In the middle of May, the Northern Army began to besiege the city of Richmond from the east, and Żychliński detailed various facets of army life during the campaign. These ranged from the political intrigues surrounding McClellan, to his own regimental duties. He also included other issues such as the polyglot communications affecting the command, hot air balloon reconnaissance and camp conditions. These conditions were such that privations and disease damaged the effectiveness of the army, though he greatly exaggerated how it debilitated its strength: from 96,000 to 46,000 able bodied men fit for service.

It was hot and always muddy and Żychliński repeatedly uses the latter term to describe the wretched conditions the armies dealt with during the siege. Since they slept in the open no matter the weather, it magnified the poor conditions and the "indescribable poverty" in which they lived that fostered diseases: "The muddy region in which we camped, and the rank odors at night, were reasons why we had about 150 sick with fever in some regiments. Typhoid began to appear and thousands of sick soldiers were sent to field hospitals." Rations were another matter that exasperated the misery because the troops subsisted on salted meats and fatback with dried biscuits and dirty water.[40]

During this period, Żychliński was able to give an eyewitness account of the early days of aerial reconnaissance. He admitted that he was "deeply amazed by the inventive shrewdness of the Americans" in their use of hot air balloons. From these, he related how "from an extreme height," General McClellan "could observe the movements and fortifications of the enemy." He described the balloon's construction being of silk with an attached "small rubber gondola" that held two men. One was an engineer equipped with a telescope and other accoutrements and another was charged with the navigation of the craft.[41] Thaddeus Sobieski C. Lowe, a scientist and inventor from New Hampshire, led the military aerial reconnaissance project as head of the balloon corps for McClellan's army. Partly named in honor of Polish military hero, King Jan Sobieski III (though not Polish himself), Lowe would later become the Union army's chief aeronaut.[42] It was a positive military development reported as such in the press:

> During the whole of the battle of this morning, Mr. Lowe's balloon was overlooking the terrific scene from an altitude of about 2,000 feet. Telegraphic communication from the balloon to General McClellan, and in direct connection with the military wires, was successfully maintained … Every movement of the enemy was obvious, and instantly reported. This is believed to be the first time in which a balloon reconnaissance has been successfully made during a battle, and certainly the first time in which a telegraph station has been established in the air to report the movements of the enemy, and the progress of a battle. The advantage to Gen. McClellan must have been immense.[43]

Witnessing such technological developments bolstered Żychliński's confidence in the army as a whole as well as his faith in its commander. Such observations of military innovation stressed his admiration for American ingenuity and the ability to apply new ideas to the military. He also recognized McClellan's requirement of additional help in order to achieve his goal of taking the Confederate capital of Richmond. The Union army was besieging "the city from two sides, but because of a shortage of reinforcements and siege artillery" Żychliński declared the Union army "could not immediately conquer it." This was when he questioned the machinations of the Washington politicians and the "intrigue … fostered by those who were opposed to McClellan, undeniably one of the most capable generals in the Northern Army."[44] The general had wanted an even greater force for his Peninsula Campaign, but the administration in Washington had retained an entire corps for the defense of the capital.

In late May, Secretary of War Stanton directed the First Corps under General Irwin McDowell to march south in order to establish an independent right wing for McClellan on the north side of Richmond.

The administration then pulled the corps away—under protests from both McDowell and McClellan—fearing a threat to Washington from Stonewall Jackson's army in the Shenandoah Valley.

Żychliński's descriptions of political discussions that officers held in camp and soldiers' everyday life illuminate his European perspective. He encountered and became acquainted with many officers of other nationalities who sometimes had shared similar political and military experiences to his in Europe. Some came to America for military commissions, others as official observers and still others were political exiles. Among the Frenchmen were the Prince de Joinville, an observer, and his nephew the Comte de Paris, who was also an observer and wrote about his experiences with the Union Army. The Comte had the added distinction of being "the son of the former King Phillippe [sic]" of France. Louis-Philippe abdicated during the 1848 unrest and his son Philippe, Comte de Paris, would later serve on McClellan's staff.[45]

The Prince de Joinville was vocally opposed to slavery and concerned about the failure of the Union efforts in Virginia so far in the conflict. Like Żychliński, he was critical but fair, and willing to make comparisons between North and South. He shared Żychliński's view that the South was united in spirit and in victory would remain powerful, whereas the Northern states would be more fractious and "each of them would have an eye solely to its own interest." He was optimistic as was Żychliński, and felt that despite its setbacks the Union would prevail: "who knows how much, in a day of peril, the energy of a free people, fighting for the right and for humanity, can accomplish?"[46]

There was discord among the German element "amidst the free air and army tents of America" with regard to the sagacity and courage of their ruling class. Żychliński, at one point, decried "German rapacity" that could undermine Slavic nations "for the sake of German culture, but did not suggest that this attitude existed among his German comrades.[47] He unwittingly foretold the tribulations of the twentieth century in Europe when he concluded (and agreed with the French and Italians) that the Germans needed a firm ruler to "govern and ... allow" quiet life and sharing opinions "about liberal theories never brought to life in his [their] own country." He mentioned the "*Drang nach Osten*" *(drive to the east)* mentality, "greed for foreign property, and conceit for their own culture" that was "so ingrained in German society" that it would take centuries "before it could be removed from the minds and blood of the German tribes." This, he felt, could only be at the expense of the Poles. Such arrogance, Żychliński wrote, inhibited "sincere, friendly relations" in camp, even with native-born Americans who would equate them to the Hessian mercenaries who fought with the English against American independence the previous century. He did commend their "good characteristics and attributes" when he said that other nations should take note of the German "sense of order and diligence ... a model for all nations."[48] There is not a similar assessment of Teutonic social characteristics from Krzyżanowski, who commanded and served closely with a number of German officers and enlisted men in the Eleventh Corps.

The Russian officers Żychliński met were not imperialists, and though they were former officers of the Russian army, they became friends. The Pole learned "that the real intellectuals in Russia are not against liberating Poland from under the yoke of absolute Czardom" because "as long as Russia is not a constitutional state like the civilizations of the west, it will subjugate civilized Poland." These Russians he said, wanted to join with the Poles and put an end to Czarist absolutism.[49] In the earlier comparison to the military experience between Europe and America, he contrasted the submissiveness of the continental soldier as opposed to the feeling of freedom in the U.S. Army. This, he said, was also true in camp where "all social and revolutionary elements were present and often the officers assembled during their free time to discuss the best means by which the republican spirit could be transplanted from America to Europe."[50]

The Peninsula Campaign ended for McClellan and the Northern army on 3 July 1862 with the last of the Seven Days battles, Malvern Hill. He had won battles but "treated them as defeats" until the Confederates had driven his army back down the Peninsula, completely "unnerved" by Lee tactically. McClellan's army was safe—but so was Richmond.[51] The campaign ended earlier for Żychliński. On 18 June he was with his unit, Company E, on outpost duty when they were ordered "to advance at double time, and finally to trot" to support the brigade on word of an enemy approach. In the darkness and in deep woods, they were hit with musket fire and the Confederates "soon attacked us with bayonets." He managed to hold his platoon together, but wrote "during this confusion I fell with my whole pack and weight on a tree stump and several soldiers from my platoon fell on top of me."[52] Żychliński received a wound in the bayonet attack but referred to it as "nothing significant." More serious was the injury he incurred and the consequences from the "heavy fall" during this nighttime skirmish. The account of his recuperation included a week suffering from fever and "ague" in a tent in Williamsburg, transfer to a hospital in Yorktown (one of 3,200 other patients) where they "could not find any leeches or ice" and where he was uncertain if he "could survive the fever in such extreme heat and discomfort for more than three weeks."[53]

With the Union Army suffering setbacks on the Virginia Peninsula, Gen. McClellan began to have his wounded and sick moved north to avoid capture. General John Adams Dix (Żychliński incorrectly refers to him as the army's chief surgeon) supervised the moving of the wounded to field hospitals and the subsequent transfer of groups numbering in the hundreds by steamers downriver from Richmond and up to New York and Baltimore as reported in the newspaper the *National Republican*.[54] After the stay in the field hospital, Żychliński related the circumstances of his move to Baltimore. There he wrote that the military hospitals were so overcrowded they put him and others in tents "where soldiers with typhoid fever were lying. The manner in which the sick and the wounded were treated was barbaric, without any delicateness or service. We were not even asked if we wanted to drink or eat."[55] In addition to his descriptions of the sick bay conditions, he also offered his political view of Baltimore, the border state city that had been a thorn in the side of the Union since before the war:

> The inhabitants of the town of Baltimore did not support the government of the United States because, in general, all of Maryland supports the Confederacy. The inhabitants of Baltimore hate the Northern soldiers. They received us, the sick and wounded, without any sympathy or mercy and of course swore and reviled us.[56]

The army medical authorities pronounced Żychliński disabled and unfit for duty because of his injuries in July 1862. He then reflected upon his service and the state of his adopted country with "facts and events seen personally." He offered the admonition, "I did not want to pass judgment on the faults of the generals and administration or politics of such an unfortunate country that is crumbling from such a bloody fratricidal war."[57]

Some of the insightful entries in his memoirs involve his leave of the American Army and return to Poland to pursue his ultimate goal of resurrecting his country:

> As a military man I felt the need to go to the Fatherland and deemed myself not obligated to fight in America when in my Fatherland the blood of my brothers was being shed and in Poland I should pay my debt on the battle fields. I contacted other Poles remaining in the army of the United States in order that together we could submit a request directly to the President to be relieved of our duties.[58]

He paralleled his predecessor, the great Kościuszko, in this regard. Both were unwavering in their opposition to slavery and support for the causes of liberty in America. Both ultimately returned to Poland to fight for the freedom of their homeland.

It was nearly twenty years after the war when Żychliński wrote and published the balance of his memoirs. He gave his subjective comparisons of the Northern and Southern armies with observations that sometimes were not completely accurate. He overstated the advantages the South had in having so "many former officers and generals from" the United States' regular army. He contrasted this with the "hastily" organized Northern army of mostly volunteers "who were largely unaccustomed to soldiering." He added that the difficulties the army had in the early years of the war were compounded by the fact that the "officers and generals of this volunteer army were inexperienced and had to learn on the battlefields."[59] Actually, the Northern officers who were regular army or West Pointers generally caught a great deal of criticism, and the press and public did not hide their contempt for their tactics and "seeming slowness of movement." On the other hand, northern Republicans attacked West Point for having been a "breeding place of southern sentiment ... responsible for the defection of many officers to the rebel cause."[60] In reality, although West Point officers led both the Northern and Southern armies, about seventy-five percent of the military academy graduates remained in service with the Union. Among general officers, 217 of 583 who attained at least the rank of brigadier were West Point graduates. This number in the Confederate service was 146 of 425.[61]

Żychliński made a point of emphasizing that the American soldiers were volunteers and free citizens, were obligated to protect their country, and were not to interfere with the rights or property of private citizens. He noted how this differed from the "soldiers of the monarchial governments in Europe."[62] In the U.S., infractions were punished and justice by military court was swift. He illustrates this with an example of some men from a New York regiment made up chiefly of Irish and Germans who stole, butchered and ate a hog from a nearby Virginia farm during the Peninsula campaign:

> Under punishment of death no one was allowed to take possession of anything that was property of a citizen, nor enter the homes of the inhabitants for the purpose of extortion of any kind, even from a defenseless enemy, and especially from those citizens who do not actively take part in any battle against us.[63]

He was part of the investigation because of his linguistic skills, and found evidence of the crime, but had wished that the men had been able to cover it up. "I harshly upbraided the commander ... for not giving the order to get rid of the traces. If we had not found anything at the place, everything could be denied." This he felt would "save a few people from certain death." Żychliński asserted that despite his assistance in their defense, the military court justifiably convicted the accused soldiers. Seven were executed and the other perpetrators received harsh punishment. He also cited a case of desertion in "the enemy state of Florida" where the deserters were captured, found guilty and shot within a few hours of deliberation.[64]

The political maneuverings of the European powers with regard to support for or alliances with the Confederate and United States affected Poland as well. France, a traditional ally of the Poles, had made an alliance with the Czar as a countermeasure against Prussia. He "found out all of this from Count Adam Gurowski who advised me against going to the uprising."[65] Since Żychliński considered Russia the great enemy of freedom in the world, it is ironic that he received counsel from his fellow Pole, the Russian apologist and radical Republican Adam Gurowski, about his planned return to fight the Czarist Empire. Żychliński did return to Poland to fight the Russians in the 1863 war. He regretted not leaving earlier for the fight, but that after "being accepted onto the [army] staff as an officer" he was dropped from the ranks after his resignation. Afterwards he lost pay and his rights as an American citizen. However, he felt obligated as did other Poles who left America for Europe as "loyal sons of Poland." These men had "the further desire to measure ourselves on the battlefield with the butchers and murderers of our grandfathers, fathers, and brothers."[66]

Żychliński never lost sight that his primary allegiance was to a free Poland. Upon his return in 1863, he immediately joined the military uprising and was an officer in the *Dzieci Warszawy* (Children of Warsaw). After fighting in several successful actions, the Russians captured him in December of that year. He managed to avoid a death sentence, but the penalty he received was exile to hard labor in Siberia. After his release in 1868, he returned to Poland and took up residence in the province of Galicia (then under Austrian control). He died in 1891.

Like his compatriots Kargé and Krzyżanowski, he fully embraced the cause to fight for the preservation of the Union and his perspective of the Constitution, while never losing sight of his "Polishness." However, while they remained in the United States as citizens and pursued successful careers after the war, Żychliński returned to Poland to fight for his fatherland's freedom. He was unable to experience the final victory of the Northern army, having left for Europe after a series of defeats. Nor was he to see his dream of a fully independent and united Poland restored to the world stage.

Valery Sulakowski

Valery Sulakowski received his military training as an officer in the Austrian army, and like many of his contemporaries was a fiercely independent Pole. He had a penchant for military discipline and order, and he carried that with him to his service in the Confederate army. Sulakowski took the reins of the Louisiana Polish Brigade from Gaspard Tochman in the summer of 1861 and immediately applied his martial philosophy to the amalgam of ethnic and American-born troops that were to become the 14th Louisiana Volunteer Infantry and make their mark on the war in more ways than just the battlefield. Many of his peers considered him the "sternest and best disciplinarian in the Confederate army."[67]

Sulakowski trained and became commander of the Louisiana Polish Brigade after they originally had organized in New Orleans. His troops included Poles as well as Germans, Irish, French and Scandinavians. He was considered "a natural to lead the multinational regiment." Sulakowski was an exacting authoritarian in the European fashion and successfully led his men north from Louisiana (not without incident) to participate in the Virginia campaigns.[68] He resigned his commission a year later when passed over for promotion by an officer with less experience and seniority. He resurfaced as Chief Engineer for General John Bankhead Magruder in 1863 and participated in a secret mission to Cuba in 1864. His accolades and criticisms vary and include, "without a doubt the best colonel in the service," as well as being "despotic" while enforcing strict military order.[69]

In Europe, Sulakowski's revolutionary activities made him *persona non grata* with the Austrian authorities, and by some accounts he emigrated due to the "cruel despotism of Russia." He made his way to America and first settled in the town of Houma, Terrebonne Parish, Louisiana. He owned property and had timber holdings there on Bayou Terrebonne and also worked as an engineer in New Orleans. He made his personal reputation as an officer in the Confederate army in the first year of the Civil War commanding Louisiana troops.[70]

Perhaps the first crucial moment (at least in the public perception) for creating the reputation of these troops from southern Louisiana at the beginning of the Civil War occurred at Grand Junction, Tennessee in August 1861. The men from this state had not yet earned their battlefield sobriquet, "Tigers," but their reputation for rowdiness and raucous behavior received its initiation before they experienced their first skirmish. Moving north by railroad cars to their ultimate assignment in Virginia, the men had been in close quarters in the August heat for the nearly 400-mile journey from Louisiana to southwest Tennessee. Their priorities when they disembarked on this stop were liquor, taverns and food. There was some disgruntlement among the troops due to the feeling that they had not been issued proper arms and equipment prior to their departure. This was one reason for the start of the émeute, as the Creole bilingual newspapers in Louisiana referred to the riot. As their commander, Colonel Sulakowski wished to forestall any incidents, and

Valery Sulakowski

ordered the taverns closed to prevent episodes of unruliness or breaches of discipline.[71] His orders proved wise in theory, but the "execution of such an order proved, as often, impossible and liquor flowed freely."[72] The imbibing had begun at an earlier stop south of Tennessee in Holly Springs, Mississippi. One group of men surreptitiously had procured:

by some means ... a barrel of whiskey," from which they "drank immoderately." The worst consequences followed. The men who were traveling in box cars, indulged in the worst extravagances—even it is stated, going so far as to throw their bayonets at each other. One man was thrown from the platform, and killed by the train passing over him, cutting off an arm and a leg. On leaving the cars at Grand Junction, open mutiny broke out, and the men turned against each other with perfect ferocity, entirely disregarding the authority of their officers, until the determined conduct of Col. Soulakowski [sic] compelled a return to military rule.[73]

The reports had stated that the situation would have been much "more disastrous but for the firmness and bravery of the commander of the brigade ... who shot down some of them that refused to submit to his authority."[74] The men had actually procured more than one barrel and even had gone through a whiskey ration issued for the journey from Louisiana.[75] In addition to ordering the closure of liquor stores, Sulakowski had positioned armed sentries in front of any establishment that sold alcohol. Since many of the men were already in a state of inebriation upon arrival, this only served to rile the troops further and they went through windows and broke down doors to shops. At one saloon, the "drunkards" overpowered the sentries to force their entry. When other guards arrived in an effort to subdue the group, "a bloody brawl erupted after a guard bayonetted one soldier during the scuffle."[76] When some officers attempted to quell the disturbance—one even firing a warning shot with his pistol—the mob chased them into the Percey hotel and set fire to the building. They were oblivious to the civilians, including women and children, who also were in the hotel. The rioting soldiers "rushed in like a mob of infuriated devils, and commenced to indiscriminate destruction of the hotel furniture and everything they could lay their hands on."[77]

Sulakowski realized that his officers could not contain the situation and came on the scene in a rage and armed with two revolvers. A "commanding presence" at six feet tall with stern features, he ordered the men to return to their quarters immediately in a "voice of extraordinary power." When there was a hesitation in obeying his command, he discharged first one revolver and dropped an unruly soldier, and then another with a shot to the face. He even shot a sergeant who had failed to respond to his commands with sufficient urgency. There were seven total deaths, two immediately and perhaps five or six more mortally wounded at the spot. Nineteen others were wounded before the riot had been completely subdued. Sulakowski had quelled the disturbance and restored order by the force of his person and a couple of pistols.[78]

Discipline was of paramount importance to Valery Sulakowski. He was the perfect commander for that unruly lot that had begun as a loose-knit group of untrained Louisiana volunteers with no military skills but plenty of fight. Sulakowski was "the very incarnation of military discipline—cruel, despotic, and absolutely merciless. Nothing less could have cowed the wildest and most reckless body of men in the southern army."[79] He was furious that his officers had let the affair escalate to a full-scale riot and disbanded the 1st Company B, *Franko Rifles* from New Orleans as he considered them to be the chief instigators. He had the officers resign their commissions that September and transferred the enlisted men throughout the regiment. When the regiment arrived in Virginia, the Confederate War Department officially re-designated the Polish Brigade as the 14th Louisiana Volunteer Infantry.[80]

Sulakowski's men learned to respect and obey him as a result of his imposition of a strict training regimen and enforcement of military order. He had assumed command of the regiment from its founder and sponsor, Gaspard Tochman, and led the men to the war in Virginia. They arrived after the Confederate victory at First Manassas and their chief hope was to get into the action before the war was over. The 14th Regiment was put under the command of General Magruder on the Virginia Peninsula along with the 2nd, 5th and 10th Louisiana regiments. Much like the men in Leon Jastremski's 10th, the composition of the 14th was diverse and polyglot, and French became the language of drill and instruction. This proved to be a source of good-natured amusement for some of the soldiers from other regiments from different states who up until then had only heard their own local vernacular of southern English spoken. Occa-sionally after finishing their drill and dress parade, they had a chance to take in the Louisiana soldiers drilling. William Oates, an Alabama officer, was both complimentary and entertained when he observed:

> The Polish Legion from Louisiana, commanded by Colonel Sooli Koski [sic], a Polish officer of distinction, arrived one or two days later and was encamped near us … Each afternoon, as soon as we vacated, the Polish Legion, with its numerous drum corps, would occupy the ground. The foreign accent of Sooli Koski and the

alacrity and precision with which his men obeyed his commands, not a word of which we could understand, presented a good entertainment for the edification of our officers and men.[81]

The admiration came from other quarters as well. Colonel B.L. Farinholt of Virginia was pleased to serve as "part of the command of the famous" Colonel Sulakowski, who had "seen much service in the European wars, especially at the Siege of Sebastopol." Farinholt lauded the Pole's "sagacity and ability" and referred to him as "a most exacting military commander, disciplinarian, and organizer."[82]

Despite Sulakowski's iron-fisted rule over his men, the 14th Louisiana reverted to its riotous ways again in September en route to a mission in Norfolk, Virginia. At a stop in Petersburg and again in Norfolk, they displayed "disgraceful conduct" in "one of the most terrible affairs that ever disgraced the annals" of the fair city of Petersburg. The episode also cast shame on their home city of New Orleans. In this occurrence, it was only a portion of the regiment, maybe forty men, who were "inflamed to excess by that bane of mankind, liquor" who fought each other with "paving stones, clubs and bowie knives." They behaved as "untamed beasts of the forest, in their deadly encounters with one another" before officers were able to quell the disturbance. In Norfolk, they threatened a shopkeeper, Mrs. McCulloch, with knives. They sent her screaming for help when they broke the plate glass window of her store to steal cigars and confections before the authorities arrested several of the men.[83]

In January 1862, Sulakowski took charge of the left flank of Magruder's army on the Peninsula. During the early winter, he occupied his men with the construction of an extensive system of fortifications and trenchworks as part of the defenses of Richmond. General McClellan had assessed in his preparations for the Peninsula Campaign that the strong earthworks and trenches presented a formidable obstacle to his army. His chief engineer reported that rifle pits, trenches and parapets connected the extensive "field works" throughout, and they made use of "every kind of obstruction which the country offered." He asserted that the defensive line was "certainly one of the most extensive known in modern times."[84] Additionally, Sulakowski ensured that his men had proper winter quarters and provisions. The 14th Louisiana had the "finest winter quarters, for they were all built by military rule, there were in Virginia. When the men were not working they were drilling." At the same time, in an army and war known for its privations, "no regiment, in its wants, was better looked after, or obtained more regularly its requisitions."[85]

The defense works proved to be strong testimony to Sulakowski's engineering expertise after his departure from Virginia. As a professional soldier, he was ambitious and competitive and felt that his molding of this motley group of misfits into a well-functioning military unit merited a promotion. As an adoptive Louisianan, he wished a generalship and command of a brigade from his state. This did not transpire. As was common with many professional soldiers, he had a disdain for political appointees that were granted ranking officers' positions. Howell Cobb, a Georgia congressman, received preference over him and was made brigadier general on 12 February 1862.[86] Sulakowski resigned his commission on 15 February and Richard W. Jones became colonel of the 14th a few days later. Sulakowski addressed his men with a somewhat bitter farewell in which he expressed his resentment toward the political authorities in Richmond. Sulakowski was not the only senior officer who felt this way. His friend, Colonel Mandeville de Marigny, later resigned his command of the 10th Louisiana, also disgusted with Richmond's political favoritism. Sulakowski's resignation was "a shock," especially to Magruder, since the Polish colonel was thought of as "without a doubt the best colonel in the service."[87]

The troops were losing the leader who had trained them and made sure that they were the best provided for regiment in the army. The men admired and respected Colonel Sulakowski. They saw him "as one of the most provident and efficient commanders they ever had," despite, or perhaps because of, his stern character and strict discipline. Under his leadership the men found that it gave them an advantage in situations when they were "in competition with others in the Confederate army, about camping grounds, supplies or similar subjects of contention."[88] They did not have the same affection for Jones, who was not at all popular. As an expression of their dissatisfaction, "the men of the 14th Louisiana handled this crisis in typical style—they rioted." Officers even went to resign in protest, but the headquarters staff was able to bring the disturbance and the defections from the regiment under control.[89]

Not all of Sulakowski's officers respected and admired the colonel. Frank Schaller, who was still with the Louisianans but not in Grand Junction for the riot, felt that the colonel had been an impediment to his advancement in rank. Schaller resented that the regiment had been allowed to elect officers and complained that he was rightful commander of the 2nd Regiment. He had always looked to Tochman as a mentor, a "noble" for whom he felt "greater veneration." Schaller supported Tochman's confirmation as general and appealed to him about Sulakowski's command. He also was angry that Sulakowski was not under disciplinary action for the shootings in quelling the riot. In September 1861 he wrote to his wife, Sophie Sosnowski, that he vowed to get even if he and Sulakowski survived the war: "there will one day be a terrible reckoning between him and myself. He can dodge me by intrigue and wily conversation, but he shall not escape my bullet."[90]

Sulakowski returned to New Orleans where he spoke out against the war effort conducted by the government in Richmond.[91] He served as chief engineer under Brigadier General Jean-Jacques Alexandre Alfred Mouton in Louisiana in the autumn of 1862. There he built a defense line and constructed fortifications to keep the Union gunboats from coming up Bayou Teche and the Atchafalaya River from the Gulf of Mexico.[92] Before Sulakowski had departed for New Orleans, Magruder made an unsuccessful plea with the Confederate War Department to keep this officer of such great promise. He had been loath to lose his favorite colonel's services in Virginia. When the Confederate authorities subsequently transferred Magruder to take charge of the defense of the Texas coast in late 1862, he sought out Sulakowski. Magruder met with him and made him colonel of the artillery and chief engineer for the District of Texas in June 1863. Sulakowski set up his headquarters at Galveston and was responsible for the coastal defenses from the Sabine River on the Louisiana state line to the Rio Grande River border with Mexico.[93]

Magruder had come to Texas under a cloud of accusations about "being incapacitated for energetic attention" to his duties "by reason of drunkenness." The charges had stemmed from some Virginia parents' reluctance to have their sons serve under Magruder fearing his intemperate influence. The *Dallas Herald* reported the origin of the story and added that since then, General Magruder "has not drank an intoxicating draught," according to persons who knew him well. The newspaper opined that if that was so, "it speaks volumes for his head and heart."[94] When he was victorious in the combined naval and land battle of Galveston on New Year's 1863, he gained more respect and popularity. He also increased his authority and ability to make appointments and strategic decisions. He had taken control of the Texas coast from Sabine Pass to Galveston and "became the toast of Texas."[95]

Magruder was in need of more troops for defense of the Texas coast, and because this had a cost, he also had to gain control of the state's cotton trade from black marketeers and corrupt agents. It was the valuable commodity that he could trade for hard currency or materiel. He issued a new order for cotton exportation through Mexico in exchange for needed supplies and munitions. Sulakowski too realized that more troops were needed, specifically for the proper manning of the Galveston defenses. He requested 1,200 more soldiers to add to the garrison. The Texas legislature also had passed stricter conscription laws that required all foreigners to "take an oath of allegiance to the Confederate States, and enroll themselves as subject to military duty." If they did not pledge and enroll, they were immediately subject to dismissal from employment. Sulakowski concocted a more creative scheme for enlistment of soldiers than conscription. He was more interested in seasoned fighters than in getting the state's immigrants in line.[96]

When Poland's 1863 revolt against Russia failed, thousands of Poles who had fought in and led the army were scattered throughout Europe as exiles. Russia was the only major European power to support the Union and therefore was an enemy of the Confederacy as well as Sulakowski's ancestral foe. He envisioned recruiting a force of 5,000 from those who had fought in the insurgency. The colonel felt that these Poles would be promising recruits for enlistment if he could provide the proper incentives. The proposal was to reward service in the Confederate army with citizenship and 200 acres of land in Texas upon completion of duties. Magruder was enthusiastic in his backing of the idea.[97] Lieutenant General Edmund Kirby Smith, in command of the Trans-Mississippi Department, also was supportive of the project. He approved of payment of $80 (in cotton) for each recruit and proposed, "the Corps that Colonel

Sulakowski raises can elect officers, serve their terms and then" would be Confederate citizens "without any need for further nationalization." Smith also intended to nominate and have Sulakowski confirmed for a generalship "upon his arrival with two or more regiments." They were to enter Texas from Mexico after disembarking at the port of Matamoros to avoid Federal interference at sea. His only regret was that he did not have "full approval of the Department" for all the necessary monies since only the State legislatures could approve funding.[98]

Texas Governor Francis R. Lubbock wanted victory for the Confederacy yet was never one to think progressively when it came to creative military solutions—especially if he perceived there was a monetary cost to his state. He conveniently put the proposal documents in a place where they could be forgotten. Even with the expressed interest of President Davis and others, Lubbock in effect tabled the plan. This deed was in conjunction with his opposition to enlisting slaves and adamant insistence that Texas would never allow blacks to serve in uniform under arms within his state. Major General Patrick Ronayne Cleburne had written a cogent argument for arming slaves in exchange for freedom and citizenship. Cleburne had been successful on the battlefield as an officer in the Army of Tennessee. An Irishman by birth, he had built a successful law practice in Arkansas before the war and drew upon his legal experience to formulate his reasoning. Virginia and Louisiana had been in favor of his idea, but in Texas slaves could only serve as teamsters, cooks, laborers for construction of battlements or other menial jobs.[99]

In 1864, with the war going increasingly worse for the Confederacy, Sulakowski set out on a secret mission.[100] The Federal blockade had made receipt of any shipments impossible, except through channels in Mexico, primarily Matamoros on the Gulf coast. Magruder learned that the Confederate quartermaster had to flee inland to Monterrey "for his life," so there would be no cotton trade for what looked to be months. He wrote to Brigadier General W.R. Boggs, the Chief of Staff, describing a plan to be conducted by Valery Sulakowski. The Polish colonel proposed that he evade the Federal blockade by setting sail in the schooner *Dodge* from Calcasieu (on Louisiana's border with Texas) with 3,000 bales of saleable cotton to go to Havana, Cuba. There he planned to "purchase a steamer" for use in transport of troops and armaments. Magruder's report summarized the plan:

> The necessity of getting arms and troops is so great that Colonel Sulakowski ought to take all the facilities he requires. His plan is to buy, with the proceeds of the cargo of the schooner Dodge, a light-draught steamer, which he says he can get, to run her into the Brazos, and take out the remainder of the 2,000 bales of cotton; with this to procure soldiers and arms, and if any political consideration should prevent his success in getting soldiers, he will invest the whole in arms.[101]

Magruder thought this was the best possible plan for military aid. He also mentioned that Sulakowski had a back-up plan to approach Mexican Governor Santiago Vidaurri about "permission to colonize a portion of his territory with Polanders, his countrymen." Vidaurri was provincial governor of the northern state of Nuevo Leon and Coahuila on the south side of the Rio Grande. He had been on friendly terms with the Confederacy and this provided an alternative to the Texas land grants that had stalled with Lubbock. Magruder was certain that Sulakowski would have his request granted.[102]

In correspondence from 3 May 1864, Sulakowski wrote to Magruder from Matamoros, Mexico. First he reported on the Federal troop strength in Brownsville, Texas, on the Rio Grande, having passed through the area on the way to the Mexican port. After advising Magruder that a military assault could succeed, he described the difficulties he was having in accomplishing his mission. Initially, he was "detained three weeks at" Matamoros because the steamer *Melville* was re-routed to New York, and the Federal navy captured the schooner *Dodge* in the Gulf of Mexico. As a result, he predicted his departure to Havana for 8 May by another schooner. Another incident that made things more complicated was the interception of a friendly agent from Governor Vidaurri's staff by Federal troops (who then turned him over to pro-Union Mexicans). Apparently without trial, they executed the man by firing squad the next day:

> The Federals have covered themselves with unprecedented infamy. Without being requested, they have turned over to Cortina a political refugee, the secretary of Governor Vidauri [sic], who entered their lines ... he was shot the next day outside of the town by Cortina. It makes one's blood curdle at such infamy.[103]

Sulakowski added that even though the Federals captured the schooner *Dodge,* he was still "determined not to give up" his "project." Additionally, he gave a heartfelt assurance that he was more devoted to the Confederate cause than ever, even though he was outside the country facing an uncertain future.[104] The Federal blockade, seizure of the schooner and capture of the transport ship made completion of the mission impossible.

Later in 1864, a group of exiled Poles came up with a similar plan to provide troops for the South. Four Poles participated in an alleged plot that they proposed to Confederate government authorities in Richmond. Two colonels, who had fought against the Russians, J. Smolinski and A. Lenkiewicz, and their compatriot a major (Bninicki) and a chaplain evaded the Federal naval blockade and entered the country through the port of Wilmington, North Carolina. They made their way to Richmond and after arranging a meeting in September with Jefferson Davis and Secretary of State Judah Benjamin, they outlined their plan. Their premise was that there were thousands of Poles in Europe who were sympathetic to the Southern cause. They identified with the struggle against the Union and compared it to their own fight against Imperial Russia.[105]

The plan was similar to that of Sulakowski's in that it offered recruitment, transport to America and military service in exchange for land and citizenship. They also were to come through Mexico and then enter the Confederacy in Texas. Benjamin authorized an initial £50,000 to the South's agent in England, Colin J. McRae, to aid in establishing the recruitment network in Europe. His orders were to allow the Poles to volunteer of their own accord. The potential addition of several thousand men to the army's ranks temporarily helped inflate Richmond's sagging hopes for the war effort, though the plan never fully materialized.[106]

Years later, in 1889, a detailed account of the plot appeared in the New York *Sun.* It referred to the plan as "£250,000 for 15,000 Men" and seemingly sought to discredit the Polish-Confederate alliance and mutual sympathies. The stratagem was basically a plan contrived "to swindle the Confederates." The report declared that "President Davis and Secretary of State Benjamin were neatly hoodwinked, but Agents McRae and [his partner, James] Williams were alert and honest." The newspaper's version of the affair mentioned that the assemblage of as many as "15,000 or 5,000 foreigners into the Southern army … would have aroused a feeling of indignation" in the North. It did not make any reference to the enlistment of numerous immigrants into Union ranks. The group under Smolinski approached Sulakowski requesting his assistance in their venture. He rebuffed them and wanted no part of the association. Agent Williams cited in a letter from London dated 1 February 1865 that Colonel Sulakowski on his mission in Europe, "was repulsed by Maj. Buynicki [sic] in such a way" that he refused to "connect himself in any way to the affair."[107] At that point, the war was in its waning months and Sulakowski likely felt that the effort was futile and distrusted the motives of the perpetrators who he deemed were operating for monetary gain.

Valery Sulakowski returned to New Orleans and family life at the end of the war. He worked as a civil engineer and surveyor and largely stayed out of public life. One instance of public attention was when he testified in a perjury trial of Louisiana's Governor Joshua Baker in 1868. His testimony involved his activities in constructing fortifications on Bayou Teche, Louisiana, and his knowledge of Baker during the war. The better known occurrence, and one more fitting of his character and reputation, was on the event of the visit of Grand Duke Alexis of Russia. In his entourage was the old nemesis of Gaspard Tochman, Ambassador Bodisco. The New Orleans mayor and his staff gave the Duke a warm reception, but the crowds barely were able to catch a glimpse of him after his arrival by ship. Sulakowski, ever the opponent of Imperial Russia, "bitterly denounced the Russian," holding up a placard, but his friends kept him from attempting any possible assault on the Duke. Additionally, the mayor had the Duke "driven down to quiet and ne-glected streets to his apartments" to avoid incident. He also had police at the watch for "the apprehensions of murderous pursuers, or to escape assassination."[108] The New Orleans *Picayune* referred to the Colonel as "not only a soldier, but a gentleman possessing a bright intellect and rare literary acquirements, and was thoroughly conversant with several ancient and modern languages." He died suddenly at age forty-six on 19 June 1873 of apoplexy. His funeral was held from his residence on Carondelet Street.[109]

Perhaps Sulakowski's defining moment was in quelling the riot at Grand Junction—and for that he was most remembered. The *Lafayette Advertiser* wrote following his death that he had been a "man of great prowess and bravery." It referred to the episode as "A Heroic Act," in which "A Single Man Combats and Subdues A Hundred."[110] At that moment Sulakowski embodied the synthesis of the nineteenth-century revolutionary leader with an Old World military officer. He was a rebel quelling a rebellion. The Colonel was at the head of a multinational body of soldiers that were united for one cause in the defense of their *new* country against a perceived empire. The soldiers in his regiment represented countries and ethnic groups that had been downtrodden, and many of the men had experienced the turmoil in Europe that took place in the first half of the century. Here in America they also became revolutionaries—rebels in the eyes of the enemy and *Rebels* in their own estimation against the enforced establishment of hierarchical rule.

In some respects, Sulakowski was a dual symbolic figure who embodied Poland of that epoch and the Southern spirit. He was a firebrand, independent, and a fierce defender of his ideals, but ultimately did not achieve his full potential as an officer. Żychliński, as noted, left the American army while it had been suffering setbacks at the hands of the Confederates. In returning to Poland, he fought in the unsuccessful 1863 war against the Russian empire and had to endure Siberian exile and imprisonment. Sulakowski's last stand of defiance against Russia was his protest against the visit of the Russian Grand Duke to New Orleans after the Civil War.

CHAPTER 5

THE MODEL NEW AMERICAN OFFICERS

Joseph Kargé and Wladimir Krzyżanowski were emblematic of many Poles, North and South, who came to America with their ideals and convictions and had the courage to carry out their duties and pursue their goals—and did so successfully. Both men were exemplary in that they remained true to their ideals and duty bound throughout the war and in their careers. They both served in the field from the war's beginning until the end. In the Union army they shared many of the same trials that accompanied the ordeals of war itself. The antipathy of nativism that existed in the army as well as civilian life was a gratuitous obstacle they faced, especially in the early days of the conflict when they had yet to prove themselves on the field of battle. Unwarranted charges made by jealous underlings proved to be unnecessary deterrents to effectively fulfilling their duties as officers. Delays in receiving deserved promotions for specious reasons could wear on the morale of a leader as well as the men under his command. Despite these hindrances both officers endured, prevailed and were successful. At the same time, they adhered to their principles and maintained the ideals that had put them in their positions.

In the Civil War's second year, between the disastrous defeats suffered by the North at Fredericksburg (December 1862) and Chancellorsville (May 1863), Kargé and Krzyżanowski joined to rally support for their fellow Poles in the January 1863 uprising against Russia. Both officers also transferred with their units to serve in the western theatre, mostly in Tennessee and Mississippi. By war's end, both had achieved the rank of general. They continued to achieve and influence others in their lives in the rebuilding United States after the war. Kargé became a professor at Princeton University and Krzyżanowski went into civil service and held several positions around the country.[1]

Włodzimierz Krzyżanowski

Włodzimierz (Wladimir) Krzyżanowski came to America after the 1846 Polish insurrections, settled in Washington, D.C., and worked as a civil engineer in Virginia before the Civil War. He joined the Republican Party and supported Abraham Lincoln for president. When hostilities began, he raised troops for the Union and became commander of the 58th New York Infantry, also known as "The Polish Legion." He saw action at such major engagements as Second Manassas, Gettysburg and later in Tennessee. He eventually attained the rank of brigadier general by the end of the war. Afterwards, he remained in government service, first in the Reconstruction South in governing positions and later in the Treasury Department. He died in 1887 and was buried in New York, but later his remains were interred in Arlington National Cemetery in Virginia.[2]

Krzyżanowski had one of the most successful and distinguished careers of any of the Poles on either side before, during and after the Civil War. It is significant that after rising through the ranks, this Polish officer performed at the equivalency of a general's rank until his actual appointment to that rank by the president in the middle of the war. When the nomination expired due to Congressional inaction, he continued to fulfill his responsibilities without wavering or exhibiting any resentment. He also weathered and survived inquiries and criticisms, as well as enduring the stigma of being a foreigner in the "foreign" Eleventh Corps. The succession of actions in which he participated recorded his rise, determination and devotion to duty.

The misunderstanding of Krzyżanowski, his place in the army and his status as an American soldier—and for that matter other officers of European origin—began with his name. In the official records his first

Wladimir Krzyżanowski

name is listed as Wladimir, an anglicized version of the Polish spelling, and sometimes even "Waldimir," an obvious misspelling.[3] The *Historical Register and Dictionary of the United States Army* lists his place of birth simply as "Poland" and his entry into the army from New York. It lists his service as:

> Colonel 58th New York Infantry 22 Oct 1861; Brigadier General Volunteers 29 November 1862; appointment expired 4 Mar 1863 and reverted to Colonel 58th New York Infantry; Brevet Brigadier General Volunteers 2 Mar 1865; Honorable Muster out 1 Oct 1865; [died 31 January 1887.][4]

Krzyżanowski's regiment was under the command of General John C. Frémont at the Battle of Cross Keys against Stonewall Jackson's Confederates and again as part of General Carl Schurz's Division in the campaign of Second Manassas, in which he commanded a brigade as part of General Franz Sigel's First Corps. He was not directly involved in the actions at Antietam or Fredericksburg. However, he and his men met Jackson again on the battlefield at Chancellorsville in May 1863 where he "shared in the disaster which befell Joseph Hooker's right when it was overwhelmed" by Jackson's famous flanking attack. He was in the thick of the fighting at Gettysburg, then transferred to Tennessee to serve under General Hooker yet again, leading his brigade into action at the battle of Chattanooga. He later was involved in the defense of the railroad system in Tennessee and was commander of Federal troops at Stevenson, Alabama at the end of the war.[5] Krzyżanowski, or "Kriz" as his men affectionately referred to him, embodied the traits and beliefs that would motivate and propel Poles of Southern or Northern affiliation into military service during the war.

Krzyżanowski was a regimental and brigade commander in the much-maligned Eleventh Corps that had a high percentage of first generation and foreign-born troops. The Confederates routed them at Chancellorsville and afterward the Eleventh endured accusations ranging from poor discipline to dereliction of duty and cowardice. Although they carried that stigma with them, neither the press nor their comrades in the army specifically singled out Krzyżanowski and his men with negative criticism. He and his brigade were part of the Army of the Potomac and Union army in general that had suffered a string of setbacks in the Eastern theatre that began with Manassas in July of 1861 and did not end decisively until 3 July 1863, the final day at Gettysburg. According to the official reports, he demonstrated skillful leadership and coolness under fire, and he and his men generally acquitted themselves well. As a soldier and a man, "he was an idealist who possessed the determination and courage of his convictions to risk all that he had in the pursuit of the goals he valued."[6]

He later wrote his memoirs (*Wspomnienia*), which were first published in a series of magazine articles. In his own words, it is evident that he stood on principle and honor.[7] His biographer, James Pula, infuses these ideals into the narrative and demonstrates the character of Krzyżanowski in the performance of his duties. He especially states that the Pole accepted his orders and served dutifully despite the delays and difficulties with his promotion. His personality comes forth in certain affairs after the war during Reconstruction. Even before the war, he identified himself with the Radical Republicans and the policies of Abraham Lincoln's "unswerving principle of liberty under a firm national government that reflected the ideal he had relished since the patriotic childhood stories of his native land."[8]

During the war Krzyżanowski was to experience disappointments in several areas before the cessation of combat and final victory in 1865. The events of 1863 in particular illustrate the obstacles that Poles faced in America as well as in their homeland. The notion that ethnic or foreign-born officers did not receive promotions they felt they deserved was palpable in both the Northern and Southern ranks. German and Irish officers also expressed this sentiment.[9] German-born General Carl Schurz, who nominated the Pole along with Col. Alexander Schimmelfennig for the rank of brigadier general, said that Congress passed over Krzyżanowski because no one in the Senate could pronounce his name.[10] The disastrous defeat at Chancellorsville in May added to the gloom, and his brigade was part of the Union line overrun by the Confederates in what was to be a temporary setback at Gettysburg in July. The other blow of 1863 was twofold: the Polish revolt against Russian rule in that part of their ancestral home, and the Czar's indication of support for the Union cause. Russia, the enemy of his people on the other side of the Atlantic, was now an ally of his new nation. The situation, of course, improved for Krzyżanowski and his men, for they ended up on the side of the victors and he was able to begin a post-war career.

Krzyżanowski began to exhibit his leadership ability as an American soldier at the beginning of the war. He first commanded a company of militia in Washington, D.C., then personally organized an infantry

General Alexander Schimmelfennig, brigade commander in the Eleventh Corps.

regiment in New York and obtained the rank of colonel. That regiment became the 58th Volunteer New York Infantry, comprised of men of various nationalities but called "The Polish Legion." He later became "commander of the Second Brigade (Schurz's Division)" in the Army of Virginia. It was composed of the 58th and 54th New York and 75th Pennsylvania Infantries and the 2nd New York Light Artillery.[11] Yet it is his actions and participation in major engagements that define and distinguish Krzyżanowski as an officer of the Union Army. Whether in engagements in which his troops fared well or when the Confederates were victorious, he showed himself as an unflappable leader. He served in the Eastern theatre in Virginia beginning with Cross Keys, then Second Manassas and Chancellorsville through Gettysburg. After transfer to the Army of the Tennessee, he took part in the Chattanooga and Knoxville campaigns and saw action in related skirmishes and battles in Alabama and Mississippi. His superior toward the end of the war in Fall of 1864 and Spring 1865, Major General Robert H. Milroy, considered him "a noble Pole and a most splendid officer" who should be promoted.[12]

Krzyżanowski's first assignment after the fall of Fort Sumter at the beginning of the war was in the defense of Washington as captain of a company of volunteers. For three months until mustered out in July 1861, he was with the 8th Battalion, District of Columbia Infantry, and saw minor actions and exchanges of gunfire with Confederates at Great Falls, on the Potomac River between Maryland and Virginia, and nearby Seneca Mills.[13] It was here "that the captain acquired the nickname 'Kriz' from his fellow officers," who found it easier than pronouncing his Polish surname.[14] After his term of duty expired, he received permission to recruit an infantry regiment and received a promotion to the rank of major. He went to New York City and opened a recruiting office in Manhattan "where the large population and weekly influx of immigrants proved a constant source of volunteers."[15] Although he had recruited 400 men, the authorities in New York, "encouraged by the War Department, began combining incomplete regiments into units" in order to form the 58th New York Volunteer Infantry. "The colonelcy of the new regiment went to the man who raised the most troops," and this was Krzyżanowski.[16] He "received authority from the War Department on August 20, 1861 to recruit a regiment of infantry, which he named the *United States Rifles*."[17] The regiment came to be considered the Polish Legion, at first by legend "in honor of five of its captains who served in the Polish Legion during the Hungarian Uprising of 1848." However, this was not totally accurate and may have been in "deference to the commanding officer ... and a tribute to the Poles in the regiment whose homeland still lay subdued by foreign powers."[18] The reality was that the regiment was a conglomeration of authorized but only partially completed units:

> [that were] known as the *Polish Legion* ... Wladimir Kryzanowski [sic] was appointed Colonel of the regiment. The companies were mustered in the service of the United States for three years in Nov., 1861, and, composed of Danes, Frenchmen, Germans, Italians, Poles and Russians, were recruited principally in New York city.[19]

In November 1861 the regiment departed New York for Washington. Its assignment was "duty in the Defences of Washington, D.C. till April, 1862."[20] The Army considered the 58th New York a "foreign" regiment because it was primarily comprised of "immigrants and second-generation Americans ... and segregated it into organizations of similar composition."[21] They were assigned to a brigade with Pennsylvania regiments whose men were of German extraction and their division commander, General Ludwig Blenker, was originally from Bavaria. The division itself was referred to throughout the army as the "German Division."[22]

Krzyżanowski's regiment spent the winter encamped near Washington at Hunter's Chapel, Virginia, where it endured the boredom of camp life until March 1862 when Krzyżanowski and his men began to grow impatient for action. As spring arrived the boredom of camp life stirred the men's eagerness for excitement, and they saw the possibilities with the assignment of their new commander, John C. Frémont. President Lincoln had put Frémont in charge of the newly formed Mountain Department in Virginia. With this development, they also learned that they soon would see action against the Confederate rising star, "Stonewall" Jackson in the Shenandoah Valley. As part of General Henry Bohlen's brigade in Blenker's Division, the 58th New York received orders to proceed west to Virginia's Shenandoah Valley. Frémont had complained that he needed additional strength in the Valley to confront Jackson, whose Confederate army was protecting the agriculturally rich and strategically important region. This was part of his grander plan of sweeping south through Virginia to the southwestern part of the state. If successful, this operation ultimately would sever railroad and communication ties between Richmond and the western Confederacy as well as prevent the Confederate army from concentrating against McClellan and his Peninsula campaign in the east.[23]

Cross Keys

Upon arrival in early April after their march to the Shenandoah Valley, a heavy snowstorm soon enveloped the 58th New York Regiment's quarters at Salem, Virginia. This unseasonal blizzard dampened the springtime enthusiasm of Krzyżanowski's men, and the troops' "misery was only heightened by the government's neglect to provide them with foul weather gear."[24] Additionally, the Army provided them with inaccurate maps. Such bad navigational tools led them on circuitous marches in which they "spent a good deal of time digging in and out of the impossible mire created by the incessant rain and snow." Every road was a quagmire for Krzyżanowski's troops and the going was even worse for the horses, mules and wagons. Supplies ran short because the men abandoned so many wagons and horses that were "helpless and weary or wallowed in the mud."[25] Sickness became rampant, munitions ran out, and the troops of the 58th as well the rest of Blenker's Division began to "fend for themselves" and forage in the countryside. This foraging off the farms and land was done to the extent that "Blenkering" became the term local Virginians used for looting and pillaging. The people despised these invaders all the more because they stole whatever they could and destroyed what they did not take.[26] The citizenry "learned to fear and loathe the immigrant troops, collectively termed 'Dutch' (i.e. Germans) … of Blenker's division." There were instances of glee at their misfortunes, as in receiving word of Union soldiers lost to drowning during a river crossing. Confederate General Richard S. Ewell referred to them as "miscreants" and reported "with atypical relish on the casualties he had inflicted."[27] Ewell reported officially that Blenker's division had been "notorious for months on account of their thefts and dastardly insults to women and children."[28] The spring snowstorm, rains, mud and enmity of the local people created morale-depleting conditions for the Polish Legion in the months leading up to their first major engagement, the Battle of Cross Keys on 8 June 1862.

Krzyżanowski wrote his battle report from the headquarters of the 58th Regiment at Mount Jackson, Virginia on 12 June. He stated how he formed his "regiment into line … in the middle of a large rye field, skirted by woods immediately on the right of the battery" while detecting enemy artillery fire on his right. Another account (not a battle report) by a late 20th century historian has the 58th Regiment in the rye field with Krzyżanowski being "mightily confused, wondering where the enemy was, where his friends were, and what he was to do," but does not cite any official report or witness for such "confusion" or "wonderment."[29] Bewildered or not, he sent out skirmishers to determine the Confederate advance in preparation for the action. Krzyżanowski then related how when his skirmishers withdrew back within his lines, he had his men "keep up a constant fire, which told greatly among the enemy's lines [and then] gave the command to charge

Artist's rendering by Arthur Szyk depicts Krzyżanowski leading his men at Cross Keys with a saber in hand rather than a bayonet.

bayonets, and succeeded in driving him back about a hundred yards."[30] He did not embellish his participation in the fight nor leadership as commander, even though he "distinguished himself ... when he personally, with bayonet in hand, led a successful charge on Ewell's Confederates." He did not have a sword within reach but ordered "his men to advance on the enemy."[31] His brigade commander, General Bohlen, also mentioned the charge in his official report:

The Fifty-eighth met the enemy and drove him back at the point of the bayonet. Being in danger of being cut off by two columns advancing on the right, and also by the enemy's force placed on the left, the regiment had to retire … The regiment being without any support, fell back behind Captain Wiedrich's battery in good order … From the report of Captain Schirmer, whose guns were supported by the Fifty-eighth Regiment, this regiment behaved with great gallantry, under the command of Colonel Krzyzanowski.[32]

The modern battle analysis mentioned above dismisses Bohlen's account as an "opportunity to float a grossly exaggerated report" that the New Yorkers drove the enemy back "at the point of the bayonet." It continues that the report is "unconfirmed by any observer" and "transpired in his [Bohlen's] own fevered imagination."[33] Yet, in another instance the historian shows seemingly deferential respect and writes that Krzyżanowski's reports of the same battle exhibited "atypical modesty," thereby suggesting that his usual reports were embellished.[34] This is not the case, however, since the Polish colonel's report stated that he and his men withdrew with "greatest dismay" when he saw superior enemy numbers advancing. He saw a body of fresh Confederate troops under Brigadier General Isaac R. Trimble, and reported "two regiments coming out of the woods on the right of the enemy's battery, and having no reserve to fall back on I thought it imprudent to remain any longer, and consequently gave the command orders to retire while a heavy musketry fire was poured upon my men."[35] The biographer refers to the official reports and asserts that Krzyżanowski "behaved like a professional, commanding his regiment with skill and honor."[36]

The portrayal of Colonel Krzyżanowski is one of being "histrionic" and "excitable," a commander with a "fevered imagination" who "boasted in a postwar narrative of his own bayonet charge that hurled a horde of Rebels back, saving the Union from destruction." It seems an exaggeration to state Krzyżanowski "was sure that the fate of free men everywhere hung in the balance" during the "virtual Armageddon" which was the battle of Cross Keys.[37] There is nothing in the Official Reports to substantiate such sentiments on the part of the colonel.

The Battle of Cross Keys resulted in a Confederate victory (Union losses of 684, Confederate losses 288) for Major General Richard S. Ewell of Stonewall Jackson's command.[38] His Union opponent, Major General John C. Frémont, had a two-to-one numerical superiority but began his assault on the enemy thinking that *he* was outnumbered. He did not have proper reconnaissance, and with "no supports readily on hand, the Northerners blundered into a killing frontal attack which was easily repelled. From that point on the Confederates held the initiative."[39] Frémont had decided to fight Jackson "whenever and wherever found," even though the Confederates had occupied a position that was "an amphitheatre of hills, a position so admirably fitted for defense that even double his own force could not dislodge [them]."[40] Jackson, on the other hand, had a low opinion of Frémont's tactical abilities. He "entertained a profound and not ill-founded contempt" for Frémont's military talents. The Union officers gave credit to Jackson's "military skill and boundless audacity" in achieving victory at Cross Keys' over the "sluggishness" of Frémont and in the Shenandoah Valley in general.[41]

Krzyżanowski did not catalogue the "fatiguing marches in unseasonably inclement spring weather" that had exhausted his men, nor did he mention the lack of sufficient supplies and weakened morale that plagued his men prior to the engagement.[42] Throughout the Shenandoah Valley campaign Stonewall Jackson had successfully engaged, beleaguered and defeated Union forces numbering a total of 52,000 men with his force of 17,000 Confederates. The Union General officers as a group "failed to perform well during the campaign, [but] the troops generally fought bravely when committed." Krzyżanowski wrote of the disappointments of the defeats in the Valley campaign, yet he received favorable reviews for his handling of his regiment and its conduct during their first major engagement.[43]

Second Battle of Manassas (Second Bull Run)

The reorganization of Union forces following the Valley Campaign and Seven Days Battles assigned the 58th New York to the newly formed Army of Virginia in the summer of 1862. The Polish Legion was transferred to the 2nd Brigade, 3rd Division, First Corps of the army under Major General John Pope, dating from 26 June 1862.[44] Pope had been successful in operations in Missouri and Tennessee in the western theatre, prompting Lincoln to bring him east and place him in command of a force that would operate separately from the Army of the Potomac, which was still on the Virginia Peninsula. Despite Pope's so far respectable military record, many of his fellow officers and the troops he now commanded considered him "a rude, quick tempered braggart." His address to the troops of his new command was a self-praising, self-aggrandizing speech about his successes and "a condemnation of their past efforts."[45]

Krzyżanowski's men had been disheartened by the overall failures of the army in the Shenandoah Valley but they retained a "cautious hope."[46] He was now in charge of a brigade under corps commander Franz Sigel and division commander Carl Schurz. Robert E. Lee, in command of the Army of Northern Virginia, having forced McClellan back from the environs of Richmond, now planned to turn against Pope and demolish his army before it had a chance to unite with the Army of the Potomac and thus comprise a force too large for the Confederates to handle. After maneuvers west of Fredericksburg, including the Battle of Cedar Mountain on August 9, Lee decided to divide his army and confuse Pope and his 75,000 Federal troops. Half of the Confederates under Stonewall Jackson would cross the upper Rappahannock and march north, screened by the Blue Ridge Mountains, while the other half, under Longstreet, would demonstrate along the river to hold Pope in place.

On August 26 Jackson emerged from the mountains via Thoroughfare Gap and descended on the Union rail line at Bristoe Station. By the next morning he had captured the Army of Virginia's immense supply depot at Manassas Junction. Pope immediately vacated his positions along the Rappahannock and moved north where he hoped to trap and destroy Jackson before he could be reinforced. Despite Jackson's record of success, given the fact that Lee had divided his army Pope "was exultant, and with cause. He had forty brigades of infantry on hand … It seemed to him that Lee who had less than thirty brigades—fourteen in one direction, fifteen in another … had committed tactical suicide."[47] However, as soon as Pope moved north, Longstreet's wing also marched, taking the same route as Stonewall.

For the next 48 hours the Union army groped for Jackson and his 25,000 men, who had taken up position along an abandoned railway cut in a wooded area outside the hamlet of Groveton, near Manassas. At dusk on the 28th Jackson revealed his position, initiating a brutal stand-up fight with a passing Union column. Now Pope knew where Jackson was, and hastened to gather his forces to destroy the isolated Confederate wing on the morrow.

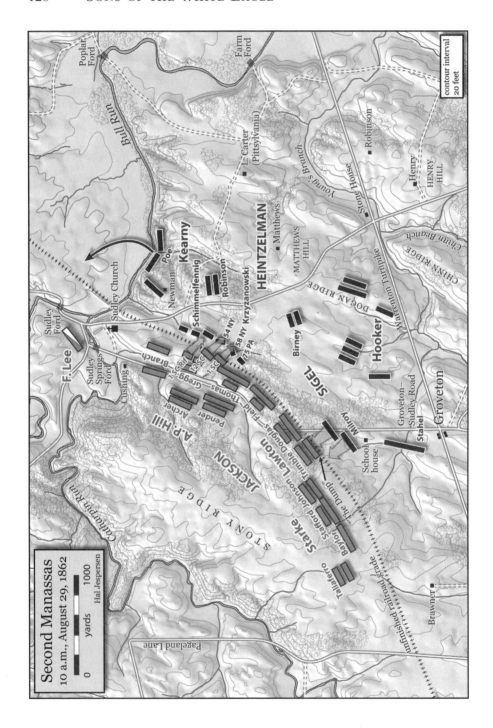

Second Manassas
10 a.m., August 29, 1862

0   yards   1000
Hal Jespersen

contour interval
20 feet

The battle began on August 29 with the advance of Krzyżanowski's brigade at 5:30 a.m. on orders from General Schurz. Krzyżanowski sent a detachment to feel out the Confederate position, and "scarcely had the skirmishers passed over 200 yards when they became engaged with the enemy ... At this time I ordered my regiments up and a general engagement ensued." It was to be a clash between the New Yorkers and Pennsylvanians of Krzyżanowski's brigade and General Maxcy Gregg's South Carolinians. The two commanders "enacted the first day's drama on Jackson's left."[48] They remained engaged until 2:00 p.m. that afternoon when Union relief arrived.

The following day Krzyżanowski's brigade went into action at 8:00 a.m. and moved into position. As soon as they had done this they "became engaged with the enemy and kept up a brisk fire." Later the colonel adjusted his troop positions as the Confederates moved. There was a brigade to his left whose name he "was unable to ascertain," but continued with "some fifteen minutes of constant firing of our two brigades" and held position. Krzyżanowski expressed some frustration and wrote that then the enemy withdrew and he had wished to pursue. Seeing this, he "consulted with the brigade commander" situated on his left flank. He reported that he implored this commander to move, "asking him to advance farther in company with me, which he, however, refused to do."[49]

In the attacks on Jackson, Krzyżanowski's men had handled themselves well. They had been engaged for more than eight hours and had taken and held a position "defended by the highly touted veterans of Stonewall Jackson's corps."[50] They also had inflicted severe casualties on Maxcy Gregg's South Carolina troops. Six hundred and thirteen of 1,500 men of his brigade were killed or wounded, not including those missing or captured. A Confederate soldier who participated in the battle said that it "raged furiously" between the South Carolinians and their Northern adversaries. "The First regiment was threatened on the right the Twelfth on the left." Fighting in woods and brush, "they pressed back the stubborn enemy [Yankees] through the thick undergrowth, killing large numbers, and losing heavily themselves."[51] For two of the Palmetto State regiments, "losses proved so severe that the 1st and 12th South Carolina each lost over fifty-four percent of their men as casualties." The majority of these casualties were the result of the actions of Colonel Krzyżanowski's brigade.[52]

Two accounts, one by a South Carolina soldier and another by a New York artilleryman with Krzyżanowski's brigade, attest to the ferocity of the battle. The South Carolinian described the storm and melee of the action:

> All the sounds of Babel roared about us; the trees and the earth were raked with balls. Standing, kneeling, lying, we fought them, so close that men picked out their marks and on some occasions saved their lives by anticipating the fire of some on the other side.[53]

However, even as the Federals put increasing pressure on Jackson's beleaguered line, the battle was about to shift drastically against them. About midday on the 29th, Longstreet's wing of the Confederate army had begun arriving on Jackson's right, prevented from attacking at first only by the presence of Fitz John Porter's corps hanging ominously off their flank. On the 30th, General Pope, fooled by some retrograde tactical shifts among Longstreet's units plus a steady stream of Jackson's wagons (probably with wounded) heading to the rear, convinced himself that Lee's entire army was in retreat. He ordered Porter to engage Jackson and a renewal of attacks along the line. It was at the height of this pressure, when nearly Pope's entire army was committed against Jackson, that Longstreet's wing launched a gigantic assault on the Federal left.

The key to the battlefield was Henry House Hill in the Federals' rear, which would dominate their escape route. But first the Confederates would have to take Chinn Ridge, along which a succession of Union brigades tried to make a stand to protect the rest of the army. When Krzyżanowski's brigade arrived at the action on Chinn Ridge, the Federal position had already become precarious. Rebel units were lapping around the flanks, and the ground was strewn with the bodies of men who had previously tried to resist. "There was no hope of salvaging anything already lost," as more and more Confederates arrived on the scene. With his brigade decimated and close to being surrounded, when Krzyżanowski conducted an orderly withdrawal of his troops, the Confederates took Chinn Ridge.[54] By then darkness was falling, however, and Union forces were able to retain control of Henry House Hill.

The Colonel asserted in his official report that his troops did well in the fighting on 30 August 1862. "The Seventy-fifth deserves again to be especially mentioned for its bravery ... [T]he Fifty-fourth Regiment suffered severely, a number of its officers and men being wounded."[55] He continued and mentioned individual officers, many of German ethnicity: "The gallant conduct of First Lieutenant Wertheimer, of this regiment, deserves to be noticed, who, while the enemy's batteries were pouring a perfect hail of lead into our lines, nobly grasped a guided flag and cheered the men to follow him … Captain Wahle, Captain Ernewein, and Adjutant Brandt, on this day again behaved bravely." He also had under his command Captain Aleksander Małuski and other fellow Poles. The report concludes with the loss of one of Krzyżanowski's aides-de-camp, "who was severely wounded in the thigh. He showed great coolness and courage." Then finally, "I was unfortunate enough on that day to lose my horse, which was shot under me."[56]

The battle as a whole was a sound defeat for General Pope at the hands of Lee, who had divided his army and confused the Northern commander. Pope at one point had been convinced "the battered rebels would now flee, and promised a relentless pursuit the next day."[57] Instead the Southerners launched an overwhelming counterattack and forced the Union army to retreat with great losses in men, materiel and further depleted morale. Despite this, Pope reported that he had not lost and had been greatly outnumbered—both assertions were false.[58]

Battle of Chancellorsville

Krzyżanowski's brigade had suffered casualties of 372 killed, wounded and missing at Second Manassas. Doctors subsequently diagnosed him with a concussion after he complained of severe headaches in the days following the engagement. His condition could have been the result of the crushing fall after his horse had been shot. He received medical leave and returned to Washington to recuperate. Nonetheless, "the anguish of his recent experiences," exhaustion and throbbing headaches "made his daily routine one of mental and physical exasperation."[59] That September 1862, with the Army of Virginia disbanded and its units folded into the Army of the Potomac, the Federals marched to meet Lee's Confederates who had crossed into Maryland. While the battle of Antietam raged, the Polish Legion and the rest of Krzyżanowski's brigade were assigned to the defense of Washington. They remained there until October when, back under Krzyżanowski, orders sent them to Centreville,

Virginia. Except for a few minor skirmishes, their next assignment was as a reserve for the Army's new commander, General Ambrose Burnside, near Fredericksburg.[60] The Union Army sustained another serious defeat there, and Krzyzanowski's men "had to spend much of their time during December digging graves for former comrades."[61]

That fall came the nomination for promotion. Krzyżanowski's division commander, Carl Schurz, proposed his official promotion to brigadier general, especially in light of the fact that the Pole had been command-ing a brigade since July 1862. Schurz wrote to President Lincoln that Krzyżanowski "had distinguished himself greatly by his bravery in the battles of Bull Run Aug. 29th and 30th 1862," in petitioning for the position.[62] The promotion stalled in the Senate and Schurz later wrote:

> Of my two brigade commanders, Schimmelfennig had been made a brigadier general, as he well deserved. Krzyżanowski was less fortunate. The President nominated him too for that rank, but the Senate failed to confirm him—as was said, because there was no one there who could pronounce his name.[63]

With the nomination, Krzyżanowski received the respect and treatment accorded a general; when the Senate "failed to confirm him, however, he reverted to the rank of colonel on March 4, 1863." There were instances of officers who resigned when denied promotions, but Krzyżanowski resolved to continue fulfilling his duties as a soldier.[64] He and his brigade would face a serious test in the Chancellorsville campaign as the war entered its third year.

Lincoln had placed General Joseph Hooker in command of the newly reinforced and revitalized Army of the Potomac. William Swinton of the *New York Times* reported that "the army, in all its aspects, material and moral, is in splendid condition ... larger than it was ever before materi-ally. The health of the troops is better than it ever was before."[65] In the new re-organization of the Eleventh Corps, Krzyżanowski's brigade now was composed of the 75th Pennsylvania, 26th Wisconsin and his own 58th New York Regiment, The Polish Legion. He and his men were also revitalized. General Hooker "exuded confidence," and in his first cam-paign intended to capture Richmond.[66] According to General Schurz, Hooker had an "abundance" of self-assurance."[67] As martial spirit soared in the Eleventh Corps, President Lincoln visited the reorganized army in

Virginia. Krzyżanowski's brigade received high praise for its appearance and well-skilled drills after Lincoln reviewed the troops.[68]

Although Hooker had performed well in the Peninsula Campaign, and had shown "tenacious courage" at Antietam, it was said that he "also drank and talked too much for his own good." He had even suggested that a dictator was necessary if the North was going to be victorious, for which Lincoln chided him in a letter on 26 January 1863.[69] In that same letter, the President told him forcefully, "Beware of rashness, but with energy and sleepless vigilance, go forward, and give us victories."[70] Despite his façade of confidence and competence, however, Hooker proved indecisive during moments of crisis and suffered defeat at Chancellorsville. Krzyżanowski's brigade as well as the entire Eleventh Corps was at the center of Stonewall Jackson's flanking attack that triggered the Confederate victory.

Leading up to the battle, his brigade had moved under orders into a position on the army's far right south of the Rappahannock River west of Fredericksburg, Virginia. While the Union Sixth and First Corps sought to keep the Confederates' attention pinned to Fredericksburg, Hooker had moved the rest of the army west and crossed the river behind Lee, placing the outnumbered enemy army in a vise. "Krzyżanowski's men fully realized the importance of their position. Morale soared with the knowledge that they had succeeded in catching the rebels off guard."[71] Hooker was well pleased with the situation and even issued an order in which he stated "the operations of the last three days have determined our enemy must either ingloriously fly or … give us battle on our own ground where certain destruction awaits him."[72] He even went so far as to claim that Lee's Confederate army was now the "legitimate property of the Army of the Potomac."[73]

Around the Federal camps and in the Northern press, the Eleventh Corps had been considered the foreign contingent of the Union Army. Its commander, General Franz Sigel, had resigned his commission due to his unhappiness with the reorganization. His replacement was a West Pointer and native-born American, Major General Oliver O. Howard. Still the "foreign" perception lingered. Howard's "straightlaced ways were laughable to men brought up amidst Continental-style free thinking and free drinking."[74] He was not popular with his men, although

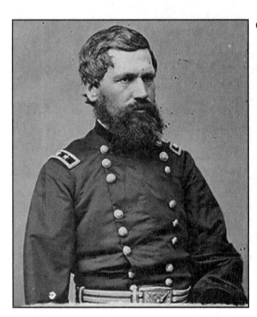

Oliver O. Howard

Schurz found him personally agreeable. His assessment was that the men regarded Howard "with dubious curiosity; not a cheer could be started when he rode along the front. And I do not know whether he liked the men he commanded better than they liked him."[75] Howard was a Maine Yankee and devout Congregationalist, a much different commander than the German-born Sigel, but the majority of the senior officers in the Eleventh Corps remained foreign-born or first generation Americans of continental European ethnicity. Besides Krzyżanowski and Schimmelfennig, three of the corps' divisions, four brigades, "twelve of twenty-six regiments, and six of eight artillery units were commanded by men with Central European names."[76] Additionally, roughly two-thirds of the corps' troops consisted of German or "mixed nationality" regiments according to Howard's official report.[77]

Caught between the two Federal forces, Lee decided to split his forces in turn. Leaving 10,000 men under Jubal Early to deter or delay the Yankees at Fredericksburg, he marched with the rest of his force, some 45,000 men, to confront Hooker. On 1 May 1863, his lead units collided with advancing Federals and held them to a standstill. Although Hooker's army had an advantage in numbers, the densely wooded terrain confined advances to a few narrow roads, thus allowing the Rebels to hold their ground. Hooker decided to pull his forces back to around the crossroads of Chancellorsville and there wait for Lee to either flee the field or attack.

That evening, Lee and Stonewall Jackson held their famous conference atop cracker boxes in the woods. It was decided that Lee would split his army yet again, this time sending Jackson with some 25,000 men, screened by 3,000 cavalry, on a circuitous march around the Federal army to hit its relatively unguarded right flank. This was the flank where Krzyżanowski and the rest of the Eleventh Corps were positioned.

Jackson's column marched all morning and afternoon on 2 May, and toward the end of the day had reached Hooker's flank as well as his rear. Arranging his divisions into three lines, Jackson launched them through the woods toward the unsuspecting Eleventh Corps. Krzyżanowski officially reported his perception of the early stages of Jackson's attack by noting that there was firing on the left of his line at 6:00 p.m. He wrote that he "discovered a part of the First Division coming down upon the left of my troops in the greatest disorder." He "inquired into the cause of the disorder, and was informed by officers and men of that division that the enemy came in such force and was pushing so rapidly that they were obliged to fall back."[78] When the Confederates completely pushed his skirmishers back into his line, he said it was "done in good order." However, he wrote that he was completely outflanked, "the consequence of which it became necessary to withdraw" and call for reinforcements. First, he received orders to withdraw further back to an area bordering the woods. When his brigade fell back to some abandoned entrenchments, he was joined by three other regiments (all or partial) and "we occupied this position for upward of one hour." Krzyżanowski then made "efforts to join the rest of the corps near a large farm house north of Chancellorsville" and was successful. On 15 May he reported his brigade's casualties to Major General Schurz as 61 killed, 194 wounded and 179 missing.[79] General Schurz confirmed these reported actions later in his memoirs:

> Colonel Krzyzanowski, the brigade commander … asked for immediate rein-
> forcements, as the Twenty-sixth Wisconsin, being nearly enveloped on all sides
> could not possibly maintain its position longer. Not having a man to send, I
> ordered the regiment to fall back to the edge of the woods in its rear, which it did
> in perfect order, facing about and firing several times as it retired.
>
> In the meantime, the enemy completely turned my left flank, and had
> not the rebel[s delayed] … a large part of the Eleventh Corps might have
> been captured before it could have reached the open ground surrounding the
> Chancellor house.[80]

Schurz continued, relating that the corps was in a battered state, and
that officers were scrambling to shore up units with what troops
could be hastily summoned from other points." He further recounted
the end results:

> When at last Jackson's overwhelming assault had wrecked the helpless
> Eleventh Corps, there was no other power of resistance between Jackson's
> triumphant force and the Chancellor house—the very heart of the position
> of the Army of the Potomac—but the remnants of the Eleventh Corps in a
> disorganized condition.[81]

The first wave of Confederates struck the "9,000 isolated troops in the
Eleventh Corps" that were basically unprepared. For the most part, their
arms were stacked and men "played cards, slept or cooked their evening
meals." Reports came in to the Union headquarters about enemy troops
on the move, but Howard in command of the Eleventh Corps had "paid
them no heed." Schurz, against Howard's wishes, had told Krzyżanowski
to reposition his brigade and thereby create a point of resistance against
the onslaught. Hooker also misread the situation and "besieged by a
multitude of such reports, became convinced that his plan was succeeding." This gave him the misperception that Lee was defeated and was
going to withdraw. Jackson, however, had maneuvered into a position
from which to cave in Hooker's flank and succeeded. Stonewall paid
for his success with his life, however, as that night he was accidentally
shot by his own men as he reconnoitered forward, looking for a way to
continue his attack.[82]

The next day, 3 May, was even bloodier as the Confederates sought
to drive the Federals out of their remaining positions. They might not
have succeeded except that Hooker ordered a tactical withdrawal from
some high ground in order to better compact his lines. It was the best

artillery position on the field, and the Rebels promptly packed it with cannon that proceeded to bludgeon the Army of the Potomac, forcing it to retreat further. After a relative pause on 4 May, during which Lee attended to the other Federal wing, under Sedgwick, that had emerged from Fredericksburg, Hooker withdrew north across the river and had his Chief of Staff, Daniel Butterfield, send the bad news to President Lincoln. In the report, Hooker laid blame all around, yet suggested he was prepared to continue the fight. The cavalry was the first group he faulted, then culpability fell to a subordinate commander: "The cavalry, as yet learned, have failed in executing their orders ... General Sedgwick failed in executing his orders ... [General Hooker has decided] that he should retire from this position to the north bank of the Rappahannock for his defensive position."[83]

Following the defeat at Chancellorsville, the Northern press, citizenry and the United States Congress searched for reasons, and ultimately looked for a scapegoat. The Eleventh Corps, given its preponderance of ethnic Germans, and European officers such as Schurz, Schimmelfennig and Krzyżanowski and the Polish Legion (though never singled out for criticism) became an easy target. Despite Hooker's mistakes, "No single man would end up being blamed for the defeat in the Virginia wilderness. Instead an entire corps would be, and by proxy, an entire ethnic group."[84] In the press, there was no restraint for the negative criticism of the corps. While a Southern newspaper, the *Richmond Examiner,* seemed reserved in its report: "The enemy finding himself outflanked, deserted his works without resistance and fled toward Chancellorsville,"[85] a Northern counterpart, The *Daily National Republican,* was specific about ethnicity in reporting: "The German regiments ... wavered on Saturday before the heavy masses of the enemy."[86] The *National Republican* also absolved General Howard of blame for the "disgraceful affair" and declared, "had he been longer in command of these men ... this stampede would not have occurred." Additionally, the newspaper report declared that "there was not one word of truth" in the report that Hooker "was whipped and driven back across the Rappahannock."[87] Compared to these accounts, the *New York Times* was unsparing in referring to the Eleventh as "the cowardly corps" that fled the field, "panic-stricken Dutchmen" and "cowardly retreating rascals." William Swinton wrote:

This corps is composed of the divisions of Schurz, Steinwehr and Devin [sic], and consists in great part of German troops. Without waiting for a single volley from the rebels, this corps disgracefully abandoned their position behind their breastworks, and commenced coming, panic stricken, down the road toward headquarters.[88]

When newspapers reached the camps of the Eleventh Corps, the troops were appalled. Krzyżanowski's men and the rest of the corps were "stunned at first," then their "reactions quickly turned to pain followed by anger." They had felt maligned as "foreigners" before, but at Chancellorsville they felt they had been "placed in a terrible position through the ineptitude of their commanding generals ... [and] had fought desperately."[89]

Krzyżanowski received numerous complaints from his men about the criticisms they felt were unfair and unfounded. There was resentment throughout the brigade and he later wrote about it in his memoirs. He was rarely stinging in his criticism of other officers but made the exception in writing about Hooker's handling of command at Chancellorsville. He reflected bitterly, recounting and questioning the occurrences in his memoirs: "*Co mogło skłonić Hookera do tego niesłychanego tchórzowskiego odwrotu?*" which translates as "What may have prompted Hooker's uncalled for cowardly retreat?"[90]

Schurz himself felt stung by the criticism in the press and from within the army. He figured his division had suffered losses of nearly one fourth and that the accusations were more bitter than even the defeat at Chancellorsville. He felt that his division had been blamed for the rout of the Eleventh Corps and that the Corps had been faulted for the total failure of the campaign. In his report to General Howard of 12 May 1863 from near Stafford Court House, Virginia, he wrote about the accusations of cowardice:

Preposterous as this is, yet we have been overwhelmed by the army and the press with abuse and insult beyond measure. We have borne as much as human nature can endure. I am far from saying that on May 2 everybody did his duty to the best of his power. But one thing I will say, because I know it: these men are no cowards. I have seen most of them fight before this, and they fought as bravely as any.[91]

Krzyżanowski agreed and stated in his *Memoirs* that the weight of the nation was on the army's shoulders, and too many officers and men had fallen "on the fields of glory (*na polu chwały*)" encouraging others to "valor and bravery."[92]

Schurz called for an investigation into the circumstances of the battle and the conduct of all the commanders in the corps. He also requested that his report be allowed to go out to the public so that the country would learn the truth. He wrote similarly to Secretary of War Edwin M. Stanton 18 May 1863, and asked permission to publish the report or have a court of inquiry publicly investigate the issue:

> The conduct of the Eleventh Corps, and especially of my division, has been so outrageously and so persistently misrepresented by the press throughout the country, and officers, as well as men, have had and still have to suffer so much abuse and insult at the hands of the rest of the army, that they would seem to have a right to have a true statement of the circumstances laid before the people, so that they may hope to be judged by their true merits.[93]

The War Department did not immediately grant this request. Schurz later lamented in his memoirs that Howard placed blame on everyone but himself as well as faulting every condition and circumstance but those that actually occurred. Howard, according to Schurz, had ignored all warnings of the impending disaster.[94] Both commanding generals, however, commended Krzyżanowski and his brigade for the stubborn resistance that bought the Federal troops some precious time in slowing down Jackson's onslaught. It kept the Confederates from achieving total victory before dark.[95] Howard wrote to Hooker later that May that "The conduct of Colonel Krzyżanowski 58th N.Y.Vols. Commanding the 2nd Brigade 3rd Division has been above reproach since I have been attached to the [Eleventh] Corps."[96]

Hooker meanwhile was maneuvering to extricate himself from the inevitable position of blame for the defeat. He lied and greatly exaggerated the number of Confederate casualties and captured.[97] In the subsequent military hearings for which General Schurz had so earnestly hoped, questions arose about the Eleventh Corps' defeat and "panic." Critics also came up with another reason inferring that the indirect cause for the rout was that they were "mostly foreigners." The result was answers such as that by Major General Alfred Pleasonton, who attributed the disaster to the terrifying effect of musketry, artillery fire and "increasing yells of the rebels" on the imagination of the already wavering troops. He "would have preferred to have sent the 11th Corps to Spotsylvania Court House" as opposed to the wilderness area where they were deployed. Pleasonton generalized that since the Wilderness mostly was "open country there and Europeans are accustomed to" fighting on open battlefields, it followed that they would have fared better fighting "in an open country than in the woods." He differentiated between the skills of the American and European soldiers with the affirmation that "our troops will fight in the woods better than any people in the world."[98]

Hooker testified before Congress that he had given explicit "instructions to be in readiness for the enemy" but his men disobeyed. He even gave damning testimony against his own Eleventh Corps' actions to the Committee on the Conduct of the War:

> The 11th corps had been completely surprised and disgracefully routed ... No disposition had been made to receive an attack, and there were no pickets on the alert to advise of the approach of an enemy. I only know that my instructions were utterly and criminally disregarded.[99]

Adjutant Theodore A. Dodge of the 119th New York was a nativist who had often expressed his disdain for foreign troops in the Union army. However, he referred to the Eleventh Corps' misfortunes as just part of the many-faceted calamity. Dodge cited the battle as "the best conceived and most fatally mismanaged of the many unsuccessful advances of the Army of the Potomac." He also referred to Hooker's testimony as an "uncalled for slur upon the conduct of his lieutenants." He especially took exception to the commander's remark, castigating his own staff, that "in all armies officers are more valiant after the fight than while it is pending," and that his "were no exception."[100]

Gettysburg

After the debacle at Chancellorsville, Krzyżanowski's brigade showed a roll call of only 1,205 men present and fit for duty. Almost half the men of the brigade who were listed on paper were suffering from wounds or disease or had returned home to await discharge. His listed strength of 2,141 did not reflect the men actually lost in the battle. He was still indignant about the accusations heaped upon the Eleventh Corps and was absolutely firm "in his belief that the results of the fighting [at Chancellorsville] ...

were produced by the prejudiced and pusillanimous natures of Generals Joseph Hooker and Oliver Otis Howard."[101] He wrote reservedly in his memoirs of his feelings as they re-crossed the Rappahannock in defeat. He was hesitant to place blame directly, "*na kogo wina jej spada?*" (On whom does blame fall?), and wanted to tell his story "with a cool head and being impartial" (*zimną krew i bezstronność*). Krzyżanowski wrote that he felt justified in "imposing [his] opinion" as one of those who was left standing after the battle, and did directly question Hooker's handling of the affairs of the battle and ensuing retreat.[102]

After Chancellorsville, Robert E. Lee decided that it was time for a bold move on Northern soil. Another victory there might force the Union to pursue a negotiated peace and lead to ultimate independence for the Confederacy. When Lee moved north it gave the Federals a chance to take the Confederate capital, but Lincoln's priority was Lee's army, not Richmond. He grew impatient and toward the end of June replaced Hooker with General George Gordon Meade.[103]

Krzyżanowski moved his brigade north with the army in the aftermath of the defeat and accusations, and their "barely repressed feelings of anger and hostility" went with them. He found that at this juncture, the worst enemy his men confronted were the other corps of the Army of the Potomac who seemed to take every opportunity to jeer and taunt the men of the Eleventh Corps. The German-Americans now heard their former boast of "I fights mit Sigel" hurled back at them as the retort, "und runs mit Schurz."[104] After crossing the Potomac River from Virginia into Maryland, Krzyżanowski's brigade and the rest of the Eleventh Corps as well as the First Corps camped at Emmitsburg, Maryland, on 29 June 1863. They were just below the Mason-Dixon line and the border with Pennsylvania, roughly thirteen miles from the small crossroads town of Gettysburg. The senior officers of the two corps took the opportunity to meet with the new commander of the Army of the Potomac, General Meade.

On the morning of 1 July, Krzyżanowski had sent Captain Emil Koenig with part of the Polish Legion scouting for Confederates in the vicinity of their camp when he received word of skirmishing near Gettysburg. He organized his brigade and began the march northward with the rest of the Eleventh Corps. They made their way around the cumbersome baggage trains, through morning thunderstorms and mired roads, into Pennsylvania.[105]

Lee had intended to converge upon and take Pennsylvania's state capital, Harrisburg. However, when he received word of Federal troop movements toward Gettysburg, he dispatched the bulk of his army in that direction. General Howard had ridden ahead of the Eleventh Corps, which was following the First Corps in converging on the town.[106]

Krzyżanowski's brigade had covered the march from Emmitsburg in four and a half hours. As they drew closer to the sounds of battle, they reached the outskirts of Gettysburg at 12:30 p.m. The local residents gave them a warm greeting with cheers and encouragements. Many brought the soldiers water or loaves of bread as they marched through the streets. It was a welcome relief from the jeers of their comrades of the other corps. Special greetings came to the 75th Pennsylvania's Lieutenant Harry Hauschildt, a resident of the town who was to become a battle-field victim of an artillery shell in later fighting.[107]

Howard gave his orders to the divisions of the Eleventh Corps. He intended to hold the northern and western lines on the outskirts of the town until the rest of the army arrived that evening. Krzyżanowski's regiments were on the northern edge of Gettysburg and could hear the action growing closer as they deployed. They were "determined to cleanse their record" as they were keenly aware of how significant this Confederate incursion into northern territory was. Krzyżanowski himself "resolved to fight as never before."[108] He positioned his men to the right of Schimmelfennig's old brigade, now under General von Amsberg, as enemy artillery situated on Oak Hill began to find its mark. They were in the open and Confederate "shells howled, shrieked and plunged through the air like infuriated demons … Again and again the jagged fragments of iron sweep destructively through the ranks, but there is no wavering."[109] General Barlow moved his division to the right of Krzyżanowski as Union batteries moved forward to bring some relief to the infantry positions.

Confederate General Jubal A. Early recognized an opportunity and ordered his men to attack the extended Union right flank where Barlow had deployed. He sent General Gordon's Georgians against Barlow, while the brigade of George Pierce Doles was simultaneously challenging skirmishers sent ahead by Krzyżanowski, who was moving more troops forward to deal with the threat. He was making an effort to turn Doles back and his men were able to contain that brigade's advance—at least temporarily. Schurz was now in command of the corps with Howard having moved up to take charge of both the First and Eleventh Corps, after the First Corps' John Reynolds had been killed. General Schurz found that leading a corps was "much different than commanding a division." When he saw that Barlow's division was on the verge of being overrun, he dispatched Krzyżanowski's brigade to shore up the position. Krzyżanowski's men hoped "to take Doles's brigade in its right flank, but Gordon's Georgians hit them in *their* right flank instead, and the remainder of the Federal line" collapsed.[110]

Just as at Chancellorsville, the Federal troops of the Eleventh Corps were in a weak tactical position. Additionally, they had many new officers in key positions since that battle in May. The attackers, by comparison, were "commanded by one of their army's best division commanders and by competent brigade commanders." Early's division was positioned so well that it appeared as if the encounter engagement could have been planned. Early was able to "strike Schurz's brigades one at a time with superior force, in retrospect, the result" seemed as if it were "preordained."[111] The Southern charge routed Von Gilsa's regiment from its position and pushed them back into the town. Gordon's troops repelled a bayonet attack and beat down the 17th Connecticut Infantry in hand-to-hand combat. They then staged a frontal assault on Krzyżanowski's brigade that had the 75th Pennsylvania and 119th New York regiments in the center of its line. Doles' Georgia brigade struck from the left at the 82nd Ohio, and General Harry Hays' Louisianans crossed Rock Creek and struck the 26th Wisconsin on the right flank.[112] To Krzyżanowski the melee was a "portrait of even hell itself" ("*to obraz piekła, to piekło samo nawet*").[113] With his men outnumbered but fighting obstinately, he "spurred his horse back and forth behind the line, shouting orders and encouragement to his men." As he and his mount went over "an intervening fence," the horse was shot, "reared into the air," then fell with "its weight landing on Krzyżanowski's left side and chest." The Polish Legion's assistant surgeon and other aides "carried the unconscious colonel to the rear."[114] Harry Willcox Pfanz gives a slightly different account.

He relates that the horse emitted "a scream of pain and reared high into the air, pitching the colonel hard to the ground. Even though breathing was painful for him, Krzyżanowski remained on the field and conducted the remnants of his brigade to the rear."[115]

Lee's army badly battered two Federal Corps that afternoon before the survivors of those corps managed to escape to Cemetery Hill. Schurz estimated that he had 14,000 active troops engaged against about 30,000 Confederates "without the slightest advantage of position."[116] General Howard was "at the cemetery with the ghost of Chancellorsville haunting him" and "the phantom of another disaster to deal with," so he sent a deceptive report to his superior, General Meade. He had ordered them to retreat, yet stated that, when outflanked, the First and Eleventh Corps had withdrawn to a "stronger position."[117] On the first day of the battle, Krzyżanowski's brigade had suffered severe casualties: the 75th Pennsylvania lost 73% or a total of 137 men, while only 92 of 236 officers and men who went into action from the 82nd Ohio made it to Cemetery Hill that evening. The 51% losses of the 119th New York equated to 8 officers and 144 enlisted men out of 300 who had started the day. The 26th Wisconsin made it to the hill with barely half its troop strength.[118]

During the early daylight hours of 2 July 1863, Krzyżanowski's brigade remained in the cemetery and was able to hear the battle raging on the Union left from Little Round Top to the Peach Orchard to Cemetery Ridge. In mid-afternoon the Confederates opened up an artillery barrage on Cemetery Hill, employing fifty-five guns with good accuracy from long range. To compound the anxiety and damage to men and horses done by continual shell bursts and shrapnel, snipers sought Northern officers as they moved about giving orders. One artillery shot took out twenty-seven soldiers from the 119th New York regiment.[119] The *New York Times* reported, "the rebel sharpshooters have been annoying our batteries and men all day from the steeples of the churches in Gettysburgh [sic]," they "persistently blazed away at officers and artillery horses."[120] Among the victims from the original Polish Legion were Krzyżanowski's adjutant, Lieutenant Louis Dietrich, from shrapnel, and Captain Edward Antoniewski, felled by a sniper.[121]

As darkness fell just after sunset, Generals Schurz and Howard were conferring when they heard a tremendous commotion from the battery

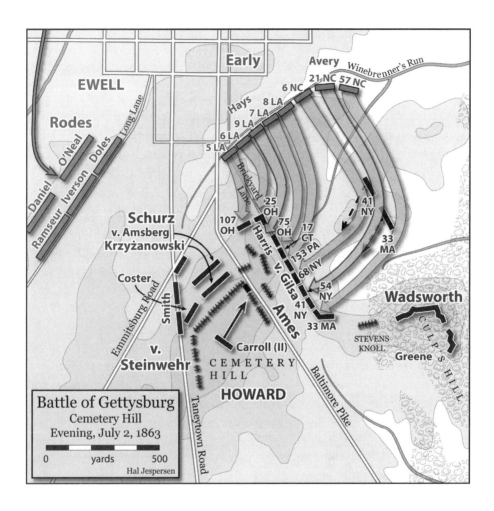

Battle of Gettysburg
Cemetery Hill
Evening, July 2, 1863

0   yards   500

Hal Jespersen

emplacements to the right of Cemetery Hill. Isaac Avery's North Carolina infantry and the famed Louisiana Tigers under Brigadier Harry Hays overran the ten guns manned by Wiedrich's and Rickett's men. Schurz knew the gravity of the situation:

> The enemy was attacking the batteries on our right, and if he gained possession of them he would be able to enfilade a large part of our line toward the south as well as the east, and command the valley between Cemetery Hill and Culp's Hill, where the ammunition trains were parked. The fate of the battle might hang on the repulse of the attack. There was no time to wait for superior orders … I took the two regiments closest to me, ordered them to fix bayonets, and,

> headed by Colonel Krzyżanowski, they hurried to the threatened point on the double-quick ... the cannoneers defended themselves desperately. With rammers and fence rails, hand spikes and stones, they knocked down the intruders.[122]

Krzyżanowski determined when he arrived with his men at the struggle that firing into the engaged mass of combatants "would indiscriminately strike down friend and foe alike." As a result, "they rushed into the fight like infuriated demons," and what ensued was hand-to-hand combat. An officer from the 8th Louisiana Infantry attested that there was hand-to-hand fighting and "it was dark & we couldn't tell whether we were shooting our own men or not" when they reached the Union battery. Their color bearer, Captain Charles DuChamp, was wounded and another "carried the colors up to the battery and planted them on the breastworks, he was then wd[wounded] or taken & our colors lost."[123] It ended with the 58th and 119th New York in control of the artillery positions and Confederates withdrawing back down the hill.[124] Major Benjamin Willis, an officer of the 119th New York, was involved in the melee and wrote directly to Krzyżanowski in his after-action report. Willis affirmed that the colonel led the counterattack "in person and with ... courage it met the foe, drove him back, saved the position, and thus secured the whole Army from irreparable disaster."[125]

At the end of the day, despite suffering another 10,000 casualties, to the Confederates' 6,800, the Union army still controlled the high ground. Krzyżanowski's brigade managed to redeem the reputation of the corps to some extent, and even the frequently unsympathetic Washington press corps gave them credit. Though overestimating the strength of the Southern attack, the news reports no longer referred to the "panic stricken Dutchmen" of the Eleventh Corps:

> General Howard's Eleventh Corps, which broke and ran at Chancellorsville, dashed in to regain their lost laurels, and most nobly did they repulse these two veteran corps of the rebel army. The repulse was so complete that no further attempt was made by the enemy during the balance of the day, and night closed with our holding the position chosen by the enemy to give us battle from.[126]

Most of the following morning of 3 July, Krzyżanowski's men remained in position on Cemetery Hill. They endured occasional artillery bursts and fire from sharpshooters, but no enemy attacks. Shortly after

1:00 p.m., the "greatest artillery bombardment yet heard in the Western Hemisphere" began. The signal came at 1:07 p.m., and then followed "a screaming barrage of iron." The main concentration of Confederate fire was the Union position on adjacent Cemetery Ridge. The Federal guns' "secondary mission is counter-battery fire." They expected a major infantry assault after the "bombardment from massed artillery." That oncoming mass of Confederates was to be their primary target.[127]

Krzyżanowski spent most of that morning keeping order among his troops and offering encouragement as they remained in their position on Cemetery Hill. Although the afternoon cannonade focused on the ridge to their left, they had to undergo occasional shell bursts and enough sniper fire to keep them attentive as well as anxious. When the climax of the battle occurred with "Pickett's Charge" on Cemetery Ridge, the brigade was relieved that "the assault was directed at another portion of the line." The colonel and his officers were able to observe and hear the tumult from their hill, the immense "life-or-death struggle" between the two armies. Krzyżanowski "sighed with relief as the disorganized remnants of the once powerful rebel host recoiled back across the fire-swept fields." The charge was Lee's last attempt, with two and a half divisions, to break the Federal lines on the ridge and push them from the field.[128]

The following morning of 4 July 1863, Krzyżanowski had two patrols survey the empty battlefield and go into the town. They returned with prisoners of Confederate stragglers, but there were no more snipers in buildings and barns. Their reconnaissance discovered that the town was empty and "Gettysburg lay devoid of hostile Southern troops." Schurz later went into the town with his staff, and to his surprise found the missing General Schimmelfennig who had been hiding in a pigsty for three days to avoid capture. In the confusion of directing his retreat from the town on the first day, he had been separated from his command and chased by Confederate infantrymen who "caught hundreds of them in houses and cellars."[129] He emerged safe but with a curious story.[130]

Krzyżanowski's brigade had seen continuous action during the first four days of July at Gettysburg with their most difficult travails occurring on days one and two. On the first day they had been in a difficult position flanked by two enemy brigades on whom they inflicted serious casualties while receiving a battering themselves. The second day involved the hand-to-hand combat to save the artillery in a grave fight that helped keep the Union army in control of Cemetery Hill and its front from being split in two. The brigade's five regiments were still not at full strength when they marched north after the losses at Chancellorsville. The 669 additional casualties listed at the end of the Gettysburg battle were 75 killed and 388 wounded, with missing or captured at 206. The death toll climbs to 155 when counting those who subsequently died from their wounds or the adjusted number verified with later muster rolls.[131] The official after action reports recounted the contribution of the New York regiments, though later historians tended to ignore them for the most part.[132] The Northern press gave some credit to the Eleventh Corps as a whole for its performance during the battle. The *New York Times,* at least for the moment, credited the corps for redeeming its reputation.[133] The regional Pennsylvania newspaper from Clearfield, the *Raftsman's Journal,* cited the "havoc" and losses of the battle and stated that the Eleventh Corps was "nobly rescued from the suspicion which rested on it before" from previous accounts.[134] The journal put the battle in a larger, more glorious context—at least from the Northern perspective—comparing it to the original American Independence day and calling it "The New Fourth of July" that reaffirmed the nation:

> On the one day America resolved that she would arise, and take her place among the nations; on the other, having arisen to all that her wildest dreams could have embodied, she proved she was too great to fall. In that event she asserted her rights; in this, she revealed her power. All that was gained on that day, was on the other preserved ... The anniversary of the day of Freedom was an inspiration to our armies, and enflamed them with a fiercer ardor.[135]

After the close of the Gettysburg campaign, the army sent the Eleventh Corps west under the command of General Hooker. They were to defend the area around Chattanooga, Tennessee, and the Union army there that was under threat from Generals Braxton Bragg and Longstreet and in "imminent peril of capture."[136] Prior to the departure to the western theatre of war, General Schurz felt he should take up the case for Krzyżanowski's promotion to brigadier once again. The rank had expired in March 1863. General Howard took up the case to restore the promotion to rank as appointed by President Lincoln. He wrote that he recommended the "restoration of [Krzyżanowski] to the rank to which the President appointed him," gave reasons of "gallantry," and cited that he had commanded the brigade for fifteen months. He had his letter of support endorsed by Generals Hooker and George H. Thomas and forwarded it to General-in-Chief Henry Halleck. Only congressional inaction had forestalled the initial approval. However, even with Howard's endorsement for the colonel's accomplishments as a brigade commander, the generalship was not forthcoming.[137]

The Chattanooga Campaign

The serious Union defeat at the Battle of Chickamauga, stemming partly from the participation of two divisions under Longstreet from the Army of Northern Virginia, was the reason for the transfer of the corps to a different army. The men of the Army of the Potomac were likely pleased to have the Eleventh Corps and all its foreigners leave, and the men in the departing corps were probably relieved to have a new assignment. They never felt fully accepted in that assemblage of regiments that spanned back to Pope's first army that had fought at Second Manassas in 1862. The Twelfth Corps accompanied the Eleventh in the move to the new Military Division of the Mississippi that included all of the departments west of the Appalachian Mountains. In forming this division, President Lincoln also made Ulysses S. Grant its commander. The movement of the two corps to Nashville was, up to that time, the single largest rail transport of a military force in history. In addition to the men, there were 4,400 horses and mules, forty-five artillery pieces, 717 wagons and all the necessary accoutrements that travel with an army.[138]

That fall of 1863 was difficult, yet Krzyżanowski was stoic in his approach to accomplishing the tasks at hand. He had hopes accompanied by an optimistic outlook while he kept abreast of developments in Poland and carried out his duties. The Poles were fighting the Russians for independence, and though he had been from the Duchy of Poznan in Prussian Poland, Krzyżanowski had fought for Polish freedom. He was now in the struggle to preserve the Union and the American Constitution in which he believed. In his new assignment, he was once again in charge of a brigade under the command of General Hooker, under whose command he had suffered in one of the most crushing Union defeats of the war at Chancellorsville.[139]

The first major action of the new campaign was in an advance at the foot of Lookout Mountain, Tennessee. The Confederates held the high ground and were able to harass the brigade's advances with descending artillery shells and repeated skirmishers. Krzyżanowski was pleased that his men were now experienced from the earlier campaigns in the east, and with discipline of movement and return fire, they skillfully skirted the enemy and reached their destination. This was Brown's Ferry on the Tennessee River where they awaited further orders. He was not pleased to be in a vulnerable position very similar to that at Chancellorsville. Once again, the Union army waited while no precautionary orders regarding preparation for the advancing enemy arrived from headquarters. General Braxton Bragg, who had been victorious at Chickamauga, was on the offensive.[140]

Now that they had found themselves in a part of the country new to them, more than a few of the officers were surprised at the primitive living conditions of some of the populace. The rural people were civil and well mannered, clean and hardworking. Yet they were unaware of happenings outside their immediate surroundings. Carl Schurz wrote that he had met many "Southern country people in Virginia and Maryland" and had been surprised that they were ignorant of things that "among the rural population of the North, were matters of common knowledge." He added that his experiences in the hill country of Tennessee, northern Alabama and northern Georgia "were far more astonishing still." These people were amazed to find that he and Krzyżanowski and many of their men were from a far off land across the ocean, the existence of which they had only a faint conception.[141]

While the officers were surprised at the lack of sophistication of the local inhabitants, they were equally perplexed at the confusing actions of one of their own, General Hooker. Krzyżanowski's brigade and the two other brigades of Schurz's division were advancing as planned to assist a body of the army engaged with the Confederates at Wauhatchie, Tennessee when they received conflicting orders. Krzyżanowski's brigade was to turn about and escort prisoners back to Chattanooga and a second brigade was to hold its position. Hooker evidently had forgotten "or did not realize that Krzyżanowski's Second Brigade was part of Schurz's division." A third brigade was going to continue on to assist

General John W. Geary when everything changed again. Hooker rebuked Schurz and asked him why his entire division had not gone to the aid of Geary. Rather than argue about the reversal of orders, Schurz asked if he now could proceed with his division that had been "held back by his [Hooker's] superior orders." Hooker replied that he had already told Schurz, Krzyżanowski and the other brigades to do so "two hours before." At this point, the officers were completely dubious as to whether Hooker "was in his senses."[142]

Despite the confusion, the Eleventh Corps did well in rescuing their comrades at Chattanooga. For this they received commendations from Generals Sherman and Thomas. Prior to this, when they had been in the Eastern Theatre of the war, the men had been accustomed to nothing but negative criticism. They remained encamped in the shadow of Lookout Mountain for the first three weeks of November 1863 and served as protection for the Union supply lines. Their only threat was the occasional shelling from Confederate artillery on the mountain. It created a heightened level of anxiety in the ranks, but the men became inured to it as it caused little damage. One shell actually struck Schurz' mess tent while he was partaking of a meal with his officers. It did not explode but "caused a momentary sensation and a rapid scattering of the diners."[143]

Krzyżanowski was happy to receive praises for the actions of his men and the entire corps. He also wrote humbly in his memoirs that the fame of winning at Chattanooga was "wrongly attributed solely to Grant," when other leaders had played a great part. He specifically mentioned Rosecrans and Sherman. Grant did, however, garner from it additional cachet with Washington and the press corps covering the war in the west. Krzyżanowski did not look askance at how it helped his army's commander-in-chief (his term) when he reasoned: "*zapewnił mu jednak olbrzymią wziętość,*" which translates as "however, it earned him tremendous popularity" and it would enable him further successes later.[144]

The beginning of 1864 brought new issues to the army. Most of Krzyżanowski's men, especially those of his original regiment, were entering their third year of the war in the same unit. The army instituted a program to retain its experienced soldiers by offering cash bonuses and a leave of thirty days for re-enlistment. Considering the long marches, skirmishes, hardships of camp life, battles and general privations of war, he felt that they had developed solid bonds in serving together and were firmly united in fighting for a just cause. Krzyżanowski decided that if his men were not with him, he would resign his commission. He appealed to his men in an assembly and they agreed that they only wanted to continue to serve under him and responded with almost unanimous re-enlistment.[145]

In late January, Krzyżanowski and 350 of his men in the 58th Regiment as well as 200 men of the 68th returned to New York City to take advantage of their leave. The *New York Times* reported that the "re-enlisted heroes" were treated to a lavish welcome reception after marching from the railroad station to Atlantic Garden on the Bowery. The mayor and members of the city council congratulated them on their service and "safe return," and Krzyżanowski gave a brief oration in which he spoke for himself and his men and their wish to continue to serve in a manner that would "meet the approval of the City authorities and the whole country." The entertainment included music, excellent foods such as which they had not seen in quite some time and sufficient libations. It was considered the finest of receptions for returning soldiers:

> a fine band of music was in attendance, and the best of cheer was had. Of the many receptions of returned volunteers, the honors done yesterday to the Fifty-eighth and Sixty-eighth regiments exceed them all, not possibly in splendor of "turn-out," but in genuine hearty welcome.[146]

After living the army life for such a long time, Krzyżanowski considered himself in paradise for the duration of the leave. He described it in his memoirs: "*Psuci przez kobiety, fetowani przez wszystkich, spędziliśmy dni 30 wśród prawdziwego Edenu,*" or "spoiled by the ladies, celebrated by everyone, we spent 30 days in the midst of a genuine Eden." It did not last, because just as the original Eden was temporary, the time to bask in the light of praise after Chattanooga was coming to an end. Official reports were portraying their actions in the Chattanooga campaign in a negative light.[147]

General Hooker had gone to great pains to shield himself from blame after the defeat at Chancellorsville in May 1863. At Chattanooga he had sent conflicting orders to Schurz about how to deploy his division. When he had needed to protect Geary's position, send reinforcements and keep the roads and lines of communication open, he did not have his troops operating in unison, and even had Krzyżanowski's brigade in the process of leaving for Chattanooga as a prisoner escort. Hooker placed official blame for the delays on Schurz and even though the Union army was the victor, there was an inquiry. Schurz wanted to be exonerated and called for a Court of Inquiry. Hooker had missed out on opportunities for glory in the rescue of Geary's division because of his indecision, and Schurz was found without fault. Krzyżanowski, who was at one point told to be heading to Chattanooga, did go to Geary's aid. He had been standing in Hooker's presence when Schurz had attempted to clarify orders. Krzyżanowski carried out his orders and his men had performed well, though he could not have felt that the inquiry and examination of his division and corps commanders and an action in which he played a significant part was going to hasten the return of his brigadier's commission.[148]

On this subject, the Polish Colonel was correct. The Court's statement confirmed that "as soon as Colonel Krzyżanowski received the order to march to Chattanooga, he dispatched an aide to General Schurz to advise him of the order." These orders were countermanded and the Second Brigade did move to reinforce Geary's division. The Court decided that Krzyżanowski's decision to halt his brigade for a time, even though it was due to conflicting orders, was neglect on the Colonel's part. The Court absolved Hooker of blame for the delay, Schurz was exonerated, but the blemish was on Krzyżanowski's reputation. He had not been part of the inquiry, nor had he been asked to testify. He was not even present. The conclusions at which the Court arrived with regard to Krzyżanowski's participation were "more than absurd," and could be considered "criminal."[149]

In the spring and summer of 1864, Krzyżanowski and his men were charged with keeping supply lines secure for the army preparing to march into Georgia. The primary assignment was guarding the railroad between Nashville and Chattanooga. He still had his old brigade with his new headquarters at Whiteside, Tennessee. He also received orders from General Oliver O. Howard to be on guard for raids since scouts had reported that there was still a Confederate cavalry regiment on Lookout Mountain.[150] Howard commanded the Eleventh Corps until mid-April 1864 when there was a reorganization that included a disso-lution and consolidation of the Eleventh and Twelfth Corps in the army of General Sherman.

A noticeable factor in the reorganization was that the army had "Americanized" the new corps by gradually removing the German senior officers with reassignments and relocations. The new formation was the Twentieth Corps that came to be under the wing of none other than Joseph Hooker by instruction of his Special Field Orders, No. 105. This was significant in two ways: Schurz, who had been a staunch supporter of Krzyżanowski, was no longer part of the organization and was without a command, whereas Adolphus Buschbeck still remained as the token "German." Buschbeck had been instrumental as presiding officer in directing the Court of Inquiry that absolved Hooker and be-smirched Krzyżanowski. In the case of Hooker, General Grant himself had preferred to be rid of him, but deferred because he had "just been sent here by the President." Months earlier, Grant actually had felt that Hooker's "presence" as part of his command was "replete with both trouble and danger" for the army's operations. The other key element in this development was that the disbanding of the so-called "foreign" corps was a thinly veiled triumph for the nativists and Know-Nothings. These anti-immigrant and anti-foreign detractors who were peppered throughout the army and federal government had been opposed to the formation of ethnic regiments and the promotion of "foreign" officers since the outset of the war.[151]

It was fortuitous for Krzyżanowski that yet another reorganization took place. This made him part of a new department charged with protection of the Nashville and Chattanooga railroad and the surround-ing areas. His new commander was Major General Robert H. Milroy, with whom he had served at the start of the war in the Shenendoah. Krzyżanowski spent the rest of 1864 primarily administering his department and directing his men in skirmishes and reconnaissance mis-sions. During that period, Sherman had captured Atlanta and Savannah and had laid waste to Georgia before veering north into the Carolinas. Simultaneously, Milroy undertook the mission to have Krzyżanowski returned to the rank of brigadier (Schurz also continued in his efforts in this area).[152]

By the spring of 1865, Krzyżanowski had served in the Union army for just shy of four years. Most of that time, he had carried out the duties of a brigadier general whether it was as a nominated general or when he had reverted back to colonel. Finally, on 2 March of that year, he received word that he had been brevetted to brigadier. Not completely passive in the quest for his promotion, he had acknowledged and freely expressed his gratitude for the influence of his supporters. He wrote to Milroy that he "did not want to be hasty" in accepting these latest congratulations because he had been "confirmed once before, and in the last moment thrown overboard." He especially was thankful for the letter delivered to the president. Krzyżanowski, the Polish American, concluded, in his words: "It will always be the height of my ambition to serve my adopted country in the future as I have done heretofore."[153]

Milroy had written to President Lincoln of Krzyżanowski's merits and expressed his concern with the fact that his friend's promotion had been long overlooked and even ignored:

> Permit me to call to your attention the long standing, meritorious & much neglected claims of Col. W. Krzyżanowski of the 58th N.Y.V.V.I. for promotion. The Col. is a noble Pole, who espoused our glorious cause at the outbreak of the Rebellion, as a private, with all the zeal that actuates his unfortunate countrymen in their love of Liberty & Free Government ... He was Educated at a Military Institution of high reputation in Europe. Was one of the leaders in the Polish Revolution of '48. Has a splendid military experience. Has a high order of intellect. Is brave, energetic. A stern disciplinarian. In short, he possesses all those qualifications ... that make him every inch a soldier and qualify him for an able and accomplished General.[154]

Milroy was unreserved in his endorsement and cited Krzyżanowski's Polish background and standing. He pointedly linked it to Poland's plight at that time after the failure of the 1863 uprising and the Polish love of freedom and liberty. In a barely concealed slight of career officers who received favorable consideration over volunteers, Milroy added that his comrade would have been a Major General by now had he been "a West Pointer, with one fourth of his merits and qualifications." Officially brevetted brigadier general on 2 March, and nominated for the second time, Krzyżanowski signed his oath for that rank on 1 July 1865.[155]

Krzyżanowski had been a staunch supporter of Lincoln, and as a loyalist he was shocked and suffered great remorse at the President's assassination in April 1865. He referred to the assassination as "the murder of Father Abraham" (*o zamordowaniu Ojca Abrahama*), and later reminisced about the sorrow that permeated a nation that should have been celebrating a great victory. He was of the opinion that the Northern leaders had been magnanimous in the terms of surrender and had "conducted themselves with compassion and noble generosity." The authorities had only "disarmed General Lee's army," allowing them to return to their homes. On the other hand, after all the "disasters" and suffering of the war, there was still an element in the South that wished to further their cause with "a nefarious plot of murder and treason." Krzyżanowski ascribed this to a hypothetical plot that placed Jefferson Davis "at the helm" of a "murderous conspiracy" aimed at Lincoln and his cabinet ministers in Washington. He was just one of many Unionists who held this view.[156]

The ascendancy of Andrew Johnson to the presidency to succeed Lincoln did nothing to please Krzyżanowski, and the succession of pardons that Johnson awarded to former Confederates incensed him further. As a Lincoln Republican, he was in agreement with the moderate policy of conciliation toward the South. With the assassination and the subsequent pardons and liberal terms given by the Johnson administration, he began to drift more and more in the direction of the Radical Republicans. This was the political wing of his countryman and agitator, Adam Gurowski, as well as Senate leader Charles Sumner and Thaddeus Stevens in the House of Representatives. In Stevens and the Radical Republican faction, Krzyżanowski saw a parallel to the humanitarian, social and democratic principles which he had espoused in the reform movements and insurrections in Poland in 1846.[157]

Even though he had been in America for years and had served the entire war in the Union Army protecting the interests of the Republic, Krzyżanowski only officially became an American citizen in Washington, D.C., on 18 March 1868. In his oath of citizenship, he declared that indeed he was a native of Poland but pointedly denied any allegiance to the Kingdom of Prussia. This comprised documented evidence of his deep-seated opposition to that imperial entity which still ruled his old homelands in northwestern Poland.[158]

In 1869 Krzyżanowski became an official of the Reconstruction government after Ulysses S. Grant became the re-united country's president. His new position was with the Treasury Department as Supervisor of Internal Revenue for Georgia and Florida. As neither state had yet been readmitted to the Union, he oversaw a federal district from his offices in Macon, Georgia. During this period some of his most interesting observations came about from his dealings with local Southerners reacting to their occupation by Federal troops, and the covert, and frequently violent, operations of the Ku Klux Klan.[159]

Many Southerners were furious with Grant's election and panicky at the thought of further losing political control of their jurisdictions. As Krzyżanowski viewed it, the extremists abandoned using legal channels to achieve their goals, so they resorted to the means in which they had "already proven their lofty capabilities" during the war. Though now in the aftermath, they did not form an army, but a secret paramilitary organization. One of the goals of these secret cells was to "deter the blacks from voting, first by threat and intimidation, then the lash and finally by murder," as they deemed necessary. He equated these self-styled "knights" with oppression and termed them snake-like "constrictors of liberty and freedom." They were the brigands who were "the tools of tyranny and wickedness," cloaking their identity with white robes and dark masks and riding "with two revolvers at the waist."[160]

In Georgia he also faced some of the myths perpetrated by propagandists during the war and espoused by a good number of citizens. One of them was the idea of Southern purity and chivalry, fighting hordes of European mercenaries descending from the North. Krzyżanowski had encountered nativism in the army and in the Northern states generally. He knew firsthand how unfounded many of their views could be. In an exchange that centered on noble roots versus peasant immigrants, he had to remind one young Georgian of who actually had settled the American colonies. The young man insisted that they were the scions of "aristocratic Huguenots (*szlachetnych Hugonotów*)," whereas the Northerners were the product of the "dregs and outcasts" ("*zlepków i wyrzutków emigracyjnych*") of European immigration. Krzyżanowski reminded him that his state actually was founded as a sort of penal colony for debtors escaping England, and that in reality, most French Huguenots settled in the Carolinas. The Pole, who in fact was of noble background in Europe, may well have reflected on his times in the army with officers such as Captain Dodge and other nativists and Know-Nothings who shared those same beliefs.[161]

Despite the resistance from certain elements of the population, Krzyżanowski believed in and endeavored to promote the concept of one country, the *United States*. He avoided the regional chauvinism practiced by so many Reconstructionists from the North because he realized how it alienated so many Southerners who regarded them as occupiers. Even though he became more conciliatory over time, unrest sometimes boiled over into violence and illegal activity. On several occasions, Krzyżanowski had to summon detachments of the U.S. Cavalry to aid in administering legal and civil order. The series of scandals that plagued the Grant Administration eventually affected the Treasury offices in Georgia. When Reconstruction ended in that state in the fall of 1871, guilt by association with the administration and the resurgence of the landowners who had held sway before the Civil War were sufficient to have him recalled from his position.[162]

Krzyżanowski received a new assignment to New Orleans where he worked as a special agent for the Treasury until 1873. His investigations took him to all the ports of southern Louisiana as well as the city. His memoirs contain no mention of any interaction with ex-Confederates Sulakowski, Szymanski or other Poles who resided in the state. He stated that his participation was just a minor part in the story "about the liberation of the blacks." The full story, he declared in his memoirs, would have required an epic telling worthy of the pen of Homer or Tacitus.[163]

The Treasury Department eventually transferred Krzyżanowski to the Pacific Northwest where he worked in the Washington territory and then served in the same capacity in Alaska. He later settled in San Francisco with his family and became active in the Polish Society of California. Eventually returning to New York, where he had first arrived in America, Krzyżanowski lived there until his death in 1887. His old comrade and advocate, General Carl Schurz, delivered the eulogy at his grave. Fifty years later, President Franklin D. Roosevelt praised him in a radio address delivered as his remains were moved from

New York to his final resting place at Arlington National Cemetery. The General's re-interment was on Virginia soil, across the Potomac River from Washington, on the grounds of what had once been Robert E. Lee's home.[164]

Joseph Kargé

Joseph Kargé came to America from Europe in 1851 after being part of the Wielkopolska Uprising against Prussia in 1848. He had perhaps "the greatest career" of any Pole in "the armies of the Union."[165] Much of his success as an officer was the result of his personal and professional growth from impulsive revolutionary to calculating tactician. When he was a young officer in the Prussian horse guards, he was a firebrand who mutinied against military orders and authoritarian royalty for his ideals. Gaining experience and narrowly escaping imprisonment and death afforded him new perspectives. As an American officer, Kargé learned that he could be decisive and take the initiative but not be rash. He favored the tactical maneuver over the rushed encounter with a chance for glory.

Kargé had the characteristic attributes of a European military officer that, in the early months of training, could sometimes be overbearing for his subordinates and enlisted men. This was a quality exhibited in foreign-born officers on both sides. He emphasized discipline and strict adherence to military rules that did not often sit well with volunteer recruits and conscripts. Yet Kargé "almost single-handedly contributed two-thirds of the cavalry effort of the state of New Jersey to the winning of the Civil War."[166] He was on the faculty at Princeton University in New Jersey, and after his death an obituary stated that "Professor Kargé led an eventful life. He was born near the city of Posen [Poznan], in the Grand Duchy of that name, a Polish dependency of Prussia, on July 3, 1823. His father, an accomplished soldier, had served as a colonel of cavalry under Napoleon."[167] In the Polish army allied with the French, he "served Napoleon as a colonel of cavalry in the invasion of Russia. After the Emperor's disastrous retreat from Moscow, Colonel Jacob Kargé returned to his estate near Poznan."[168]

Kargé's post-Civil War life as a professor at Princeton was not as eventful as his time in the army. At Princeton he was listed as "General

Joseph Kargé

Joseph Kargé, Ph.D., Woodhull Professor of Continental Languages and Literature."[169] In his war years as a cavalry commander, he led his troops in the Virginia campaigns and later in what was considered the Western theatre, in Tennessee, Mississippi, Georgia and Alabama. It was in these campaigns where he achieved the distinction of defeating the South's "invincible raider," also known as "The Wizard of the Saddle," Confederate General Nathan Bedford Forrest, in 1864. Up to that time, Forrest "had as yet never tasted defeat."[170]

Kargé's origins in Prussia, though he was Polish, lend to the identity confusion that occurred with so many Poles who emigrated to America during the Partitions. His gravestone says that he was born in Posen, Prussia (Appendix C). While one can interpret this as technically accurate since that area of partitioned Poland had been incorporated into Prussia, *The Civil War Dictionary* states that his birthplace was "Germany" which is technically not accurate.[171] There was no official, organized nation of Germany in existence at that time surrounding Poznan. Even his actual immigration papers say that his original nationality is

"German" (Appendix D). Some additional confusion arises from the family name itself, which suggests that it is Polonized French. However, the French rarely use the letter "K" except for foreign words, and the Polish language does not use the accented "é." "The surname Kargé is of French origin, although the family resided in the Polish province of Poznan for generations." Kargé would always list "Poland as his place of birth ... [and] never recognized the partitions." In official correspondence to the War Department, Kargé stated repeatedly that he was a "native of Poland."[172]

He arrived in New York in 1851, "at once declared his intention to become a United States citizen," and was naturalized in 1856 after the required five-year residency.[173] In America, Kargé quickly adapted to the ways of his new country. He remained fiercely proud of his Polish origins, but became a patriot in the U.S. as well. He was willing to give up his position teaching modern languages, and at the age of thirty-eight re-entered military life. Kargé responded to President Lincoln's call for volunteers "with the same deep patriotism and devotion to liberty that he had displayed earlier on behalf of his native land. His military experience gained him a commission as lieutenant colonel of a New Jersey cavalry regiment."[174]

The first appellation for the regiment was Halsted's Horse, named for its organizer, William Halsted. A former New Jersey congressman, Halsted raised 1,100 men for the regiment, but at almost seventy years old "did not possess the physical stamina for arduous duty with the cavalry, nor ... the military experience to organize and train a large body of soldiers." He had no experience with camp organization, military drills or discipline. Dealing with undisciplined and often insubordinate citizen soldiers in a poorly organized camp became the first challenge Kargé faced in his command. Having been a Prussian cavalry officer, "Kargé understood the need for organization, training and discipline. He drilled his regiment hour after hour, and on Sundays too. At times he became exasperated over the reluctance of some men to submit to discipline." This, he felt, was an unacceptable attitude for soldiers and "an indication of mutiny against his efforts to establish order." He was unyielding and stressed orderly military procedures at all times. For some of the men, especially officers who felt privileged and were unused to strict military discipline, the reactions ranged from indifference to deliberately hostile. Kargé, in later months, would confront the officers' deep-seated "bitter feelings" that "would flare up and cause him much pain and embarrassment."[175]

Kargé effectively took command of the regiment, instituted formal cavalry training and "set to work to make soldiers of the officers and men." His first move was to put the "inefficient" and malingering officers before the Examining Board in Washington. This spurred the others into activity and "implanted" a "soldiery spirit" in the men.[176] With incessant daily drilling, men and horses began to respond to order and discipline within a span of five weeks.[177] As was the case with many officers who had trained in Europe, the volunteers under them were not often pleased with the methods of their superiors. Headquartered in Northern Virginia, the regiment's camp was near Alexandria. In December, he was able to meet Colonel Wladimir Krzyżanowski and other members of the 58th New York, or "Polish Legion." Krzyżanowski hosted a dinner at which about sixty officers attended. The occasion, as the *New York Times* reported in its headline, was a "Feast in Commemoration of the Polish Revolution of 1830 … Col. Krzyżanowski Presides." A Captain of German origin gave a toast to his fellow officers and lauded them as fighting for freedom in their "adopted land." The *Times* reported the details:

> The 29th of November is an ever-memorable day in the history of liberal Poland. Thirty-one years ago on that day, at 7:00 p.m., the students of Warsaw gave the signal of revolt, and drove fifteen thousand Russians from the city. For about a year the war for independence raged with fury, until discord among the leaders extinguished Poland's political existence.
>
> To commemorate this event, Col. Krzyzanowski, Fifty-eighth N.Y.S. Volunteers, invited the Poles of the army, and the German officers of his regiment, about sixty in number, to meet at his headquarters.
>
> At 7:00 p.m. the company had assembled, and was soon seated at table in a large wooden building erected for the occasion … Col. Krzyzanowski, who presided, now toasted the company, the officers who had served in the Revolution of 1830, and drank to Poland again to become a nation.[178]

The evening with Colonel Krzyżanowski and the other New York officers had been enjoyable, but training resumed in the ensuing weeks. The resentment of Kargé's harsh discipline surfaced at the end of December when a subordinate made accusations against him for transgressions

Captured after leading a reckless cavalry charge, Colonel Percy Wyndham, an Englishman, had replaced William Halsted to command the First New Jersey Cavalry. Kargé succeeded him.

that included making the men drill on Sundays. After review, the army dismissed the charges as "frivolous." He faced further difficulties with vindictive or uncooperative officers until the governor of New Jersey had

"Halsted's Horse" reorganized as the First New Jersey Cavalry in February 1862.[179] Halsted himself was mustered out and an Englishman, Colonel Percy Wyndham, replaced him. This move boosted morale and with the "change of name there came a change of character" in the regiment. The regiment remained on duty in the "defences of Washington" until May 1862.[180]

In the spring of 1862, General George B. McClellan prepared the Army of the Potomac for the Peninsula Campaign. On St. Patrick's Day, Monday 17 March, he began moving his massive number of troops south by water from Alexandria to the Virginia Peninsula. McClellan had wanted even more troops, but President Lincoln had decided to hold back a "sufficient number of soldiers to insure the safety of Washington." He eventually released McDowell's army to move south toward Richmond in support of the Campaign, but they went overland and not farther than the area around Fredericksburg.[181]

With the beginning of the Peninsula Campaign Kargé's newly formed regiment was to come under the authority of a fledgling commander. The U.S. Senate had confirmed Brigadier General George D. Bayard of the 1st Pennsylvania Cavalry on 29 April. Kargé's newly reorganized regiment became part of Bayard's Cavalry Brigade and moved south with McDowell's army until they received orders after crossing the Rappahannock River on the way to Richmond. They were to reverse direction and return north and northwest to the Shenandoah Valley with 20,000 other troops in order to confront Stonewall Jackson's Confederate army there.[182]

The Shenandoah Valley

Kargé's first engagements on the American continent would prove formative in his development as an officer and in his leadership decisions. Early on he learned to move aggressively but with calculation, and that heroic exploits were not the ultimate goal. On 31 May the cavalry brigade arrived at Front Royal, Virginia, in the Shenandoah Valley after traveling the roughly seventy miles from near Fredericksburg. To the west near Strasburg, General John C. Frémont was engaged with Confederates under General Richard S. Ewell. During their approach they could distinguish the distant sound of artillery:

Far off among the mountains, with multiplied reverberations that shook the air around us, the sound of artillery struck upon our ears, in a continuous roar of battle. For the first time we heard the sound that heralded our entrance into action, and with one impulse the men erected themselves in their saddles, their eyes lighting up with new excitement. The first fight was at hand, and the men longed for it, as they never desire the second.[183]

Kargé's first assignment came on 2 June. Under orders from General Bayard, he took a cavalry battalion of 200 men to perform reconnaissance in the Strasburg area. When he reported that no enemy was to be found, he moved into the town with the support of infantry. These were the Pennsylvania Bucktails, riflemen from the mountains in the western part of that state. His regimental commander, Colonel Wyndham, joined him and Kargé "urged an immediate pursuit of the enemy." They were facing the troops of Jackson's cavalry commander, Turner Ashby, and his supporting artillery. Ashby, whose home was in the Shenendoah, had received a promotion to brigadier general on 23 May, although he was killed in battle before it could be confirmed by the Confederate senate.[184] When the Federals moved forward, the Confederate cannons opened fire from a distance.

After the Union artillery moved up to return fire, Wyndham "ordered an attack on the rebel batteries." In a headlong rush, Kargé led the Second and Third Battalions directly at the Southern artillery position and caused them to withdraw into a wooded area.[185] A second charge was intended to "flush out the enemy" but drew new opposing artillery fire and resulted in a brush with disaster for the Lieutenant Colonel. When Kargé stopped to rally a group of stragglers, he had his horse blown from under him:

The fight now was between the opposing artillery, and the missiles shrieked through the air, or came crashing among the trees which sheltered our men. The explosions were startling, but inflicted little injury, a few men being slightly wounded, and one or two horses killed. One of these missiles struck beneath the lieutenant-colonel's horse, as he stood in his place in line. The explosion threw horse and man into the air, tearing the animal to pieces, but the rider came down unhurt, and emerged from the cloud of smoke with no blood upon him but that of the horse.[186]

Kargé officially reported the "loss of a horse, which was shot under me by a shell bursting between the forelegs, shattering the former and cutting off entirely one of the hind legs; also lacerating his chest."[187]

A violent thunderstorm and nightfall brought an end to the day's action, and Ashby withdrew without significant damage on the Confederate side.

On Thursday, 5 June, Bayard's cavalry brigade crossed the Shenandoah River and the following day approached the outskirts of Harrisonburg. Kargé wrote that they "advanced in proper battle array, the artillery and infantry in the center ... the cavalry on the flanks."[188] Bayard had Wyndham and Kargé take the regiment and four other companies of horse from the New York Fourth Mounted Rifles to "attack and scatter" enemy cavalry in the area, but not to engage infantry. What ensued was precisely what Bayard had wanted to avoid. Kargé's report afterward to Bayard said that Wyndham "through some unexplained reasons ... gave the order forward" after receiving scouting reports about enemy cavalry "on the other side of the woods in front" of them. Wyndham's orders were to reconnoiter the Southern positions and pull back against serious opposition.[189] However, according to the *New York Times* report, he "was inclined to a daring exploit that might win fame," with "valor lacking its better part, discretion, or good judgment." In pushing forward, they were challenged on three sides in what appeared to be a perfectly prepared "ambuscade."[190]

Kargé's report told of the cavalry going forward in good order "about 3¼ miles, partly by platoons, partly by fours, as the nature of the ground would allow it, when a sudden fire" struck them from the right. Colonel Wyndham was in the vanguard, another division of platoons followed, and Kargé brought up the rear with the rest of the regiment. Suddenly "the roar of musketry" opened up on them from both flanks. He judged that there also was opposition in front when "the first two platoons suddenly emerged from the woods." This added threat, he feared, would "throw the rest of the column [that was following] in confusion." He and Wyndham dismounted to dismantle obstructing fences so that they might lead the men into "a belt of woods" to shelter them from the onslaught. At that point, Wyndham "disappeared" and Kargé was "left alone among a headless mass of men and horses." He went on to say that, in his judgment, the officers "behaved bravely" in their failed attempts to rally the troops, but the men "retreated without order and in the greatest confusion—for the most part panic stricken." Besides 32 casualties among the cavalry, they also lost the regiment's standard "and 63 others" as prisoners.[191] The Confederates captured Colonel Wyndham as well as two of the company captains. Wyndham, with a "grating tendency to pomposity," had made it known publicly that he was "eager to capture the gallant" Rebel cavalry leader, or as he had put it, "bag Ashby."[192] Henry Pyne succinctly put the action into perspective in his account: "If a cavalry charge is glorious, a cavalry rout is dreadful." He described the chaos that erupted when they drew fire, seemingly from all sides:

> Pressing upon one another, strained to the utmost of their speed, the horses catch an infection of fear which rouses them to frenzy. The men, losing their places in the ranks, and all power of formation or hope of combined resistance, rush madly for some point of safety upon which it may be possible to rally. Each check in front makes the mass behind more dense and desperate, until horses and men are overthrown and ridden over, trampled on by others as helpless as themselves to rescue or to spare. The speed grows momentarily greater. Splashing through the pools of mire, breaking down fences, darting under trees, with clang of sabres and din of hoofs, officers wild with shame and rage, shouting themselves hoarse with unavailing curses, and the bullets of the enemy.[193]

The *New York Tribune* charged Wyndham with "rashness and unskillful conduct" as well as "neglect or disobedience of orders," and listed him among the killed, wounded and missing. The *Tribune* backed up General Bayard's report that censured Wyndham "severely."[194] However, in a follow-up infantry assault by the Bucktails, the Confederate side lost its renowned cavalry leader Turner Ashby, who "had covered their retreat with admirable audacity and skill" and was urging his men to charge as he was felled by a bullet.[195]

The defeat at Good's Farm was still a humiliation for the cavalrymen from New Jersey, and it would be another lesson for Kargé in combining boldness with rationality. The campaign itself would prove to be the outset of a good working relationship between him and the brigade commander, General Bayard.

Kargé subsequently distinguished himself in action at the battle of Cedar Mountain (9 August 1862) only to face court-martial charges from a subordinate. Suffering from illness, Kargé had placed Major Myron C. Beaumont in charge of the regiment after Bayard had ordered the colonel to an ambulance. Despite this, he returned to the field at intervals when the battle became heated. Beaumont and some fellow officers charged Kargé with "cowardice" and petitioned for his removal from the regiment (circumventing army regulations in the process). These charges possibly stemmed from the prior difficulties that had occurred with the disciplinary issues during the formation of the regiment. Kargé's foreign birth may also have been at issue, just as earlier criticisms had been leveled at Englishman Percy Wyndham for receiving command. The Nativist attitudes of some Union officers had often fostered resentment of foreigners, evinced in correspondence and sometimes in the media. New Jersey's *New Brunswick Times* had criticized Wyndham's appointment but agreed with his qualifications, citing that he was an experienced officer from "Italy."[196] Chaplain Pyne's personal accounts attribute definitive action and resolve by the Pole, even when he had been ordered away from the field of action:

> Colonel Kargé, who had, for the past two days, been suffering from the symptoms of bilious fever, and had only been kept in the saddle by the strength of his will, now turned over the command to Major Beaumont, and retired, until the action should commence, to the ambulances of Assistant Surgeon Dayton ... At the first discharge Kargé was again with us ... took advantage of the concealment to shift our position ... With great delicacy, declining to take the command out of the hands of Major Beaumont ... not until the regiment was withdrawn ... could he be persuaded to obey the orders of General Bayard and retire from the field.[197]

General Bayard dismissed the charges as spurious, politically motivated and made by novices who had little wartime experience. He staunchly defended Kargé as a Pole who had seen action in Europe and already had proven himself in service with the regiment. The charges were dismissed immediately, and Beaumont admitted they were rash and without substance. Indeed, Kargé had commended Beaumont's conduct during the battle in his official report, while receiving praise from his superior officers for his "restraint and tolerance" in handling the matter of charges by a subordinate. Kargé's reputation was enhanced and the Third Corps chief of staff, Colonel Edmund Schriver, felt the accusing officers themselves deserved court martial for their behavior. He also recommended they apologize.[198]

Operations in Central Virginia

In the next significant action for the regiment, Kargé exhibited anything but the pusillanimous leadership of which Beaumont had accused him. Near Brandy Station Virginia, in August 1862, Kargé employed his dismounted cavalry to impede Confederate skirmishers harassing the First Maine and Second New York cavalry regiments. He quickly moved his men into flanking position and forced the enemy to "give way." In this engagement with elements of Confederate cavalry leader James Ewell Brown ("Jeb") Stuart's cavalry, the First New Jersey also checked the advances of the Confederates and covered the withdrawal of the Union regiments.[199] A Confederate cavalry attack caught a regiment of Union horsemen by surprise with "a ferocious charge" and caused panic among the Second New York. Kargé made a move to reverse the situation and gave his men the order to charge. Inexplicably, only three men followed him.[200]

In separate accounts, Kargé's actions were seen as decisive. The *New-York Daily Tribune* described "desperate hand to hand" fighting in which "the commanding officer of the Rebel cavalry was shot by Lieut.-Col. Karge" who then attacked with only a few men, "surprised a party of Rebels and charged them, driving them back into the woods. While retreating a pistol was fired by one of the party, the ball taking effect in the leg of Lieut.-Col. Karge."[201] Pyne related the incident also, "Kargé with his adjutant … charged a party of fifteen, and drove them before him; but a bullet from one of their pistols took effect in his leg and forced him to give up the chase."[202] General Bayard's official report stated:

> Colonel Kargé from his flank position had a fine opportunity to cut the enemy to pieces, and gave the order to charge, but he was followed only by his adjutant, Lieut. Penn Gaskell, and Lieut. William Bayard, my aide-de-camp. They rode into the scattered enemy, and here Colonel Kargé was shot through the leg making a painful and serious wound.[203]

The three accounts attest to Kargé's willingness to take the initiative as an officer and personally confront the enemy. The conflict with General Beverly H. Robertson's Confederate cavalry had been costly for the First New Jersey, even though they had assisted in the protection of the overall Union withdrawal from the area. Robertson reported that the charge of his Twelfth Virginia Regiment had "routed the federals." Forty New Jersey troopers were missing, and Kargé's injury would put him out of action for five weeks. He returned at the end of September, albeit somewhat prematurely, at the urging of General Bayard who was in need of cavalry commanders. His arrival prompted a hearty welcome from the officers and men of his regiment.[204]

Two episodes occurred that fall which contrasted with the image that Kargé's political rivals portrayed of him: early on, a stern, heavy-handed European disciplinarian, later, unfit to be their commanding officer. The irony is that on one hand, men such as Beaumont questioned his military abilities, yet on the other they bristled under his strict command. After his cavalry had taken the town of Warrenton with little resistance, they came upon Virginia civilians who were surprisingly friendly, as well as, in the wake of the horrific battles of Second Bull Run and Antietam, numerous Confederate wounded soldiers, paroled prisoners and stragglers. Kargé reported nearly 1,400 in all that were quartered in nearly every home in the town under deplorable conditions.[205] His official report of 1 October 1862 shows his concern for the sick and convalescing as well as his regard for the local Southerners, who were nominally the enemy. He lamented the hospital accommodations in which the sick and suffering were relegated to "the bare floor" without blankets or pillows. The Colonel described makeshift hospital wards in houses where "the sick and wounded were literally decaying in their own filth," wanting of proper care. Kargé reported that the scene he witnessed was beyond belief:

> The wounds were mostly of a very serious character, and amputation of legs and arms were very frequent. The number of deaths amounted, daily, to 50, caused no doubt by want of proper care, nourishment, and medical stores. Of the two latter they were perfectly destitute, so far so, that some of the ladies of high respectability expressed to me the wish that the United States authorities, having taken possession of the place, would do something to alleviate the sufferings of both the sick and inhabitants.[206]

He observed that even though the war was just into its second year, the Southern countryside and residents were in a difficult way because "the country is stripped of everything in the shape of provisions, and starvation stares the people in the face." Kargé went on to say that the paroled prisoners were eager to receive their official papers, be free of military duty and swore they would not "take up arms again against the Yankees." He paroled 1,200 "sick and wounded rebel soldiers" at Warrenton.[207]

Kargé received a nomination for promotion to brigadier general from division commander General Julius Stahel in October 1862. Though his comrades and general officers who knew him favored this consideration, Kargé was refused the rank at the time. Army of the Potomac cavalry chief, General John Buford, denied the promotion because he was unfamiliar with Kargé's performance. This denial illustrated the "undercurrent of resentment between Regular Army and volunteer officers." Buford and his fellow regulars would have had a tendency to defer promotions of volunteers and especially political appointees. There is no evidence of Kargé's response to the failure of the promotion's approval at that time, and he continued to carry out his duties efficiently with "unswerving devotion."[208]

During this same period, the lighter side of this serious officer surfaced in his handling and reporting incidents involving some of his men on night picket duty. In one, an inexperienced corporal fired a shot in the middle of the night. Kargé thought it was a warning of approaching enemy troops and ordered his bugler to wake the camp and take up arms. When his men brought the corporal to him and Kargé learned that it was a shot intended for some errant pigs, the Pole was furious. He unleashed a torrent of colorful language and followed with a symbolic *coup de grace* from his boot. As the hapless corporal fled the furious colonel, Pyne reported Kargé's lament that "the scoundrel didn't even bring the pigs as atonement" before ordering the men back to sleep.[209]

A more serious occurrence was near Dumfries, Virginia, when rear outpost sentries from the First New Jersey sustained serious casualties from a surprise attack. The loss of six men, 16 horses and assorted weaponry resulted in the recommended dismissal of Second Lieutenant Jacob H. Hoffman for "the disgraceful neglect of duty on an outpost, by which he and his party were surprised." The cause was a supposed "drunken party of the enemy's cavalry." Kargé wrote his report after receiving the account of five of the men who had escaped capture. He related that Hoffman had not positioned his forward scouts well:

> [He] allowed his men to lay aside their arms, went, at about 6:00 p.m., according to the custom of many of our patriotic officers, to provide for his belly, in a neighboring house, leaving his command to the care of Providence. It is further stated that the inmate of this house is a young and attractive female, whose husband is a captain in the rebel army, and who was seen by one of our posts returning to her house on horseback about 4:00 p.m., just about the time when our vedettes were relieving one another … were attacked both in front and rear and the same time

> ... through a premeditated plan, the clew of which was furnished by the culpable negligence of the officer in command of the outpost. The result was, that of 14 men the whole were either captured or scattered without firing a shot. Among the former is the worthy lieutenant, who certainly has not neglected his duty as a gallant man, so far as the fair sex is concerned.[210]

Kargé's facetious tone in describing Hoffman's dereliction was apparently too flippant for one of the generals, who nonetheless approved the recommendation for dismissal. It is probable that he used this tone because he felt disillusioned by criticism for his military strictness from some quarters at the same time that others were questioning his knowledge of command. The sequence of events likely would have increased the stress and difficulty for the Colonel that autumn and early winter. The battle wound to his leg, the slow healing process hindered by a somewhat hasty return to action, dealing with the insubordinate Beaumont's charges, and denial of promotion compounded by the duties of command and combat would have weighed heavily on Kargé.[211]

On 18 December, General Bayard died after being struck by an artillery shell. He had been a friend and comrade in arms, who in his reports had praised Kargé for "gallantry" and being "always ready and valiant." The Polish colonel had requested leave to recuperate and avoid losing his leg from his prior wound. After not receiving an answer in what he felt was a timely manner, Kargé tendered his resignation just before Christmas 1862 to be with his family in New Jersey.[212]

Army of the Tennessee

In the spring of 1863, Kargé returned to active service with the authorization to raise a regiment of cavalry. In June, the governor of New Jersey gave him the rank of colonel with the position of Chief of Cavalry of the state militia. He began his new recruitment efforts from his office in Trenton and even had the same headquarters used by General Casimir Pulaski for a time during the American Revolution. He became colonel of the Second New Jersey Cavalry and quickly regained the reputation of a strict officer who tolerated neither dereliction nor desertion. A report that detailed forty of his troopers under guard with shaved heads illustrated his methods of discipline. However, he accepted the service of previously dismissed Jacob Hoffman, who returned with the colonel's approval. Kargé offered him another opportunity and Hoffman achieved the rank of lieutenant within a year.[213]

After undergoing requisite training, the regiment moved south to Washington in October 1863 making its temporary quarters across the Potomac River in Virginia. In November came a transfer to the Army of the Tennessee and they relocated to Mississippi, Tennessee and the Western theatre of the war under General William Tecumseh Sherman. Their brigade commander was Colonel George E. Waring, Jr.[214]

Upon arrival, Kargé's regiment immediately became involved in Federal efforts to take control of northern Mississippi and western Tennessee. This meant they had to nullify, destroy and break the Confederate cavalry under Nathan Bedford Forrest. Forrest had effectively remained in control over this area while Sherman's corps commander, General Stephen A. Hurlbut, proposed to suppress him. Hurlbut had overwhelming manpower with 20,000 troops, including 7,500 cavalry "scattered from Columbus, Kentucky, to Corinth, Mississippi." In this grouping was the Second New Jersey, which was part of General A.J. Smith's division. Hurlbut set up a "strong cordon, ten thousand men" to hold the territory for the North in opposition to Forrest's "army" of four artillery pieces and and an initial force of roughly three hundred men.[215] While the Union commanders made little haste to strengthen their positions, and their preparations were described as "leisurely," Forrest recruited volunteers and received reinforcements. He was able to swell his ranks to about 3,300 from within this territory that was nominally under Federal control.[216]

Just before Christmas 1863, the Second New Jersey moved south from Union City with Waring's brigade in vain pursuit of Forrest in Jackson, Tennessee. After a short recuperation in that town, they resumed under awful weather conditions. Sub-freezing temperatures, icy roads, snow and sleet storms took their toll on men and horses. During and after this fruitless pursuit, Kargé objected to the "misuse of cavalry" by senior staff. At one post, after being under temporary command of a Missouri infantry regiment, he compared the infantry colonel's knowledge of cavalry to that of a goose's facility with astronomy. This was his critique of being ordered on a mission to subdue a band of horse thieves with a contingent of 500 mounted troopers. He had looked at the mission from a practical standpoint and deemed that "the work could have been done by a sergeant with twelve men."[217]

In February 1864, Kargé and his New Jersey cavalrymen became part of General Sherman's Meridian Expedition. Twenty thousand men under Sherman were to bring the war to the Southern people in a 130-mile march from Vicksburg due east to Meridian, Mississippi. The method was to wage war in "the most efficient, least fatal" way that would sap the enemy's will and capability to fight.[218] The mission had two goals: destroy the Confederate railroad system in northern Mississippi and subdue Nathan Bedford Forrest, "who with an irregular force of cavalry, was constantly threatening Memphis and the river above, as well as our routes of supply in Middle Tennessee."[219] Sherman had decided that a destructive campaign waged against Southern "property, hearts and minds" with minimal casualties would be more effective in ending the conflict than conventional warfare. He differed in his viewpoint from Kargé and some other officers with regard to this aspect of the war. In his "destructive war against the hearts and minds of Southern society," Sherman did not include "the destruction of slavery."[220]

It was in this campaign that Kargé and his regiment directly met Forrest in combat. He was with Waring's brigade under the generalship of William Sooy Smith and his Division of three brigades, seemingly proceeding south from Memphis without distinct precision. Smith himself was "vacillating in his orders, and a little anxious in his demeanor." Though he could be steady under fire, Kargé eventually had reason to question his leadership.[221] The first endeavor was a setback for the Union forces at West Point, Mississippi. When Smith's division encountered the outnumbered Confederates after long pursuit and Forrest turned to confront them, Smith had his men withdraw. This was despite his exhortations to the men, and claims that he would attack and fight wherever he could find Forrest. The withdrawal baffled his officers, and in doing so, Kargé and his men primarily fought from a defensive position in a holding action.[222] Although the decision to retreat was his, Smith faulted the slow movements of his New Jersey and Pennsylvania regiments for the reversal. Waring's report differed and he praised Kargé and the Second New Jersey. Kargé in turn castigated General Smith for the foolhardy conduct of the operation and received a three-day confinement to quarters for criticizing a superior officer. The *New York Times* disputed the resolve of General Smith because "he did not make an earnest attempt to get through," and his retreat was unnecessary. The failure was "more likely attributable to want of pluck and dash in its Commander."[223] Kargé for the second time in the campaign was critical of what he considered poor leadership and decisionmaking on the part of his senior officers.

Waring worded his summation in a similar tone when he cited that they had had "fair opportunity for dispersing the most successful body of cavalry in the Rebel service," however:

> Our commander had evidently no stomach for a close approach to the enemy and his injunctions … to 'Fight at close quarters!" Go at them as soon as possible with the sabre! And other valorous ejaculations, were in singular contrast to the impressions he evinced as the prospect of an actual engagement drew near.[224]

General Sherman's conclusions were in line with those of Kargé and Waring when he wrote in his memoirs that "General Smith never regained my confidence as a soldier" despite his appeals for relief of "censure."[225] In his frustration, Sherman went up the chain of command from Smith and included his officers in Memphis, accusing them of "timidity" and singling out General Hurlbut for replacement.[226] From the Confederate point of view, while Sherman's infantry had succeeded in reaching and sacking Meridien, the failure of his cavalry wing to join him—turned back by Forrest—meant that he had no remaining option save to retrace his steps back to Vicksburg.

While Sherman restructured, Forrest continued to range freely in this region of Mississippi as well as western Tennessee. In addition to engaging Union forces, attacking garrisons and worrying Sherman's plans for moving east to capture Atlanta and subdue Georgia, Forrest was recruiting men, adding to his stores and generally strengthening his contingent. In the spring, Kargé became temporary commander of the First Cavalry Brigade, with Waring now as his division leader, in a renewed attempt to quash Forrest. They set out from Memphis under their new cavalry commander, Samuel D. Sturgis, who had replaced Benjamin C. Grierson, who was on temporary leave. Kargé moved east toward Bolivar, Tennessee, with his group of seven hundred troopers including four hundred of his Second New Jersey, the Tenth Missouri and two artillery pieces. He located a force of Forrest's Confederates that were entrenched just west of the town.[227]

Perhaps due to the lack of effectiveness of previous maneuvers in the Meridian expedition, Kargé decided to attack. Whether or not Forrest's "invincible" reputation added motivation is not part of the Polish colonel's reports. Even Forrest's comrades had noted in their official correspondence that the Yankees were "frightened at every mention of the name Forrest."[228] Kargé decided against a headlong charge against the entrenched Confederate position. Instead, he put his two artillery pieces to use to shell the enemy, then engaged them in an exchange of fire. Forrest himself came upon the center of action, together with his escort company, and led a "furious charge" at Kargé's position but was driven back. Kargé began to move his men forward with tactical maneuvering in order to put pressure on the Confederates and force them out of their trenches. When he felt he had the advantage, he ordered a direct charge on the fortifications, at which point the defending Southerners, overwhelmed, "abandoned their positions and retreated in confusion toward the town [Bolivar]."[229] Afterwards, a combination of weather, rising streams with damaged bridges, and delays of moving infantry on the part of General Sturgis kept Kargé from capitalizing further on his success.[230] Sturgis described the action from the reports he received about Kargé's encounter with Forrest:

> Colonel Kargé … met the enemy with a force equal if not larger than his own, commanded by Forrest in person. After a sharp engagement of nearly an hour's duration he had succeeded in dislodging the enemy from the earth-works and rifle-pits, which had been thrown up there before, and finally drove him through the swampy bottoms in the direction of Pocahontas and Middleton, not however, until the bridge over the Hatchie River had been destroyed. Our loss in the engagement was 2 killed and 10 wounded. The enemy's loss was much heavier, owing to the determination of our troops and the superiority of our arms and artillery, which the enemy was not at all provided with. Among his wounded were several officers, including Forrest's adjutant-general, whose arm was shattered by a carbine ball.[231]

The report from the Second New Jersey Cavalry was succinct as it confirmed Kargé's victory over the vaunted Forrest:

It being ascertained that a force of the enemy held the town of Bolivar, on the Hatchie River ... Colonel Kargé, commanding the First Cavalry Brigade, was sent forward with a force consisting of 200 of the Tenth Missouri Cavalry, 400 of the Second New Jersey cavalry, and a section of guns belonging to the Tenth Missouri Cavalry. Starting at 1.30 p.m., we made a forced and very rapid march, and found the enemy, 800 strong, under command of Major-General Forrest, in position behind strong intrenchments [sic] and fortifications, about 1 mile from Bolivar. After a severe engagement of two hours' duration we routed the enemy and drove them from their intrenchments and through the town, and but for the lateness of the hour (it being after 8:00 p.m.) and our utter ignorance of the country through which the enemy retreated, would have captured or destroyed the entire force.[232]

The triumph at Bolivar was not a victory in a major battle that decided the outcome of the war in the western theatre, nor even the possession of western Tennessee or northern Mississippi. Indeed, the Confederates maintained that all they had intended was to buy some time to allow their wagons and a column of unarmed conscripts to cross the bridge over the Hatchie, after which their fighting men withdrew, burning the bridge behind them. However, Kargé's nominal victory over the previously unbeatable Forrest was the spark needed by the Northern press to light a motivational fire. The *New York Times* headlined an article, "The Rebels Driven From Their Intrenchments Near Bolivar" and referred to Forrest's men as a band of "Cut-throats" trounced in the two-hour fight.[233]

There is no evidence of Kargé embellishing his reports with self-praise for pushing Forrest's men out of Bolivar. Indeed, he was able to bask in favorable light only for a short period before the Battle of Brice's Crossroads marked the disastrous end of Sturgis' command.

In early June, Sturgis set out with his forces into northern Mississippi again endeavoring to defeat Forrest. Kargé was given a raiding and reconnaissance mission: disrupt and destroy railroad operations, wreck the trestles at Rienzi, obtain Confederate telegraph transmissions and gather as much information of their movements and troop strength as possible. On 5 June after reaching Salem, Mississippi, Forrest's boyhood home, Sturgis sent Colonel Kargé with 400 men on the assignment: "to Rienzi, via Ripley, with orders to destroy the railroad, &c., then move up to Danville and seize and hold the bridge over the Tuscumbia."[234]

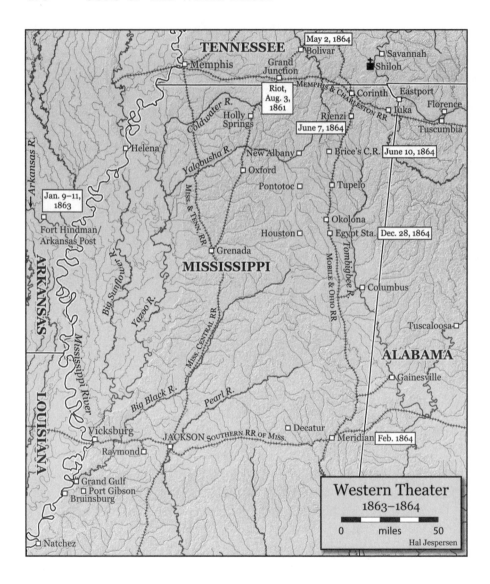

They arrived at Rienzi on the morning of 7 June, but left hurriedly after "burning the depot and destroying a few yards of the railroad track." At one point two of Forrest's brigades surrounded Kargé's detail, but they were able to escape. When pressed, they had moved onto an island in the river guided by a local citizen they had coerced into service. Giving the man a threatening warning "that his life would be forfeited if he betrayed" them, Kargé's men "spent about as miserable a night as one could imagine." The next morning, they were fortunate to find an unguarded gap in the enemy's lines and Kargé swam his cavalry across the river unharmed.[235] Once safe, they proceeded back to meet the main body of the expedition near Ripley, Mississippi, and the mission was accomplished. Even before Kargé rejoined the main column, Sturgis was thinking of abandoning the expedition. He went so far as to admit in his official report that he had "a serious question in his mind as to whether or not" he should continue. He hardly exhibited the confidence of a commander sensing victory when he wrote that "the bad condition of the roads," due to incessant rains, the spent horses, the "overwhelming force" of opposing Confederates (vastly overestimated at 15,000–20,000 with 12,000 engaged in the battle), and the "utter hopelessness of saving our train or artillery in case of defeat" all spelled doom.[236]

Having entered "Forrest country," Sturgis dreaded defeat and in conferring with his officers, they concurred with him about what would be the end result. In all probability the only outcome would be disaster. Had Kargé been present and not on his mission to Rienzi, he may not have made the opinion unanimous considering the success of his raid. Sturgis wrote in his official report that since he "had abandoned a similar expedition only a few weeks before … it would be ruinous on all sides to return without first meeting the enemy." It was with this defeatist attitude and a pervasive expectation of doom spreading among his staff due to the "sad foreboding of the consequences," that Sturgis resolved to press onward. Forrest had been "denied his Tennessee raid," and was about to descend with "full fury" on the "luckless Sturgis."[237]

General Cadwallader C. Washburn, now commanding the Army of West Tennessee from Memphis, wrote that "the causes of our failure" included General Sturgis' expectation of defeat, and that he "had no confidence in the success of the expedition, a feeling which could not fail to have an important bearing upon the actual results."[238]

In his after-battle report, Sturgis praised Kargé for his successful but exhausting mission, but wrote to Washburn from Ripley on 11 June 1864 about the difficulty of the fighting in which they had engaged:

> Our loss in killed and wounded is very heavy. We have lost most everything, including a number of wagons and artillery, with ammunition. I have fallen back

to this point. The enemy will probably try to cut me off … If possible please send me a brigade of infantry to help me. Please send a train of forage and some commissary stores to the railroad terminus."[239]

The *Indiana Herald* reported on the "disaster" of the Sturgis expedition but lauded the raid conducted by Kargé and his cavalry:

Nothing of interest occurred until the expedition passed Salem, Miss., on the 5th, when 300 men went in advance. Passing through Ripley they captured several small parties of the enemy, and moving directly upon Rienzi and Danville, destroyed the railroad and burned the depot at the former place—constantly skirmishing with a considerable body of the enemy. They rejoined the main column on the 8th with 25 prisoners.[240]

In planning for the engagement, Forrest indicated that he intended to attack Sturgis at Brice's Crossroads, on the road to Guntown, just south of a narrow bridge across Tishomingo Creek. He would draw him in and fight on his own terms. Forrest felt that with a swift strike through wooded terrain, the Yankees would not know just how few in numbers were the Confederates they faced. His first movement was to strike and "whip" the Union cavalry that had come across the creek three hours in front of the foot soldiers. Forrest predicted that "as soon as the fight opens they will send back to have the infantry hurried up. It is going to be hot as hell and coming on a run for five or six miles over such roads their infantry will be so blowed we will ride right over them."[241]

The *Indiana Herald* continued with the account of the battle at the Crossroads with emphasis on the notion that the Federals were outnumbered:

On the 9th the main column passed through Ripley, moving southwest. On the morning of the 10th the cavalry moved in the direction of Guntown … encountered the enemy's pickets, and soon came upon a large body of the enemy, in position, and the battle became general. The cavalry dismounted and drove the enemy some distance, when the latter were re-enforced, and our men fought four hours against great odds. When the infantry came up, the cavalry retired. At 3:00 p.m. another large body of the enemy arrived on the railroad, in sight of the battle, which was raging furiously, all our forces being engaged. It was soon evident that we could not withstand such attacks as were being made by such superior numbers, and our men began to fall back, contesting every inch of ground. The colored troops fought with desperation, and were the last to give way. The column retreated to Ripley, a distance of 25 miles, that night, after burning a large portion of the supply train, and destroying ten pieces of artillery, which they were unable to move through the swamps.[242]

Nathan Bedford Forrest who routed Sturgis at Brice's Crossroads was considered the "Wizard of the Saddle."

Forrest initially held in check the Union cavalry that had crossed Tishomingo Creek, and as more and more of his men rode in he began to get the upper hand. At that point the Union infantry arrived, exhausted after their hard march, and Forrest began to slash their line with his patented flanking attacks. They gave away, but a huge traffic jam developed on the lone bridge across Tishomingo Creek, blocking their retreat and causing panic within their ranks. Confederates followed, firing into the throng, and on horseback crossed the creek themselves to mount a pursuit throughout the night all the way to Ripley.

The "disaster" of the Battle of Brice's Crossroads warranted a military board of investigation that convened in Memphis at the end of June 1864. Under questioning, Sturgis confirmed Kargé's reconnaissance mission with "400 select cavalry." He also attributed some of the difficulties of his own expedition and communication with his superiors to having sent his telegraph operator with Kargé to assist with "intercepting any communications that might be passing from the enemy, and afterward destroying the lines."[243] The telegraph operator, Fred W. Snell, wrote a scathing retrospective years later in the *Chicago Daily Tribune* that charged that the conduct and failure of the expedition was a "crime" unparalleled in the war. He went so far as to state, "had General Sturgis been a Confederate officer in disguise, he could not have more successfully turned over to the Rebels these immense stores and 3,000 veteran troops."[244]

Brice's Crossroads was a setback for the Union operations in Mississippi, but Kargé's cavalry missions and defensive work were the bright spots in the otherwise failed expedition. Forrest achieved victory with only 492 casualties to his available force of 3,500 men against what he reported as 10,252 opposing him on the Union side (in reality, some 8,300). He felt "the victory may be justly considered one of the most complete of the war" and cited Union killed and wounded of more than 2,000 plus another 1,618 captured (including three musicians) as well as the force's complement of artillery pieces and a wagon train of supplies and ammunition.[245] General Samuel Sturgis remained without assignment for the duration of the war and Joseph Kargé emerged with a more lustrous reputation as a tactical cavalryman. General Sturgis himself singled out the Polish cavalry colonel despite the debacle, and expressed his "high appreciation" for "the valuable services rendered by" Colonel Kargé, whom he termed an "excellent and dashing officer." Sturgis specifically cited Kargé's "reconnaissance to Corinth, and his subsequent management of the rear guard, during a part of the retreat, fighting and defending the rear during one whole afternoon and throughout the entire night following."[246]

In the subsequent reorganization of the division, Kargé received command of the First Cavalry Brigade.[247] He participated in another expedition to target Forrest with his brigade consisting of the Second New Jersey, Seventh Indiana, First Mississippi (U.S.) and Nineteenth Pennsylvania cavalry regiments. By 17 August 1864, he had taken charge of the Second Cavalry Division and was recipient of the continual demands from General Sherman that Forrest must be destroyed.[248] Under General A.J. Smith the deployment of the cavalry was contrived and deliberate. Though he had four times the number of troops that Forrest had in the field, Smith displayed no aggressiveness. Periods of inaction and Smith's recalcitrance when it came to obeying his orders allowed the Confederate cavalry leader to avoid entrapment. Even after Forrest had conducted a surprise middle of the night incursion into Memphis (the location of Union army headquarters), there were missed opportunities in which Kargé's division could have confronted him fully. After an artillery exchange, "the engagement continued until we gained possession" of the Confederate position. The Seventh Indiana Cavalry prepared for a charge, only to have their orders countermanded even though "the enemy seemed to flee precipitately." In another instance, "the men and officers" worked "with great zeal in hope that the corps would at least aid in punishing the enemy, then reported to have made a daring raid on Memphis," and were then ordered to remain in camp.[249]

In the winter of 1864–65, Kargé took part in a raid led by General Benjamin Grierson on the Mobile and Ohio railroad. Confederate General John B. Hood was then conducting a strategic march into Tennessee to draw Sherman's forces away from Georgia and his planned march to the sea. The purpose of the raid was to disrupt and cut supply lines and communications that were vital to Hood's army as it advanced toward Nashville. The main railroad was the Mobile and Ohio, and Colonel Kargé was to lead his cavalry on a wrecking mission from Tupelo south to Meridian, Mississippi.[250]

At Egypt Station, Mississippi, the Confederates occupied fortifications and awaited reinforcements on the railroad that the Union cavalry had been working to decommission. Working in clear, dry late December weather as opposed to negotiating knee-deep mud and washed-out roads, Kargé's force made good progress and began an attack on the Confederate defenses and an actual, well-positioned stockade. After pushing back the front line skirmishers, Kargé ordered an assault on the stockade itself. The ensuing charge "broke down the gates, and, after some vicious hand-to-hand fighting, forced the Rebels to surrender."[251] Three factors enabled their success: they were armed with Spencer repeating rifles that gave the Northern horsemen superior firepower, the speed of the cavalry attack overwhelmed the defenders, and Grierson was able to delay the arrival of enemy infantry support. The *New York Times* reported that Kargé's assault accomplished "the garrisson [sic] of 500 rebels captured, whilst Gen. [Franklin] Gardner was in sight with 2,000 infantry, which Gen. Grierson held at bay, while Col. Kargé's brigade charged the stockade on horseback." The report also catalogued the destruction of Hood's supply lines going north that included wagons, munitions, horses and mules, and provisions for his campaign in Tennessee.[252] The damage to the actual railroad system recorded in the pro-Confederate New Orleans *Daily Picayune* press was "about forty bridges and trestles burned, forty-one cars destroyed, several station houses ... one and a half miles of track turned over, and some twelve to fifteen rails bent." The *Picayune* added optimistically that it was surprising that considering the extent of the damage that the system would be up and operating in a week.[253]

As the war came to a close in late winter and spring of 1865, Kargé's brigade continued to serve under General Grierson with whom he had developed a close friendship. They participated in the Alabama campaign to seize control of Mobile Bay and capture the city of Mobile, the Confederacy's remaining port. With the April surrender of Robert E. Lee's army in Virginia and Joseph E. Johnston in North Carolina, the war effectively ended. There was some preparation for deployment when word arrived that President Jefferson Davis had fled with his entourage from the capital of Richmond to avoid capture. However, Davis' capture in Georgia in early May 1865 put that to rest. Kargé had had a string of successful operations leading a regiment, a brigade and a division, and Grierson felt that the Colonel was deserving of his general's star. He recommended the promotion and declared that Kargé was "one of the most valuable officers" and his services "entitle him to the rank of full Brigadier General." He was promoted to that rank dated from 13 March

1865 and in his acceptance affirmed that he was a native of Poland.[254] In Grierson's memoirs he noted that Kargé:

> … was an excellent officer, brusque and impatient under restraint, but soldierly in bearing, energetic and efficient in the performance of duty. He was always successful in accomplishing orders in any task assigned him while serving under my command. Some years after the close of the war, he became a member of the faculty in Princeton College as professor of languages, a position he continued to fill up to the time of his death."[255]

Joseph Kargé served on the Princeton faculty as Chair of Continental Languages and Literature for twenty-two years. He was well-liked by students and colleagues who had great respect for "Professor Kargé's perfectly transparent, trustworthy, honorable and cordial character."[256] After his death on 27 December 1892, his gravestone in Princeton, New Jersey memorialized him as "A gallant soldier, an accomplished teacher, a true friend."[257]

CHAPTER 6

UNDYING GREY AND DYED BLUE

As the youngest of the Poles examined in this book, Leon Jastremski and Peter Kiołbassa were also the most American. Though both were born in Europe, they arrived in the United States as children who had emigrated with their parents. They had not been the product of the revolutionary movements that had stirred the emotions and fueled the political thinking of the generation that preceded them. Both of these men grew up learning American ways through a European lineage and in communities that had strong ties to the Old World. Kiołbassa came to Texas with his parents and settled in an established farming community of Silesian Poles. He learned to be a frontier Texan: riding, handling livestock and doing farm work, but he was firmly entrenched within his ethnic group. The Catholic church was central to his community and he kept his ties with clergy throughout his life. Jastremski was born in France and grew up in the mostly Francophone area of southwest Louisiana. The church also played a part in his life growing up, and later when he settled in Baton Rouge, and through his regiment's chaplain during the war.

As young men, both Kiołbassa and Jastremski had ties to their homes and community and were raised with the traditions of their families and Old World heritage. They differed in that one, Kiołbassa, came from a peasant background whereas Jastremski's familial roots were aristocratic on both sides. In the war, both men began their service with the Confederate army. An enthusiastic eighteen-year-old who joined the 10th Louisiana Volunteers and stayed true to his commitment throughout the war, Jastremski did not have a political stake in the Southern cause but answered the call to defend his state and home. Kiołbassa began the war in the Texas cavalry and switched sides to serve with Union troops from Illinois. He held to his principles but veered from his allegiance to the army. Jastremski was steadfast throughout his four years of ordeals. The war itself was the cause of the radicalization of both men and it was where their paths diverged. Their experiences leading up to the war, their exploits as soldiers, and the directions they took afterward illustrate that they transferred the spirit and determination learned from their predecessors to their military service and beyond. The factors that combined to influence and build their character enabled them to apply their ideals to their actions.

Peter Kiołbassa and the Silesian Poles of Texas

Peter Kiołbassa came from the Polish community in Karnes County, Texas by way of Upper Silesia in Prussian Poland. The oldest permanent Polish settlement in America had its origins in that part of the partitioned homeland. An emigration of Polish Silesians to Texas took place in the 1850's and was precipitated by "difficult social and economic conditions" in the southwestern section of the Kingdom of Prussia. The "conditions" were such that despite the cost and sacrifice, the journey across the ocean to a land completely different, and to a country in which they did not know the language, was worth the risk. The exodus consisted of landowning peasants who were individuals of good standing in their community and had accumulated sufficient wealth to afford the voyage to the western hemisphere. They were established citizens who owned property, paid taxes and were "permanent constituents of an old social order." These Poles were not part of the gentry, but they were, by class, a much higher rank than the landless peasants or laborers. The local government even officially expressed regret at the loss of good citizens and a somewhat wealthy segment of the population.[1] This was also the sentiment in the Polish press in Kraków in the Austrian part of Poland. The commentary in a Polish language newspaper *Czas* expressed concern that the Polish Silesian population was receding:

Each week more of the Polish population in Silesia disappears: the wealthiest segment is departing for America, encouraged in their hope of establishing a separate Polish settlement, while the poorest element left behind perish like flies from hunger and misery, the rest degenerates: first customs, then language and sometimes even religion.[2]

The local German property owners did not necessarily share this sentiment. These landholders, who were the minority population, felt they could find ample replacements from other areas of Prussia for the departing Poles. They were of the opinion that Germans they would bring in to recolonize vacated land would be better workers.[3]

Peter Kiołbassa

Even though the Polish Silesians had the wherewithal to enable their emigration, they were not immune to the social and economic conditions that set the stage for leaving home. Increases in the cost of goods, especially food, and high taxes caused resentment among the populace. Grain imports from Russia had stopped because of the Crimean War, and a potato blight had seriously depleted that local staple crop. With the food shortages also came outbreaks of typhus and cholera. These factors all contributed to growing conditions of poverty in the province.[4]

There are four key elements in understanding the character of the Silesians who settled in Texas: their background in Europe, their decision to undertake the ocean odyssey to America, the overland journey from Galveston to the interior of the state, and the establishment of their settlement in Karnes County. In the early 1850s, Leopold Moczygemba, a Franciscan priest, came to south central Texas to minister to the Germans who had settled there. He knew well the situation of his people in Prussian Upper Silesia and saw promising possibilities for a new colony of Poles in Texas. He started the process by the acquisition of a large tract of land at the confluence of the Cibolo and San Antonio rivers.[5] Moczygemba had arrived in Texas in September 1852 with three other Franciscans from his province to attend to the Catholic parishes. Assigned to be pastor of two parishes, he began his pastoral work first in New Braunfels then moved to one in Castroville in February 1854. Observing the freedom of the society and the potential to establish open communities that could prosper, he began to write letters home to family and friends in Upper Silesia. His correspondence went so far as "suggesting and even urging" his fellow Poles "to come to a place he was preparing for them in Texas."[6]

Moczygemba's persuasive dispatches from Texas were pivotal in creating the mindset for leaving among the Silesians, who would circulate the letters throughout their communities. However, two circumstances really set the stage for the emigration. One was a tangible physical disaster, the other consisted of the unacceptable substandard social conditions. In 1854 the worst flood in over fifty years struck the Odra River and all its tributaries. That August, continual heavy rains inundated the area and every river and stream overflowed its banks. The floodwaters wreaked havoc with the unharvested crops, and what had promised to

Father Leopold Moczygemba, Franciscan priest who helped found the oldest Polish settlement in America.

be bountiful yields of wheat, barley, rye or potatoes were either washed away or left to rot in muddy, inaccessible fields. Homes and villages were flooded and roads became impassable. The late summer deluge coupled with the economic conditions were the physical motivators for emigration, but social discrimination also made many long for a "better life elsewhere." The Poles were the majority of the population in Upper Silesia, but the inequality of the system under the minority Germans had them relegated to the status of second-class citizens.[7] Furthermore, even though the 1848 insurrections failed, many Silesians had lost any semblance of the feudal attitudes of their forbears and were unwilling "to accept a hopeless future." They became more inclined to weigh their options and consider taking their chances in America.[8]

Stanisław Kiołbassa, Peter Kiołbassa's father, was a farmer and civic activist from Świbie who had been elected a deputy to the Prussian parliament in Berlin. He served in the Reichstag's 1847–48 sessions, and the German newspapers generally considered him a liberal. Even his constituents were not always pleased with him; a young man from his district actually attacked him physically. On a visit home from parliamentary sessions, the man accosted Kiołbassa, blaming him and the parliament for drafting him into the army. Military service beginning at age twenty with active duty for five years, then reserves until the age of forty in the Prussian army, was compulsory. Conscription was another grievance the Silesians held, and it contributed to their reasons for leaving. After his terms in Berlin, the elder Kiołbassa returned home to Świbie where he met Father Moczygemba. The Franciscan was visiting Kiołbassa's parish and substituting for the local priest for several months in 1851.[9]

Moczygemba's later letters from Texas again would have circulated through Świbie and other villages in Silesia. Other letters from Silesians who had already begun a life in America painted a picture of Texas as a land of opportunity where one could own livestock and raise profitable crops such as cotton and wheat. The letters seemed to omit the hardships of the journey and the tribulations of establishing a settlement in a virtual wilderness. From Cieszyn, also in Austrian Poland, the *Gwiazdka Cieszyńska* (Cieszyn Star) reported that the settlers were doing well in Texas, and "the letters coming from there sound quite laudatory." The article suggested the possibility that the writers may have wanted to "lure others from home." The *Star* added that the Polish Texans had "bread, fish and plenty of coffee daily," good hunting was freely available, and they often had game on their tables. The winter climate was mild with only occasional "severe frosts" and summer was "simply very hot." The soil was fertile and the settlers grew potatoes, cucumbers and pumpkins, and had lush pasture grass.[10] From Cieszyn and also *Czas* in Kraków, the report was that more than five hundred people from Upper Silesia had emigrated, mostly to Texas:

> While emigration from Germany to America has generally diminished every year, it has continually increased in Silesia. In the current year especially it seems

that the numbers were unforeseen. From the beginning of April until now [22 May] already more than 500 villagers of Polish origin have departed.[11]

The Kiołbassa family was part of this emigration that traveled by train to the North Sea port of Bremen and boarded the ships *Weser* and *Antoinette* to sail to Galveston, Texas. From there they made their way inland toward San Antonio. They established Panna Maria and other settlements in Karnes County and the San Antonio environs.[12] Panna Maria became (and is) the "oldest permanent Polish settlement in America and home of the nation's oldest Polish church and school."[13]

The new arrivals built simple homes and a church, and settled into an agricultural life similar to what they had lived in Europe. The Texas subtropical climate was markedly different from the temperate continental climate with relatively long winters to which they had been accustomed. They raised livestock and farmed grain, corn, sweet potatoes and cotton, a new crop which they discovered was very profitable. They endured hardships, but the frontier life inured them to difficult conditions and prepared young men such as Peter Kiołbassa for life during the war.[14] One of the dangers unique to their experience was potential exposure to hostile Indians. The communities in that region were always on alert to such possibilities, but grew and developed with some degree of prosperity. After running a report from local Texas newspapers about an Indian attack on a group of German settlers, editors in New Orleans and New York considered it sufficiently notable to acknowledge the Polish settlement:

> "Panna Maria" is the name of the new town built up near the confluence of the San Antonio and Cibolo rivers, in Karnes County, by Polish emigrants. The town contains one hundred and thirty families. The Texan says they are energetic and are fast acquiring our language.[15]

When Texas seceded from the Union on 2 March 1861, it was the harbinger of four years of hardship for the Polish settlers. Those who went to war faced the difficulties of military life, and those who remained behind had to deal with privations and uncertainty. The Silesians had little stake in the war because none of them were slaveholders and their community was fairly isolated from San Antonio and other population centers in the state. Nonetheless, a company of them assembled on the

Cibolo River with three other companies to drill under L.B. Russell. The fourth company was "entirely composed of Polanders commanded by Capt. Joseph Kyrish." This group achieved "the highest honors of the whole battalion," and Russell attributed this to "their military discipline in the old country" and to their willingness to adhere to strict military conduct that was not appealing to the other Americans.[16]

At the age of twenty-three, Peter Kiołbassa joined the Panna Maria Grays, one of the companies raised in Karnes County "made up of Anglos and Poles." He took the oath to the Confederacy as a loyal Texan and signed up as a bugler for the cavalry unit. The Grays' duties in the early months of the war were primarily for security of the local area. They patrolled and provided protection from potential incursions by Union troops, Mexican bandits and marauding Indians.[17] In the spring of 1862 he was with the Texas Lancers in B.F. Fly's K Company in Carter's Brigade of the Texas Mounted Volunteers. Kiołbassa had his horse, which the army listed at a value of $150 and his equipment listed on the muster roll at $40. This company later became Company I of Wilke's Regiment of Texas Lancers (see Appendix A). There were other Poles from Karnes County, including two of Father Moczygemba's brothers, sent to Arkansas later in the year with his regiment.[18]

Arkansas Post and Capture

In 1685, while the territory was still part of Louisiana, the French had founded an outpost forty miles up the Arkansas River from the Mississippi. On this site the Confederates built Fort Hindman, or Arkansas Post, "a square, full-bastioned fort" on a horseshoe bend in the river, and armed it with twelve guns, among which were three nine-inch Columbiads, and a garrison of "about 5,000 men." In the outlying area, it had the additional protection of a ring of rifle pits dug about one and a half miles before the fort. Generals Sherman and John McClernand considered Arkansas Post a threat to Federal supply lines and an obstacle in the Union's plan to take control of the Mississippi River.[19]

General McClernand described Arkansas Post as "a small village … situated on elevated ground, above the reach of floods" and the most prominent feature on the river's bank for several miles. It was "50 miles above the mouth of the river, 117 miles below Little Rock, and is surrounded by a fruitful country, abounding in cattle, corn, and cotton." In order to justify his campaign to his commander, General Grant, McClernand cited eight reasons for the importance of his expedition to take this Confederate stronghold. He received permission and in the beginning of January, McClernand set out with his force of 30,000, supported by the Mississippi Squadron of fifty transport boats with additional gunboats and three ironclads under Admiral David D. Porter.[20]

Earlier in the previous fall, orders arrived that at first angered, then later demoralized Kiołbassa and his fellow Texans. The 24th Texas Cavalry became the 24th Texas Dismounted Cavalry. A report from the Union side confirmed that "so scarce is subsistence for horses that they [the Confederates] have dismounted a large part of their cavalry force … including the Twenty-fourth Texas, Colonel Wilkes, and the Twenty-fifth Texas, Colonel Gillespie." The Confederates were urgently "cutting and stacking prairie hay on the railroad … and procuring corn from the bottom-lands on the lower bank of the Arkansas River, bringing it up by boats to Little Rock." The Texans had grown up with horses and were proud of their role as cavalrymen, so they were understandably displeased at being "dismounted." The only slight consolation was that they were in comfortable quarters at Arkansas Post for the winter of 1862–63.[21]

The comfort did not last and on 9 January 1863, the Northern forces mounted their assault. Brigadier General Thomas J. Churchill, commandant of the Post, "was informed by [his] pickets stationed at the mouth of the cut-off that the enemy, with his gunboats, followed by his fleet of seventy or eighty transports, were passing into the Arkansas River" with the objective of attacking Arkansas Post. Churchill reported that he had about 3,000 effectives and that he was facing the (an exaggerated estimation) "overpowering foe of 50,000 men, who were pressing upon them from almost every direction." The next morning the gunboats began their shelling at 9:00 a.m., easily driving the infantry manning the rifle pits back to the fort. Churchill had just one battery "of field pieces, of 6 and 12 pounders," and he "did not return their fire." The guns in the fort could not give artillery support because of "some defect" in the gunpowder. At 2:00 p.m. "a large body of [Union] cavalry and artillery" began a flanking movement and "advanced cautiously." The next morning the firefight continued with artillery duels and the Union gunboats falling back.[22]

After a short time the gunboats returned, as Churchill continued in his after action report, which sometimes conflicts with other accounts:

> Four ironclads opened up on the fort, which responded in gallant style with its three guns. After a continuous fire of three hours they succeeded in silencing every gun we had with the exception of one small 6-pounder Parrott gun which was on the land side … that gallant band of Texans and Arkansians [sic] having nothing to rely upon now save their muskets and bayonets, still disdained to yield to the overpowering foe of 50,000 men, who were pressing upon them from almost every direction. Just at this moment, to my great surprise, several white flags were displayed in the Twenty-fourth Regiment Texas Dismounted Cavalry, First Brigade, and before they could be suppressed the enemy took advantage of them, crowded upon my lines, and not being prevented by the brigade commander from crossing, as was his duty, I was forced to the humiliating necessity of surrendering the balance of the command.[23]

The other Confederate units had not surrendered yet. Churchill attached no blame to the men, but felt there had been some sort of malicious betrayal: "No stigma should rest upon the troops. It was no fault of theirs; they fought with a desperation and courage yet unsurpassed in this war." He expressed his hope and was certain that "the traitor will yet be discovered, brought to justice, and suffer the full penalty of the law." He waxed hyperbolic when he stated that, "in no battle of the war has the disparity of forces been so unequal. The enemy's force was full 50,000, when ours did not exceed 3,000 and yet for two days did we signally repulse and hold in check that immense body of the enemy." Churchill reported about 60 killed and "75 or 80 wounded." He did not give the number of captured.[24]

There are differing accounts of what was a disastrous surrender. One describes the capitulation as if the men involved were unaware of what was happening: Churchill "surrendered the fort when a white flag mysteriously appeared in the ranks … [T]he men from the fort blamed him for their capture and resented being ordered to serve under him." Even in his later assignments Churchill had to endure men under his command who complained because of his bad reputation.[25] Colonel Robert R. Garland of the 6th Texas, commanding a brigade, reported that the fort's guns had been silenced, and the Union "batteries and gunboats had complete command of the position, taking it in front, flank, and rear at the same time, literally raking our entire position." At that time the men were caught in a "terrific cross-fire," Garland was shocked "by the cry of 'Raise the white flag, by order of General Churchill; pass the order up the line,' and on looking to the left" he was greatly astonished to see "quite a number of white flags displayed in Wilkes' regiment (Twenty-fourth Texas Cavalry, dismounted)." Garland felt he was slighted in Churchill's report, was not sure if the order had actually been official, and demanded "a thorough and immediate investigation."[26]

The surrender and capture proved to be the turning point for Kiołbassa as well as many of his fellow Texans. One of his Texas comrades-in-arms later wrote an account of the battle from the soldier's point of view that could easily have paralleled Kiołbassa's perspective. L.J. Caraway related that McClernand's initial move was positioning the gunboats in front of the fort's batteries and opening fire "simultaneously with all their instruments of destruction, and such a noise" that was greater than anything he had ever heard. Their infantry made several charges, reforming each time for another assault. The defending Confederates were able to repel them initially with "deadly" volleys that were "thinning their ranks" each time. When the Union gunboats opened fire, they ignited the fort's powder magazine, enabling the infantry to storm and take the fort and seize all the "siege pieces." The Federals then turned some of the guns on the Confederates and swept their "line of battle its entire length. They disabled all the cannon of our battery and killed all our artillery horses, as their cannon were directed by a man with much skill." He portrayed the ending and actual surrender with some relief:

> Things were growing hotter and hotter, and it was plain to see that the Confederates could not endure the great odds they had to fight much longer. The Union side then formed for the next charge, four deep, and to the great relief of our army the white flag was hoisted without orders from one end of our line to the other. It has always seemed providential to surrender just at that time, as the next charge would have annihilated us.[27]

After their capture and subsequent disarming, conditions took a turn for the worse:

> A terrible snowstorm added to our disasters and it turned intensely cold. We were thinly clad, having left our clothing in camp … we boarded three transports … [and were] sent down the Arkansas River to its mouth … The change of climate was about the worst thing for us—from mild to frigid. When we got off the

[railroad] cars after eleven hours without a spark of fire, we were all nearly dead. Some of our boys were chilled to death.[28]

Kiołbassa survived the transport by boat down the Arkansas River, up the Mississippi River to Alton, Illinois, then by railroad boxcars to Camp Butler, near Springfield, for internment. He, like the others doing the fighting at Arkansas Post, had left his winter clothing behind and was dressed in utilitarian garb for battle. He had scant winter clothing for January in central Illinois. He likely was unaware that the Federal officers were considering exchanging prisoners, especially those conscripted Confederates of foreign birth, soon after their capture.[29] Additionally, he undoubtedly would have heard stories of prisoners who had been shipped even farther north to spend the upcoming winter months at places such as Camp Douglas in Chicago, or Johnson Island in Lake Erie off the Ohio shore between Toledo and Cleveland. Even in the early confinement at Camp Butler, Confederate prisoners died of exposure. Exchange agent Robert O. Ould wrote a complaint to his Union counterpart:

> Some dozen of our men captured at Arkansas Post were allowed to freeze to death in one night … I appeal to our common instincts against such atrocities in humanity.[30]

After a short time at Camp Butler came the offer of a different possibility. Colonel W.I. Lynch and some detachments of the 58th Illinois Volunteers had been assigned to prison guard duty at Camp Butler during that period. He observed in his report of 4 February 1863, that "nearly one-half of the prisoners confined" had been conscripts who had been "pressed into the Confederate service." Moreover, they were "foreigners, Germans, Polanders, &c." who might take the oath of allegiance and join the Union army. The quartermaster for the 58th Illinois, Lieutenant George Sawin, reported that the Confederate prisoners were Texans, but many were "Irish, German and Polish nationality" who had said they were conscripted. The battle of Arkansas Post was their first engagement, but now they were willing to "take the oath of allegiance and fight for the Union." The Northern officer felt that they were with them in spirit and would have been with them in body, "but for the misfortune of locality."[31] Many other prisoners of Polish and German extraction, as well as Kiołbassa, were allowed to "leave the prison camp only a few days after they had arrived." He was sworn in as a corporal in the Union army.[32]

Not all of the Silesians that were fighting alongside or captured with Kiołbassa accepted the Federals' offer. Many of his countrymen from Karnes County served out the war with the Confederate army—whether they volunteered or went through the draft. Alexander Dziuk and Martin Dugi would exchange stories with themselves and others for years after the war. Dziuk said he was drafted at age eighteen and served "in the Confederate army till the end of the war." He added that when he returned to Panna Maria after the war, he was so gaunt that his own mother was unable to recognize him. Dugi often spoke of the hard times and squalid conditions he endured as a prisoner of war. Dziuk became a prominent and successful farmer in the area who lived until 1924 and died near Panna Maria at the age of eighty-one. His place of birth was listed as "Silesia, Europe" on his death certificate (see Appendix F).[33]

Illinois Cavalry

Peter Kiołbassa went in another direction. He started his new military career with Company D of the 16th Illinois Cavalry. Peter served with the 16th Illinois for nearly two years as a sergeant.[34] Peter Kiołbassa's first two languages were his native Polish and German, which he learned in Silesia at the state school he attended. He did not learn English until he was seventeen and had arrived in Texas. The Sixteenth Illinois Cavalry had a good number of Germans and his knowledge of the language proved useful in serving as a sergeant, and later an officer in that regiment. When on leave he often traveled to Chicago, where he met other Poles and began to establish contacts and friendships there in 1864.[35]

The 16th regiment participated in the Battle of Atlanta, where in the aftermath, Kiołbassa again—just as with the 24th Texas in Arkansas—had the distasteful experience of serving as "dismounted" cavalry. After the battle, the 16th Illinois with the 12th Kentucky was part of a defensive array under Major General Oliver O. Howard in the Army of the Tennessee.[36] They were later remounted in time to face Nathan Bedford Forrest's cavalry in Tennessee. On the approaches to Columbia, they narrowly escaped being overwhelmed while taking part in a rear guard action along with the 14th Illinois Cavalry in November 1864. Forrest's advance and flanking movement had them in a situation in which they "could not reload while mounted." Kiołbassa and the cavalry had been supplied with Springfield rifles, "which after the first volley were about as serviceable to a cavalryman" who was surrounded and fighting at close quarters "as a good club." The only recourse was to retreat before capture.[37]

In the last year of the war, Kiołbassa received a captain's commission to lead a company in the United States Colored Troops. He took command of Company E, 6th Regiment U.S.C.T. at Lexington, Kentucky, on 18 January 1865. Since he was from a Southern state, he had experience living near and interacting with blacks even though there were no slaves in his immediate community. Once again he saw service in Arkansas, this time in a blue uniform. He was mustered out at Devall's Bluff, Arkansas, on 15 April 1866, one year after the war had ended. Peter Kiołbassa finished his military service on the opposite side from which he began, just fifty miles north of where he had been captured as a Confederate.[38]

Settling in Chicago

After the war, Kiołbassa married a Polish girl who resided in Chicago. She was also a fellow Silesian who had come to Illinois at about the same time the Kiołbassa family settled in Panna Maria. He immersed himself in the affairs of the local Polish community and began planning the building of the first Polish church in the city. Kiołbassa had been a cattle rancher and farmer in Texas and served in the cavalry of both Confederate and Union armies. He had grown up performing farm and home chores then served in the military. He preferred an active life, so after the war he became a Chicago policeman. Knowing three languages was a definite asset in that city which had a growing immigrant population.[39]

In 1871 he went back to Texas for a lengthy visit and worked as the Postmaster for almost three months. While in Panna Maria, he was able to persuade Father Adolf Bakanowski to come to Chicago to serve as pastor to the Polish church there.[40]

Kiołbassa returned to Chicago, started a job as a clerk in the Customs Service and began to take an active role in local politics. He had affiliated himself with the Republican Party after the Civil War. It was a logical association since he was now a resident of Illinois, President Lincoln's home state. Kiołbassa urged his fellow Poles (estimated to be 2,000 families in Chicago) to become politically active, and he encouraged them to support former General Grant for president in 1872. After working in the Customs Service for four years, he won election to the Illinois state legislature in January 1877.[41]

Peter Kiołbassa kept his job at Customs while serving his term in the legislature. In 1886 a Democrat was elected chief Collector of the Customs Service in Chicago. Kiołbassa was said to have pledged to his new superior that he was going to switch parties and "become a Democrat." This only served to infuriate the new boss, who fired Peter Kiołbassa as well as others who were not of the Democratic Party.[42] To support himself, Kiołbassa became a notary public and dabbled in real estate and insurance out of an office on Division Street in Chicago.[43] What had appeared to be a self-serving gesture was not as significant as his transfer of allegiance from Confederate army to Union, but it was equally expedient. While the military choice appeared to be a genuine change of heart and mind, the avowed change of political affiliation in order to retain employment exemplified only toadyism.

In 1888 the city reorganized its ward system and Kiołbassa ran for the office of alderman in the newly formed sixteenth ward. The majority of the voters in the sixteenth ward were Polish, and actually had preferred a different candidate put up by the Polish National Alliance, August Kowalski. Yet the political "manager" of the rival Polish Roman Catholic Union was Father Vincent Barzynski, the Resurrectionist priest, who staunchly backed Kiołbassa. The priest had known his candidate since the pre-war days back in Karnes County, Texas, and touted his friend as the "ideal Pole." His opponents wanted Polish unity and felt that this "Texas" coalition was dividing the community with the less popular of the two candidates. Kiołbassa lost the election and actually had made a surreptitious switch of parties to the Democrats. It seemed that it had not been just a ruse to keep his job at Customs. It was very probable that he resented "the growing anti-Catholic and anti-foreign" leanings of the Republican Party. He became part of the immigrant and first generation ethnic movement toward the Democratic Party.[44]

Significant ancillary work with which Kiołbassa involved himself was the formation and development of Chicago's first Polish Catholic Parish, St. Stanislaus Kostka. The parishioners, 150 families who had come to Chicago from Poland, moved that the church should be only for the Polish community. Kiołbassa recruited his friend and another former Panna Marian from Texas, Father Adolf Bakanowski, to serve as pastor, and for a time, the Polish nationalists had control of parish affairs. Kiołbassa was the leader of the Polish Catholic organization and a founder of the pre-eminent Catholic church in the city.[45]

Polish Americans were still a small minority among the ethnic voters in Illinois when Kiołbassa was elected to the state legislature. Prior to that he had been encouraging political activism from the estimated 2,000 Polish families in Chicago. Another important development and milestone was his election as city treasurer.[46] He became the earliest successful Polish-American politician in Illinois, and as a politician he recognized the importance of coalition building. Though he did not have an advanced education he was worldly and had been exposed to diverse cultures and ethnic groups. When he served in the Union army, his knowledge of German had been useful. As a politician, he worked "to unite Democrats, [and] spoke Czech at a meeting of Bohemians trying to join Bohemians with Poles against Germans."[47]

As city treasurer, Kiołbassa controlled municipal bond issues and dealt with the major banks in the state of Illinois. He was involved in disputes with the Chicago city council with regard to payment of the police force with funds directly from the treasury. Despite his emphasis on his Polishness, he sometime incurred the wrath of his countrymen along with his political enemies. Another Chicago "Polish Alderman" from Kiołbassa's sixteenth ward, John Dahlman, denounced his purported switch from Republican to Democrat: "Kiołbassa is not a Democrat. He is a time-server and a contemptible fellow … He will not carry his own ward. The Poles despise the fellow."[48] Just as in the war, when he fought on both sides, he found Poles on his side and against him. This proved true when the Polish National Alliance denounced him in 1892 for claiming to be a leader in their community and circulating a fictitious pamphlet:

> … knowing him to be a whining, shifty, crawling politician, who has frequently changed his politics to get office. Not only has the Polish alliance refused to accept Kiołbassa as a leader, but its members have repudiated and rebuked him … This pamphlet, it was intimated, had the sanction of the Roman Catholic church. This was of course an impudent fiction.[49]

In 1898 the U.S. Congress was moving to pass an immigration restriction bill. The amended law was to have "unusual education" requirements to make an immigrant eligible to enter the United States. Kiołbassa led the Polish Roman Catholic Union of the U.S. in the charge to defeat the legislation. One of their tenets called upon the Congress to recognize Poland's role in history:

> In view of the great services rendered to humanity in general and in defending civilization against barbarians for centuries our nationality, notwithstanding its technical political extinction as a nation should receive some consideration at the hands of the representatives of this great and free republic.[50]

The appeal went on to affirm that Poles who came to America were doing so to work and ensure that their children would have "better education than they could acquire under the restrictions of the three nations now controlling Poland." Kiołbassa made a point throughout his career to promote the causes of the Polish community in Illinois and nationally. In this vein, he rallied 5,000 Poles in protest of a U.S. treaty with Russia that potentially could have allowed extradition of émigrés accused of crimes by the Russian Imperial government. He declared that they "object to the broad scope of the treaty, which will enable the Czar to exercise his tyranny on men who have been guilty of no just law and who have escaped from his dominion." In this regard he shared the anti-Russian sentiments of Polish Southerners Tochman, Sulakowski and Szymański, and the Union Army's Żychliński.[51]

Peter Kiołbassa differed from the other Poles discussed previously in this study in that he changed sides in the middle of the conflict. He had left his native country for the new world of Texas and become an American. At Camp Butler, he betrayed the oath to the Confederacy he had sworn and joined the Union army. Leon Jastremski was fiercely loyal to the Confederate cause and kept his oath as a soldier to the extent of always returning to his regiment after release from imprisonment. He even went to the extent of escaping from a ship's hold in New York and making his way back to Louisiana to rejoin the army at the war's end. Kiołbassa chose to side with the North after his capture. He may have embraced the concept of fighting for freedom, the abolition of slavery and preservation of the Union, but while doing so he also deftly avoided confinement in a prisoner of war camp. Returning to Texas after his defection to the Northern side would have been difficult, so he opted to remain in Chicago, pursue a career and raise a family. One of his daughters actually married and resettled in San Antonio, Texas, the major metropolitan center near her father's old home of Panna Maria. Peter Kiołbassa, however, started a new life far removed from the Poles with whom he was raised. He was successful in Chicago and whether political or professional, he was efficient in all the positions he held.[52] After a nine-week illness, he died at age 66 in St. Mary of Nazareth Hospital in Chicago on 23 June 1905. He had contracted blood poisoning that came about as a result of a foot injury.[53]

Leon Jastremski

In considering that Gaspard Tochman achieved most of his accomplishments in America in the years leading up to and at the beginning of the Civil War, Leon Jastremski was quite the opposite. Jastremski entered the Confederate service at age eighteen from Lafayette, Louisiana, where he was raised. He had been born in France, and his family had settled in Louisiana after emigrating from Europe.[54] His father had fought in the 1830 Polish war against Russia, as did Tochman, so Leon was of the next generation and thus was a more naturalized American culturally and philosophically than Tochman would have been.

Leon's father, Vincent Jastremski, had been from an area of southeastern Poland that was under Russian dominion when he was born in 1806. He fled to France with a Czarist price on his head and settled in the Mediterranean city of Montpellier where he attended medical school and earned his degree in 1836. In 1838 Vincent Jastremski married Ernestine de Pointes, of a local French aristocratic family, and had two sons. His younger son Leon was born 17 July 1843. They moved the family to Vermilionville (now Lafayette), Louisiana in 1845. Dr. Jastremski later became "an eminent physician" in the state, and Leon attended school in Lafayette before the family moved to nearby Abbeville.[55]

After his parents died, Leon Jastremski worked as an apprentice at the small local newspaper, the *Abbeville Meridional*. After Louisiana seceded in

Leon Jastremski, General, United Confederate Veterans, ca. 1900

January 1861, he entered the Confederate service as a seventeen-year-old private in the 10th Regiment, Louisiana Volunteers,[56] which was organized 22 July 1861 at Camp Moore. He was in the Louisiana Swamp Rifles (Company E) and within four days of his induction, the regiment departed for Virginia under orders to join the forces defending the Virginia Peninsula.[57]

The first months on the Peninsula were spent primarily in drill and training. Jastremski echoed the emotions of soldiers throughout history in his complaints about the dull routine of camp life that began each day at 5:00 a.m. reveille and concluded with bedtime at 9:00 p.m. He described the daily routine after morning roll call as breakfast, "guard mounting," parade, drill, "fatigue duty," and "when there is no digging to be done, we have to clean up Quarters. After which we are free until 6 o'clock. Then dress parade" and dismissal for supper until "tattoo beats and all are sent to bed like a parcel of school boys."[58]

Later, their time would include construction of defense works that included batteries and trench fortifications. They undertook this work under the command of Jastremski's fellow Pole, Colonel Valery Sulakowski from New Orleans. He had taken charge of the Seventh Brigade, composed of the 10th and 14th (Polish Brigade) Louisiana Regiments. The troops, under orders from General John Bankhead Magruder, enlisted the aid of black slave labor supplied by local Virginia landowners.[59] Magruder, "known in old army circles as 'Prince John,'" developed a good personal and professional relationship with Sulakowski.[60]

The enlisted men also soon learned the ways of hard labor. As Jastremski wrote, in addition to their drills and training, they used spades and axes for constructing earthworks and cutting trees for fortifications. This caused some of the men to reflect on the lot of the slaves working with them there in Virginia as well as in the past in Louisiana. They had become unexpectedly "experienced in an art so extremely fatiguing and unprofitable" that it reminded them of slaves "felling timbers for their masters."[61] Although they may not have been directly involved in slavery growing up prior to the war, it gave them great appreciation for their present labors—as disliked as they were. Additionally, with the experience of their martial drills, some expressed sympathy for the drudgery and work the slaves had to endure.[62]

Though he came from a Polish military family, Jastremski's birth in France and schooling in south Louisiana made French his everyday language, as indeed it was for the 10th Louisiana Regiment. Many of his wartime letters written to his brother at home were composed in French. The company would drill to commands issued in that language from Colonel Mandeville de Marigny, who had been a cavalry officer in France. Marigny utilized the French army's organizational methods in forming his units and had under his command men of more than a dozen nationalities. This multi-national character made French the *lingua franca* of the 10th and certain other regiments from Louisiana.

The 10th Louisiana "seemed to be an army from Babel, with the strange bewildering jabbering of its members," and it made communication with the officers from outside somewhat difficult in the early goings of the war. General Lafayette McLaws, after meeting with Marigny and his adjutant, wrote that while admittedly they spoke English, it was "indifferently well." McLaws added that the adjutant spoke "but two words" and more than likely did not speak English at all.[63]

The Army of Northern Virginia

The first major action that Jastremski saw with his regiment occurred when the army had to confront McClellan's juggernaut advancing up the Peninsula toward Richmond. He and his men faced Ludwik Żychliński and the *Enfans Perdu* from New York at the Battle of Williamsburg (see map on p. 85). During the daylong battle in which the Federal troops captured the Confederate earthworks christened Fort Magruder, the Southerners delayed the enemy advance and both sides claimed a victory of sorts. Despite the confusion and miserable conditions of the battle in fog and rain, the regiment fought well as a unit, confirming that the months of training had been useful. The elements combined severally against the soldiers. The exhausted men were depressed by "the rain, [and] the sight of the wounded," had no immediate signs of reinforcements, and had waves of "smoke and rain" being "driven by the wind into" their faces. The Union side suffered greater casualties at 2,239 as opposed to 1,703 for the Confederates.[64] There would be no more combat for Jastremski in this campaign until the culmination of the Seven Days Battles at Malvern Hill on 1 July.[65]

During this campaign, the intensity of enmity between the Southern and Northern armies seemed to intensify. The effect on the young Jastremski had to be palpable. Questionable deeds of conduct occurred on both sides, with some bordering on the criminal. An occasion in which "Yankee scoundrels" who were described as "blackhearted vandals," fired on Confederates supplying water to Federal wounded in the field went well reported in the newspapers. They also left their dead "scattered over the whole field *not having buried a single man*" for days.[66] On the other side, the Louisiana troops had already earned the nickname "Tigers" and deserved the reputation on more than one level. As an eighteen-year-old private, Jastremski undoubtedly would have felt the influence of and often been party to some of the behavior that defined the Louisiana Tigers. They were characteristically fierce fighters when summoned to battle, and brawling, marauding, spirited and often fun-loving at other times. Even the chaplain of the 10th Regiment, Father Hippolyte Gache, wrote that the "Louisiana boys" had gained a reputation of "general loutishness." Courageous but reckless fighters, they struck fear in the enemy and even their fellow soldiers from other non-Louisiana units expressed their fear of them.[67] A Virginia soldier related perhaps the most atrocious episode associated with the Tigers that occurred after the Williamsburg battle. The infantry had stacked their guns and were resting their columns at the roadside:

> [I]n a common on the outskirts of the town, resting and awaiting orders, when a number of wounded Federal prisoners were brought up in an ambulance and laid temporarily on the grass, while a field hospital was being established hard by. Among them was a poor wretch, shot through the bowels, who was rolling on the ground in excruciating agony and beseeching the by-standers to put him out of his misery. There did not appear to be anything that could be done for him, at least not in advance of the coming of the surgeons, so I was in the act of turning away from the painful spectacle when a couple of Tureos, or Louisiana tigers, the most rakish and devilish-looking beings I ever saw, came up and peered over the shoulders of the circle of onlookers. Suddenly one of them pushed through the ring, saying: "Put you out of your misery? Certainly, sir!" and before any one had time to interfere, or even the faintest idea of his intention, brained the man with the butt of his musket; and the bloody club still in his hands, looking around upon the other wounded men, added glibly, "Any other gentleman here'd like to be accommodated?" It is impossible to express my feelings. I fear that if I had had a loaded musket in my hands, I should have illustrated the demoralization of war a little further by shooting down in his tracks the demon, who suddenly disappeared, as a gasp of horror escaped the spectators.[68]

The lighter side of Jastremski's Louisiana comrades also shone through on occasion. During winter camp in Virginia, men from the Dreux battalion "proposed to give the denisons [sic] of that region an idea of what a Mardi Gras celebration was" like in New Orleans. The soldiers wanted to brighten up winter before the Lenten season began. They enlisted help from some local people from Williamsburg, and "some two hundred of the New Orleans boys got up a wonderful procession … [and] closed with an entertainment to Gen. Magruder and his staff at an inn in Williamsburg by the members of the battalion."[69]

Chaplain of the 10th Louisiana Infantry, Father Louis-Hippolyte Gache

Such episodes and the growing notoriety of the Tigers augmented Jastremski's development as a soldier, as well as his subsequent promotions and eventual elevation to the rank of captain. These early experiences of soldierly life certainly hardened him for the capture that awaited him after Malvern Hill and steeled him for later imprisonment. At this final battle of the Peninsula Campaign the Louisiana troops distinguished themselves, especially the 10th Louisiana. The Confederates had successfully withdrawn up the Peninsula with a succession of battles that were technically victories for the North but strategic successes for the South in protecting Richmond. McClellan had positioned his army on high ground, on a roughly mile-long plateau called Malvern Hill east of Richmond. The Federal infantry occupied the sloping hillsides of the plateau and behind them on the heights was well-positioned artillery.[70] The Southerners felt they still were in good stead. A Louisiana soldier confidently wrote, "The great struggle for Richmond has been fought and won, after six days battle, or six different engagements." He added that in all of them they had been the winners, "the enemy have been driven to the wall."[71]

Despite the sequence of tactical moves and engagements in which he advanced up the Peninsula, where it appeared that the Army of the Potomac was positioning to capture Richmond, McClellan had assumed a defensive position for this last confrontation outside the city. Robert E. Lee, who was defending the Confederate capital, instead assumed the aggressive role and decided to attack. There was to be an artillery bombardment of the Union positions, then "all the infantry were to make a simultaneous assault and wrest Malvern Hill from the enemy." In early movements, some miscommunication of orders resulted in a somewhat poorly organized assault, rife with "confusion and uncertainty." The result was "individual brigades advancing against the near impregnable" Union lines.[72]

Jastremski and the men of the 10th Louisiana languished in reserve as their fellow Louisiana regiments crashed into the Federal lines with little success and frightful casualties. General Ambrose R. Wright's brigade finally drove the enemy back as far as the artillery placements before having to withdraw with nearly forty percent casualties as the daylight waned.[73] Finally the 10th received orders to move out and Colonel Eugene Waggaman, a New Orleanian and one of the men's favorite officers, gave them a brief motivational speech that reminded them that their fellow Louisiana regiments had distinguished themselves while they themselves had been held in reserve that week. He also invoked the memory of the "Yankee Beast," Benjamin Butler, so despised for his harsh occupation of New Orleans, as he exhorted his men to charge the artillery position to their front. Under heavy fire, they stormed the position of thirty-six cannons and captured ten enemy guns. While engaged in hand to hand combat, they seemingly began to receive support from the rear, which Waggaman thought was from fellow Confederates. He ordered Jastremski to go back and tell them to cease their fire. Jastremski was now a Sergeant Major and immediately moved to carry out the order with authority. However, it was actually the 69th New York Infantry approaching from behind with U.S. Regulars. This small contingent of Louisianans quickly found themselves surrounded and he and Waggaman as well as thirty others were taken prisoner.[74]

The 10th Louisiana had been the only Confederates to break through the Union lines in that nighttime attack that marked the final of the Seven Days Battles of the Peninsula Campaign. Eighty-seven men were killed, wounded or missing. Among the captured were "the gallant Lieutenant-Colonel Waggaman, while heading his regiment, who it is supposed was wounded and taken prisoner," and Sergeant Major Jastremski.[75]

This would be Jastremski's first capture and internment as a prisoner of war. The Federals transferred the prisoners to Fort Delaware on Pea Patch Island, a small isolated salt flat in Delaware Bay. After a relatively brief confinement, he was exchanged and returned to Virginia and his regiment, now under the command of Stonewall Jackson, near Culpeper. Within just a few days, the 10th Louisiana would participate in the battle of Cedar Mountain.[76] However, Jastremski's return to action was short-lived. His company had been taking cover in a copse of woods awaiting orders. When they emerged and began to get into formation in order to join the battle, enemy troops had them surrounded and captured him again—a scant four days following his exchange. Jastremski had fought in five battles over the past two months and was taken prisoner by the enemy twice. Once more he was exchanged quickly and rejoined the regiment again in time for battle. This was the Second Battle of Manassas at the end of August 1862.[77]

In this decisive engagement, Jastremski and his Louisiana comrades would enhance their reputation as fighters. The 10th Regiment was now in the Second Louisiana Brigade under the command of General William E. Starke, a native of Brunswick County, Virginia, who had lived in Louisiana for years. The native Louisiana soldiers did not immediately accept Starke because they did not consider him as *one of their own*, but soon after taking charge he had the opportunity to lead the Tigers into action and gain their confidence.[78]

Jastremski and the men disabled and captured several Northern supply trains prior to the battle. The chaplain from the 14th Louisiana remarked that the convergence of an army on the disabled supply train compared to "the sacking of cities" by an "ungovernable mob."[79] However, they returned to good order and had their first fight under Starke at Groveton where they again performed well in combat. The after action reports complimented Starke and referred to the "gallant Louisianians."[80] They further lived up to this praise when, placed on an embankment at a railroad cut, they had orders from General Jackson to retain their position without fail. Starke re-emphasized Jackson's orders when he told his men to "occupy the railroad cut," and it was "to be held at all hazards."[81] After repulsing three Union attacks and practically out of ammunition, they faced a fourth assault. As the next wave of blue clad soldiers approached, they resorted to throwing stones and any rocks they could find as projectiles to repel the enemy. Colonel Leroy A. Stafford reported that when the men found themselves out of ammunition, they "procured some from the dead bodies of their comrades, but the supply was not sufficient." They then "fought with rocks and held their position." It was a combination of the rocks, clubbed rifles and bayonets that beat back the enemy's final assault and put them into retreat.[82]

The stone-throwing episode at the "Deep Cut" added to the lore that surrounded the Louisiana troops. The unfinished railroad bed had provided an ample amount of ballast as a temporary ammunition supply for the Louisianans. Some of the men chose their projectiles and hurled them on a line, just as a baseball pitcher (the relatively new game of baseball had become popular in both armies) would throw a fastball. Still others arced their rocks to cascade as if they were dummy mortar shells falling into the massed Federal troops.[83] An Alabama soldier wrote in his memoirs:

> There were a large number of flint rocks on the Confederate side of the embankment and the Louisianians [sic] fought with them. Such a flying of rocks never was seen. At last the Yankees gave way, and when they turned their backs and fled the ground was blue with their dead and wounded.[84]

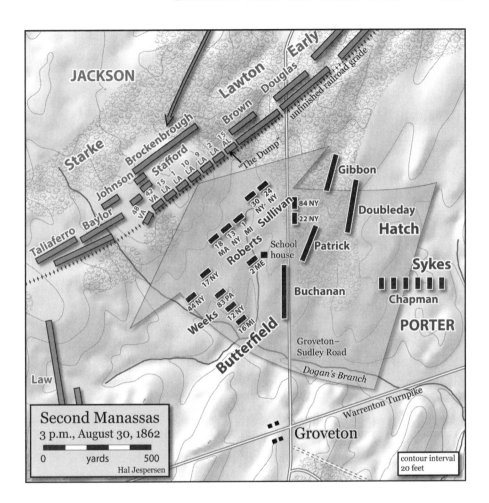

JACKSON

Lawton

Early

Douglas

Brown

unfinished railroad grade

Starke

Brockenbrough

Stafford

Johnson

2 15
LA AL

"The Dump"

Gibbon

Baylor

42 15 1 10 9
VA LA LA LA LA

Doubleday

Taliaferro

48
VA

30 24
NY NY

Sullivan

84 NY

Hatch

22 NY

18 13 7
MA NY MI

Roberts

Patrick

Sykes

School
house

2ME

Chapman

17 NY

Buchanan

PORTER

44 NY

83 PA

12 NY

Weeks

16 MI

Butterfield

Groveton–
Sudley Road

Law

Dogan's Branch

Warrenton Turnpike

Second Manassas
3 p.m., August 30, 1862

Groveton

0   yards   500
Hal Jespersen

contour interval
20 feet

The aid they received that ensured that they would overcome the Yankee charge actually came from artillery fire that enfiladed the Union lines. However, the rock-throwing defensive stand conducted by the Louisiana Brigade became legendary.[85] At this battle of Second Manassas, Jastremski with his 10th Regiment comrades and the 14th Louisiana (of the First Louisiana Brigade under Harry Hays), composed of the men recruited to form the original Louisiana Polish Brigade, were arrayed on the same battlefield against Wladimir Krzyżanowski's 58th New York Regiment. Yet a more direct confrontation between the two groups occurred the following year at Chancellorsville.

After having been the victim of two battlefield captures, the victory in the Second Manassas campaign duly lifted Jastremski's spirit. He and the rest of the men also had the satisfaction of the additional provisions with which they had supplied themselves from seized Federal supply trains and looted warehouse supplies. Not only had they stocked up on staples such as real coffee, bacon, molasses and sugar, but also canned oysters, lobsters, whiskey and wine. They also had the luxury of securing fresh boots and clothing.[86]

In early September, Robert E. Lee's Army of Northern Virginia had the Union forces at a disadvantage following Second Manassas, and he decided to push across the Potomac into Maryland. His reasoning was threefold: move the war into Union territory, gain fresh recruits in that sympathetic border state with ties to the South, and resupply his tattered though victorious army. He also thought of the diplomatic advantages of winning a major victory on Northern soil, which would afford the possibility of official recognition by England and France. The Louisiana Tigers, including Jastremski and his company, looked with greater interest at the potential resupply aspect of the new excursion. They were under orders only to secure provisions by proper means, but an incident early in the campaign involving the unlawful "requisitioning" of supplies took place in Frederick, Maryland. A civilian group of representatives went to Stonewall Jackson and charged that "foreigners" among the Confederate troops had been ransacking stores, stealing liquor and food, and behaving rudely. Jackson immediately singled out the Louisiana men, especially in light of the "foreign" accusation. Starke, who was as much a disciplinarian as was Jackson, staunchly defended his men when he learned they were not involved. A brief investigation found that the charges did not apply, and it proved to be members of Jackson's own Stonewall Brigade that were the culprits. For once the Tigers were innocent.[87]

At the beginning of the Maryland campaign and as a prelude to the battle of Antietam, Lee gave Jackson the mission of capturing Harpers Ferry (now in West Virginia). Harpers Ferry housed a major Federal garrison and arsenal and was situated at the confluence of the Potomac and Shenandoah Rivers. Jackson's corps with the Louisiana Brigade encircled the military installation and town and captured 11,000 Union prisoners as well as all their armaments and supplies with little effort expended.[88] However, after the successful operation, the corps immediately received orders to proceed to Sharpsburg, Maryland, to join Lee and the main army where they had engaged the enemy at Antietam Creek. As part of Jackson's corps, the Second Brigade marched the roughly twelve miles north to join the battle. Jastremski and many of his comrades were clothed partially in blue uniforms—some of the "fresh" clothes they had absconded with from the Federal arsenal's supplies. They entered the fight almost as soon as they reached the field, and the Brigade suffered considerable losses, with the 10th Regiment reporting casualties of 57 men killed, wounded or missing.[89] Among the casualties was the Second Brigade's commander, General Starke. Upon their arrival on the field, Starke "galloped to the front" in order to rally his men onward, He carried the brigade's standard with himself at the forefront of the assault. As soon as he entered the fray, four enemy bullets struck him and he "fell dead amidst his men." Rather than dishearten them, the sight of their mortally wounded leader spurred them "with determination and revenge, and they dashed forward and drove the enemy back." They were able to hold their position the rest of the day. General Starke, who had led these Louisianans in their heroic stand at the Deep Cut less than a month before, was dead.[90]

After Antietam the two Louisiana brigades in the Army of Northern Virginia were now "mere skeletons of their former selves." Jastremski received a promotion to first lieutenant and a transfer within the regiment to Company H, a unit organized at New Orleans that had named themselves the *Orleans Blues*.[91]

In Antietam's one-day battle, where both armies fought to a standstill, there were 23,000 casualties between the two sides. However, since Lee did not achieve the victory the Confederacy needed, he withdrew his army back to Virginia. The *New York Times* proclaimed it the "most stupendous battle of all time" and greatly over-estimated "Rebel losses as high as 30,000." The *Staunton* (Virginia) *Spectator* reported that a Confederate army intelligence officer pronounced:

> the battle a clear and incontestable victory. We pushed the enemy back while the fight lasted, and slept on the field, holding it for twenty-four hours, and then abandoned it voluntarily and without molestation.[92]

Another Virginia newspaper reported that the Confederate legislature expressed gratitude that the army had driven the Northern army from

Virginia in a series of victories. It added that the army was now stronger "than at any former period."[93]

Jastremski saw repeated action over the next few months. He spent the remainder of the autumn months of 1862 with his regiment in

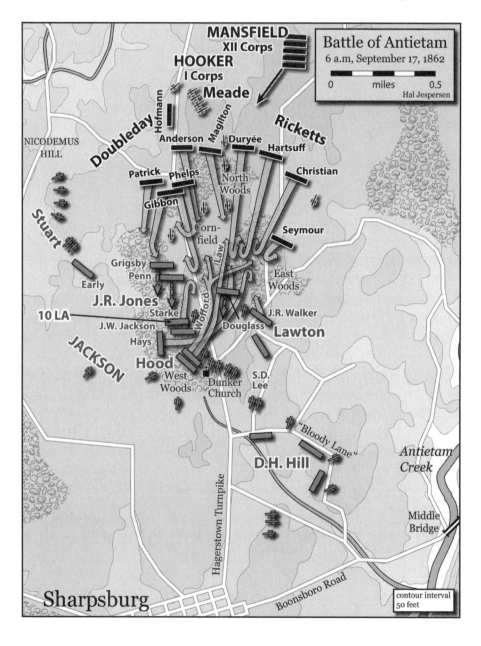

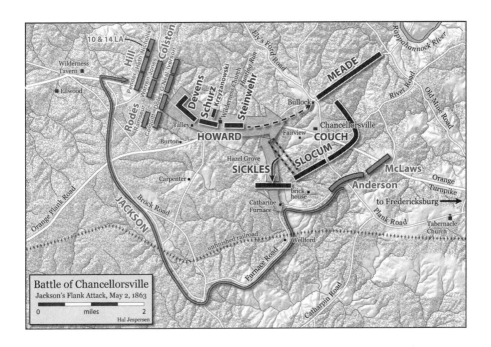

Battle of Chancellorsville
Jackson's Flank Attack, May 2, 1863

"roadblocks, skirmishes, and … delaying tactics." Jastremski was in reserve
with the Louisiana units during the Confederate victory at Fredericksburg
in December, although the brigade suffered some losses due to shelling
from Union artillery.[94] His next major battle was at Chancellorsville in
May 1863. He and the 10th Regiment were part of "Jackson's overwhelming assault [that] had wrecked the helpless Eleventh Corps," as
Union General Carl Schurz stated in his *Reminiscences*.[95]

This was Jastremski's second confrontation with Krzyżanowski, who
was now a brigade commander. In this instance, however, he was part of
a direct assault. The Louisianans were under Brigadier General Francis
T. Nicholls in the second line of attack in what was Stonewall Jackson's
old division when they struck the Union Eleventh Corps under General
Oliver O. Howard. Krzyżanowski's brigade was also second in line in
General Schurz' division when the Confederate attack began to roll
up the Union flank.[96] Both Nicholls and Jastremski received serious
wounds. Caught in an artillery barrage after the attack had completed,
Nicholls was mounted and trying to restore order amid the confusion. A
solid shot blew off his left foot and killed his horse. Later in the battle,
a barrage of grapeshot, shell and shrapnel struck the 10th Louisiana and

Louisiana Governor Francis T. Nicholls. General Nicholls was wounded and lost his left arm in the Shenandoah Valley. He later lost his left foot at Chancellorsville at the same time Jastremski received his wounds.

within minutes fifty men were lost. Jastremski "was wounded severely in the throat." Wounded at Chancellorsville, the two men became political allies after the war. In 1876 Nicholls, who also had lost an arm earlier in the war, ran for governor of Louisiana nominated by his supporters with the slogan, vote "'for all that is left of General Nicholls.'" Jastremski also became involved in Louisiana politics after the war, was an associate of Nicholls, became mayor of Baton Rouge and ran for governor in 1904 and 1908.[97]

Chancellorsville was a decisive Confederate victory but a costly one nonetheless. Of Lee's 10,281 casualties, 1,000 of them were from the two Louisiana brigades. The Confederates' most serious loss, however, occurred when Stonewall Jackson was badly wounded when accidentally fired upon by his own pickets. Jastremski was able to recover from his wounds and returned to his regiment. Jackson did not recover. Surgeons had to amputate his wounded arm and he succumbed to pneumonia shortly thereafter. The young Louisianan had served ably under Jackson in four major battles: Second Manassas, Antietam, Fredericksburg and Chancellorsville.

Upon his recovery, Jastremski returned to the 10th Regiment and was promoted to captain of Company H. With Jackson's passing, they came under the authority of a new corps commander, General Richard Stoddert Ewell, while General Edward Johnson became their new division leader. On 15 June, they participated in the capture of 1,000 Union troops in Winchester, Virginia, when they repelled a flank attack after an all-night march. This Second Battle of Winchester was a lopsided Confederate victory and only added to the mood of headiness that was pervasive in the Army of Northern Virginia after the triumph at Chancellorsville.[98] Winchester was the inaugural battle that led off the Rebels' second incursion into Northern territory and the journey to Gettysburg.

The June 1863 march into Pennsylvania was arduous due to the summer heat and dust, and in drawing near to the town the first skirmishing occurred. After initiating the clash, they again met with Howard's Eleventh Corps and drove them back and out of the town. The 10th Louisiana was subsequently involved in the struggle for Culp's Hill where Jastremski sustained a wound to the hand on the third day. They had been bogged down in an attempt to dislodge the enemy from their positions and because of heavy fire were not able to withdraw until after midnight. After the final major assault with the failure of Pickett's charge, Lee decided to withdraw his army back to Virginia. A surgeon from Hays' Louisiana brigade wrote home on 21 July with a terse account of the encounter with the Union Eleventh Corps:

> We attacked the enemy strongly … driving them through town with greater slaughter than I have ever seen, from where we attacked them to the mountain where we finally drove them, the ground was completely covered with them.

He went on to describe the difficult assault on Culp's Hill:

> On the next day we opened on the mountain where they were massed with artillery, doing fearful execution; at one time we had playing on one position over 250 [sic] pieces of cannon, this was kept up until our ammunition was nearly exhausted, when a charge was ordered; our men did nobly, charging to the top of the mountain, but were not able to hold it, and we were compelled to fall back to

the foot of it. Here we remained … Our army is in fine spirits and are eager to meet them again, to show them that if Vicksburg and Port Hudson are gone we still have an army in the field.[99]

Once again the Louisiana regiments suffered serious losses. In Johnson's Division of Ewell's Corps at Gettysburg, the 10th Regiment listed 91 killed and wounded on the third day.[100] Oddly, though, the Tigers marched away in good spirits. They "were cheerful because they knew

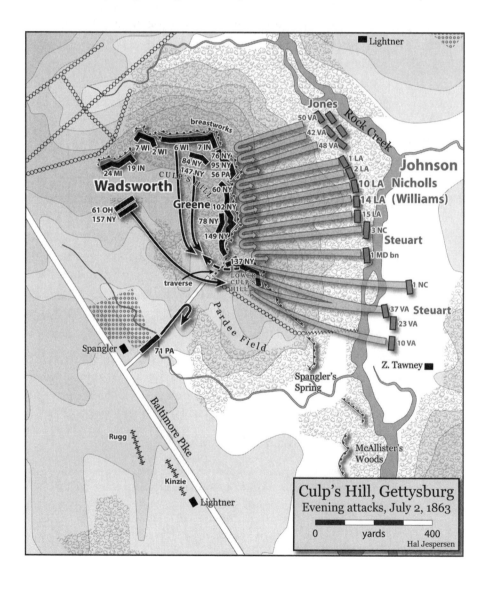

Culp's Hill, Gettysburg
Evening attacks, July 2, 1863

0   yards   400

Hal Jespersen

they had given their all against frightful odds and come away with their considerable pride intact."[101]

Captain Jastremski's company did not have a completely restful autumn and winter after their return to Virginia. He spent most of the month of September in recuperation for his hand and neck wounds in a hospital at Richmond.[102] Illness and desertion were issues that always plagued the army, but many men were getting well and some of the absent were coming back, much to the surprise of their comrades. To induce the return of those absent without leave, the company captains posted notices in newspapers at home that listed the names of deserters. The hoped to shame them and let their family and friends know their status and possibly remind the stragglers of their duty. Jastremski's fellow captain, Auguste Perrodin of Company K, the *St. Landry* (Parish) *Rangers*, sent a notice to the newspaper in Opelousas, Louisiana, and gave a group of deserters thirty days to return, or else. He wrote: *ils seront publiés comme déserteurs, et traités comme tels* (they will be listed as deserters and treated accordingly).[103]

The remainder of the winter and early spring months after the Mine Run campaign in late November/early December were spent in minor skirmishes, security duties and camp life. In the spring, the Army of Northern Virginia faced the new aggressive leader of the Union army in Ulysses S. Grant. Grant had been successful in Tennessee and Mississippi and had achieved a succession of victories, including the paramount conquest of Vicksburg to seize complete control of the Mississippi River. Now he was President Lincoln's appointed choice to challenge Robert E. Lee. The Wilderness Campaign that began in May 1864 was a series of major battles, and Ewell's corps engaged in intense fighting. It was especially fierce at Spotsylvania, where on 12 May Jastremski was taken prisoner along with 55 others from the 10th Louisiana at the "Bloody Angle."[104]

The "Immortal 600"

Jastremski again found himself imprisoned at Fort Delaware on 17 May 1864 (see Appendix E). In this, his final term as a prisoner of war, he would develop a resolve that he carried with him throughout the rest of the conflict and into his post-war career. The conditions at the prison of general poor health, disease and the rate of death were the highest of any of the Northern prison camps. Many veterans who had been imprisoned there later considered it the "Andersonville of the North." Though it was overcrowded, contemporary accounts suggested that food rations were tolerable and included beef, vegetables and even occasionally beer.[105] He wrote to his brother upon arriving at the prison to inform him of his situation, yet he did not paint as bleak a picture as many other prisoners had. Even in his later correspondence there was no suggestion of despair.[106] He did, however, tell his brother that his only clothes were nothing but tatters and asked that he send money. He also briefly described his experiences in a letter of 19 July 1864:

> I was wounded on the 3rd of May 1863 at *Chancellorsville* by a fragment of shell which struck me in the throat. It has altered my voice greatly and renders it very hoarse. I was also wounded slightly in the right hand at *Gettysburg* and lastly again slightly at *Spottsylvania* [sic]. I have participated in fifteen engagements.[107]

The prison population was well over its stated capacity and diseases ranging from dysentery to smallpox and "malarious fever" caused by unclean drinking water were rampant.[108]

Jastremski would have had a shared ethnic connection with the commandant of the camp, Albin E. Schoepf. Brigadier General Schoepf had been born in Podgorze, Poland, to a Polish mother who was married to an Austrian. He had served as a captain in the Austrian army, but joined the Hungarian "revolutionists" to fight with the Polish Legion in the insurrections of 1848, and had to flee the empire to America. Schoepf had "been commissioned a brigadier general of volunteers" in September 1861 and had fought in the western theatre of operations. After the Battle of Perryville, Kentucky, where he led a division, Schoepf and other officers fell into disfavor. Later the army transferred him east to command the prison at Fort Delaware. His military experiences in Europe fighting against imperial authority and subsequent departure from there were very similar to those of Valery Sulakowski. He also shared the same European adherence to strict discipline and inflexibility in orders. As was often the case, this did not curry favor with the volunteer soldiers under his command, nor did it gain him esteem from the Confederates imprisoned in his compound.[109]

After three months of incarceration in miserable conditions, Jastremski was among those chosen to become part of a group that the other prisoners called "The Immortal 600." The camp commandant, Schoepf, listed six hundred officers that he agreed with the authorities to send by steamship to South Carolina. These men were "to be held under fire of the Confederate guns in retaliation for the stationing of Federal prisoners in Charleston."[110] A member of the Six Hundred vehemently denied the use of Union prisoners in such a fashion because the sources for the information were completely untrustworthy:

> [The story] should not have been taken by any decent man without corroboration yet Gen. J.G. Foster, U.S.A., commanding Department of the South, headquarters, Hilton Head, S.C., accepted the word of these creatures without question, and inflicted upon helpless prisoners of war cruelties that would have shamed Nero.
>
> There never were any Union prisoners of war under fire of their own guns in any part of the South; there were never any prisoners of war treated with harshness or cruelty by order of the Confederate government authorities.[111]

The journey and transport south were an ordeal more arduous and miserable than camp existence, but it afforded Jastremski a possibility of escape or parole. It also gave him the opportunity to bond with his fellow officers who shared similar values and hopes for the future.[112]

The steamer *Crescent* "narrowly escaped a total wreck" when it struck a sandbar and ran aground near Cape Romain, South Carolina, north of Charleston. This allowed a few prisoners to escape by sea and brought charges of negligence to the ship's captain. Meanwhile the prisoners were under heavy guard, and forty of the extremely ill were removed, while a gunboat worked to free the *Crescent* from the sandbar. The heat plus cramped conditions in the hold and lack of water prompted Jastremski to refer to the eighteen-day ordeal as a "floating purgatory." They had a "passage about two feet wide" and had only "twelve inches of space being allowed to each man and two feet in the clear to each bunk."[113]

The officers disembarked under guard to Morris Island, South Carolina, where their guards positioned them in camp under fire from Confederate batteries. They were "encamped … in full range of the Confederate batteries" in an area of about one and one half acres. The shelling was frequent and was constant for more than forty days. There were numerous bursts overhead, mortar bursts would land in the stockade, and other cannon shots would strike behind them at the fort. At Morris Island there were no mail privileges and nourishment consisted of rations that were meant to punish the officers. The commandant, Colonel Edward F. Hallowell, had "an obsessive hatred for the South" and deliberately "used psychological tactics in an attempt to break down morale."[114] The Federal authorities eventually transferred them to Fort Pulaski, Georgia. Jastremski wrote three letters to his brother in Louisiana that described desperate conditions during this time, but received no word or return mail for three months.[115]

Jastremski's confinement at Fort Pulaski coincided with General Sherman's campaign in Georgia and his march north into South Carolina. This created an influx of prisoners both military and political, but mainly consisted of "spies and doubtful characters" that Sherman had ordered arrested and imprisoned. This prompted the camp commandant, Major General Q.A. Gillmore, to request that he be allowed to move the "495 rebel officers ... to a military prison at the North." He wrote this to Lincoln's chief of staff, Henry W. Halleck, and cited that the "retaliatory object for which they were originally sent" had been accomplished. He further maintained that the prisoners could be "kept by the Government at less expense and with fewer guards at one of the regularly organized prison camps at the North." Jastremski and his fellow officers were to be shipped North again.[116] The transport of "465 officers and 167 men, prisoners of war," was via the steamer *Illinois* on 5 March 1865 destined for City Point in Richmond.[117]

Over a period of seven months since their transport from Fort Delaware to the south, Jastremski had plotted escape with three other officers. It was on the return when destined for further incarceration in a prisoner of war camp that they acted on it. Jastremski had ingratiated himself to an Irish crewman who was not unsympathetic to the plight of the Southern captives. He secreted the four with rations and water in a storage place in the hold. There they could hide until the ship deposited the prisoners at the fort and proceeded to New York City. Once they arrived, they could sneak ashore for their first maneuver toward freedom.[118]

After three days and nights in the hold, the Confederate comrades emerged on deck into sunlight when they reached New York Harbor. Jastremski recounted their escape somewhat casually:

> It was with joyful feelings that we emerged upon the upper deck and in turn jumped to the wharf and walked rapidly into the city. We soon crossed Broadway and hastened to go down into a cellar saloon and eating place. We called for cocktails and had a substantial meal. We were in rags and looked like tramps. Fourteen dollars in greenbacks was our aggregate wealth. We went to a cheap lodging house and got a room under assumed names. There we gazed at each other and rejoiced at being free men again. Allen had been a prisoner for fifteen months and DePriest and I ten months. It was then Sunday, March 13, 1865.[119]

Jastremski wrote his brother that his plan was to return south and rejoin the army. He declared that his intention was to "fight for the flag of the Southern cause," and that his duty compelled him to continue to fight the enemies of his country. He and his fellow Louisianan, Lieutenant Cicero M. Allen, made their way to Baltimore then to Point of Rocks on the Potomac River border of Virginia and Maryland.[120] Ironically, this was near the spot where Jastremski had crossed with the Army of Northern Virginia earlier in the war. It was early April 1865, and Robert E. Lee had his battered Confederate army in retreat southwest of Richmond and on the verge of surrender. Since he felt that it would have been impossible to cross Union lines to rejoin his old unit, Jastremski made his way west by rail to Louisville, Kentucky, and then down the Ohio and Mississippi rivers to Louisiana. He returned home to a "ravaged land which only led to further despondency and gloom," where nothing "had been spared." The captain still reported for duty to General Richard Taylor, who granted him an immediate furlough.[121] The indomitable captain very likely was the last man from his 10th regiment to give up the fight.[122] In Jastremski's words, there was "nothing left for him in Abbeville." He had no means and no opportunity to even work for a meal. He was "too poor to buy it, too proud to beg for it, and too honest to steal it."[123] From Abbeville he made his way the 110 miles to his brother's home in Baton Rouge where his family greeted him warmly "with tears and open arms. To their horror, he was torn from his family by a company of the 93rd U.S. Colored troops and taken to Franklin, Louisiana." For one last time he was a prisoner of war, but this time the hostilities were over and he at least had seen his family.[124] The circumstances only served to strengthen his resolve and embitter him toward the Union forces occupying his home state. He eventually reunited with his brother's family and settled in Baton Rouge after receiving official parole and the end to his service in the Confederate army.[125]

Post-War Louisiana

As a wounded veteran and participant in numerous great battles, Jastremski easily found a welcoming community in Baton Rouge. He worked at his brother's drug store, attended St. Joseph's Catholic Church, and met Rose Larguier, the daughter of a local merchant there. They married 1 July 1867, shortly before his twenty-third birthday. Louisiana was under Federal military occupation, and that same year the U.S. Federal government rescinded the general amnesty that had been granted at the end of the war. Reconstruction had begun in the former Confederate states and it initially prohibited former Confederates from political activity.[126]

Leon Jastremski and his brother John both became involved in Louisiana politics as soon as restrictions eased. They secured voting rights and became actively involved with other white citizens in resisting the controls of Republicans that had been pro-Union and blacks who were seeking public office. In November 1870, under the authority of then Mayor James E. Elam, he led a company of armed volunteer firemen to ensure order during voting and "quell[ed] a riot at a polling place" where there had been disturbances between groups of blacks and white voters. This action gained Jastremski popularity among ex-Confederates, Democrats and Louisiana citizens who were working for "home rule and white control of politics." In 1876, Leon Jastremski, with the support of former members of the Knights of the White Camelia, won election as mayor of Baton Rouge and served until 1882.[127]

In the meantime, Jastremski had organized a company of Zouaves for the state militia. He put them to use in 1876 when a report of twenty-eight armed and "Belligerent Negroes" were attempting to cross into Baton Rouge by ferry. A group of alarmed citizens requested help and Jastremski and the Zouaves moved to disarm them:

> [Jastremski] rode up to them and made the demand. After a parley of some twenty or thirty minutes, some twenty of them consented, while some seven or eight

others walked back ... After the arms were delivered over, they were allowed to proceed on their way, receipts being given them for their arms, which are to be returned them whenever the citizens deem it expedient to do so.[128]

During the presidential and gubernatorial elections in November of that year, Jastremski banned liquor sales during voting and deployed extra police at voting sites. He also patrolled the polls to ensure that there was no intimidation to Democrat voters and afforded the same considerations to blacks and Republicans. He was pleased that early returns had his old comrade-in-arms, General Francis Nicholls, in the lead for governor and he won the majority by a margin of 6,000 votes. However, "Republican-controlled election boards" in parishes throughout the state altered the returns. This prompted a battle between the Southern Democrat and Reconstruction Republican factions that ended with newly elected President Rutherford B. Hayes recognizing Nicholls as governor. The President then ordered the pullout of the Federal military presence in the state, thereby giving Jastremski and his fellow former Confederates the satisfaction of seeing progress in their post-war efforts to regain power. The invaders had finally departed the sacred soil of Louisiana.[129]

As a prominent citizen and political force in Louisiana, Jastremski relocated the state capital back to Baton Rouge from New Orleans. Under Union occupation, Benjamin Butler had moved the government seat to New Orleans in 1862 after burning the old capitol building. Jastremski had the structure completely restored, refurbished and put to use. He also established a tri-weekly newspaper, the *Louisiana Capitolian,* in 1879 and the weekly *Louisiana Review,* later to merge with the *Advocate,* and served as the state's printer. One of his adopted causes was the importance of formal education for professional journalists. In addition to serving as mayor, Jastremski also was "one of the founders of the National Press Association and served for ten years as president of the Louisiana Press Association."[130]

Having virtually regained complete control of the state, ex-Confederates exerted their influence in every facet of government. Jastremski and some of his former army comrades were part of the electoral process, and he represented East Baton Rouge Parish on the Democratic State Central Committee in 1879.[131] Governor Louis A. Wiltz, the ex-Confederate soldier who succeeded Governor Nicholls, appointed Jastremski Brigadier General of the Louisiana National Guard. Thereafter, fellow citizens referred to him as "General" throughout the remainder of his career. He supported Grover Cleveland's successful bid for the U.S. presidency, and subsequently received an appointment as American Consul to Callao, Peru, in 1893. In his acceptance speech, Jastremski took an oath to defend the United States Constitution, thirty-two years after he swore his oath to the Confederacy.[132]

Leon Jastremski became active in veterans' affairs and was one of the founders of the Louisiana United Confederate Veterans. He represented the Army of Northern Virginia, New Orleans camp, at the First Annual meeting of the United Confederate Veterans held in Chattanooga, Tennessee, 3 July 1890.[133] He later was elected Major General of the Louisiana Division in 1901.[134] Jastremski even suggested that he was one of the founders of the United Confederate Veterans and that he and several other veterans had conceived the idea in 1888. He stated that he had originated the name of the organization and declared that "there is glory enough for everybody … to make the organization the superb one it has become."[135]

Jastremski ran for governor of Louisiana as a reformer in 1903, after having announced his candidacy at a Confederate veteran meeting in New Orleans. He fell short of winning the Democratic nomination to Newton C. Blanchard, who went on to win the governorship. He later challenged for the office again, announcing in June 1907. In late November 1908, Jastremski "was stricken with apoplexy" while campaigning and died a week later on the 29th. The General, as people popularly referred to him, was buried in the Old Catholic Cemetery in Baton Rouge.[136]

When Jastremski entered the army as a seventeen-year-old private he had the youthful exuberance and enthusiasm to fight and defend his homeland. His imprisonment had served to instill an even more rebellious spirit in him. The act of taking up arms to fight the North was a dutiful obeisance. His final military arrest by the 93rd US Colored Troops after the war had ended, and having been under guard by black Union troops during his imprisonment, undoubtedly influenced his perceptions of Reconstruction and the political involvement of freed blacks in Louisiana. His post-war ambitions and achievements proved to be more powerful weapons in serving the people of Louisiana and furthering his causes than carrying a musket and captaining a company of comrades in the Confederate army.

CHAPTER 7

REWEAVING AN UNEASY FABRIC

Near the end of the Civil War, Frenchman Ernest Duvergier de Hauranne reflected on earlier predictions that the conflict would be the ruination of America itself and destroy the fledgling democracy's "ideals of freedom". After the war, he first thought, it would be necessary for an authoritarian regime to take control of the country, that is, a "strong hand of absolute power" that was always "the natural and usual heir of revolutions." His new assessment, though, was that the American struggles served to make the nation stronger. The armies of both sides disbanded in an orderly fashion and the democratic institutions evinced their sturdiness, a "solidity and adaptability" in restoring the country. Such a peaceful resolution may not always have been possible with the "great military and monarchical nations of the Old World."[1]

One can attribute the same sturdiness to the characters studied in this book. These men (except for Żychliński) whether Northern or Southern, became part of the fabric of the two nations and re-wove their lives into the unified country after the war. In returning to society, they became productive citizens and retained the ideals that carried them through the war.

Ludwik Żychliński did not have a post-war life in the restored United States, having returned to Poland in 1863, but his observations of Europeans and Americans from his memoirs are straightforward, unbiased opinions, such as his admiration for the Southerners' sincere devotion to their cause. Other times his writings exhibit remarkable vision, as in his interpretation of the German "*Drang nach Osten* (drive to the east)."

That lust for more land in the east would resurface in the first half of the twentieth century at Slavic expense.[2] Adam Gurowski died a year after the war's end on 4 May 1866. He at least had lived to see the Union victorious and most of his wartime views vindicated. He also managed to continue his acerbic criticism of politicians with whom he disagreed, nearly to his final days. Accordingly, he felt, Lincoln's successor, President Andrew Johnson, was trying to undermine Congressional authority and becoming more of an absolutist. He compared Johnson to the Count's former colleague, Napoleon III of France—once a man of the people, later an imperialist. Adding to the threat, unreformed "secessionists" had filtered into Washington and were in league with Johnson's underlings in working against the Radical Republicans.[3]

In resolutely adhering to his principles, Gurowski was similar to fellow Unionists Włodzimierz Krzyżanowski, Joseph Kargé, and Ludwik Żychliński. The difference was that these three men chose to work within the system toward their goals. Additionally, they remained sworn enemies of Czarist Russia. Krzyżanowski and Kargé faced disappointments in the field, difficulty with deserved promotions, and dissatisfaction and even disobedience from subordinates, but still maintained their dedication to the army and loyalty to the country. They also maintained a devoted coterie of friends and supporters. Such perseverance was beneficial in their post-war lives, Kargé as a professor at Princeton and Krzyżanowski in civil service.

Some of their war-related experiences were harbingers of an America to come. Krzyżanowski encountered Georgians during post-war Reconstruction who fancied themselves descendants of aristocrats, while Northerners were the outcasts of European society. These reactionary Southerners mirrored the nativist views he had seen in the Northern army. To a greater extent, post-war extremist groups such as the Ku Klux Klan and Knights of the White Camelia were the precursors of the movements in the early twentieth century that were anti-immigrant, anti-Catholic and pro-temperance. Krzyżanowski was witness to American nativist attitudes that would intensify as immigration greatly increased toward the turn of the century. Such thinking moved north, took root and found its hotbed in the Midwestern states such as Indiana,

Ohio, Illinois and Michigan whose troops had been at the fore of the war effort against the South during the Civil War.

As different in social status, education and background as Kiołbassa was from the other Polish officers who fought for the Confederacy—or the Union for that matter—he had a similar trait in his idealism. The statement Krzyżanowski issued in 1898 against the proposed restrictive immigration laws reflected this. Indeed, it was an echo of a message Gaspard Tochman had sent more than half a century before.[4] Poles were believers in the principles of freedom and Poland was a symbol of the defense of civilization. Sulakowski would have shared this idea, and his scheme to recruit Polish freedom fighters for the Confederate army affirmed it.

There is a marked difference between how these individuals dealt with the issues of slavery and race that were so prevalent and divisive in nineteenth-century America. Tochman exhibited more racial bias than the others. He believed that blacks were inferior and theorized about it in his writings. Ignatius Szymański did not come forth with formal arguments on the matter, but owned the slaves who worked his *Sebastopol* plantation in Louisiana. Szymański (and numerous other Southerners) contradicted the validity of the system when he returned to a successful life as a businessman in an economy that no longer was propped up by slave labor. On the other hand, Kiołbassa came to the Confederate army from a farming community in Texas whose agrarian economy *was not* based on slavery and, later as a Union officer, commanded black soldiers in the U.S. Colored Troops. He would have had a much different attitude towards slavery and blacks in general. He and Jastremski were closer in age than the other officers, but Jastremski came from an area where there were a good number of slaves as well as free people of color. He remained loyal to the Confederacy, and after the war worked to excise his state from the grips of Reconstruction and wrest political control from the Republicans for his cadre of ex-Confederates.

In order to gain a comprehensive understanding of the American Civil War, it is necessary to examine the link between the revolutions of Europe, the concept of building nations from monarchical societies, and the upheaval that took place in America 1861–65. The inevitable realization is that the war was more than a conflict between Americans, as demonstrated by the Poles in this study, whether Union or Confederate. Americans could compare Poles and others fighting in the European insurrections of the nineteenth century to the leaders of the American Revolution. They easily would have recognized the connection to their American "unique revolutionary past."[5] This group of Poles established that connection and continued the legacy begun by their predecessors.

APPENDICES

Appendix A

Peter Kiołbassa Muster Roll card 24th Texas Cavalry

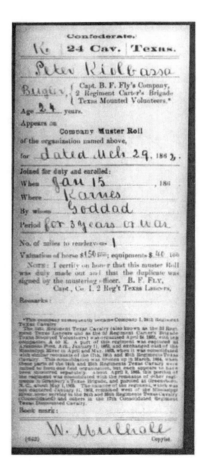

Appendix B

Peter Kiołbassa Regimental card, Captain, 6th Cavalry, U.S. Colored Troops

Appendix C

Joseph Kargé Immigration/Naturalization card stating his former nationality as "German"

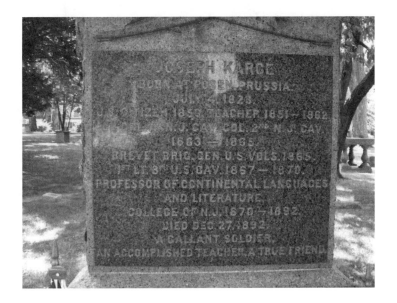

Appendix D

Joseph Kargé's gravestone denoting his birthplace as "Prussia"

Appendix E

Leon Jastremski Service Record with 10th Louisiana Regiment, 22 July 1861 to 28 February 1865

Appendix F

Leon Jastremski record of capture in Virginia 10 May 1864 and taken as prisoner of war to Fort Delaware

Appendix G

Texas Pole, Alexander Dziuk's death certificate showing his place of birth as "Silesia, Europe"

NOTES

Introduction and Chapter 1: Bearing the Standard in America

1   André M. Fleche, *The Revolution of 1861: The American Civil War in the Age of Nationalist Conflict* (Chapel Hill: The University of North Carolina Press, 2012), p. 8.

2   Florian Stasik, *Polish Political Émigrés in the United States of America 1831–1864* (Boulder: East European Monographs, New York: Dist. Columbia University Press, 2002), pp. vii–viii. Arthur L. Waldo, *The True Heroes of Jamestown* (Miami: American Institute of Polish Culture, 1977), pp. 82–88. Jan Drohojowski, *Poles in United States* (Warsaw: Krajowa Agencja Wydawnicza, 1976), pp. 9–10.

3   André M. Fleche, "The Revolution of 1861: The Legacy of the European Revolutions of 1848 and the American Civil War" (Doctoral Dissertation, University of Virginia, 2006), p. 11.

4   Alphonse de Lamartine, *Histoire de la Révolution de 1848,* Vol. 1 (Brussels: Kiessling et Comp., 1849), p. 162.

5   Fleche, *The Revolution of 1861*, pp. 2–3.

6   Although Delaware was a slave state and the District of Columbia had legal slavery, they were not considered actual threats to join the Confederacy. Slavery was a relatively insignificant element in Delaware's economic and social structure and Washington was the capital city and seat of government in the District.

7   Shelby Foote, *The Civil War: A Narrative, Fort Sumter to Perryville* (New York: Random House, 1986), pp. 51–53.

8   Sigmund H. Uminski, "Poles and the Confederacy," *Polish American Studies,* Vol. 22, No. 2 (Jul.–Dec., 1965), pp. 99–106.

9   David S. Heidler and Jeanne T. Heidler, eds., *Encyclopedia of the American Civil War: A Political, Social and Military History* (Santa Barbara, Denver, Oxford: ABC–CLIO, 2000), Vol. IV, p. 1036.

10   Ibid., pp. 822–823.

11   Anne J. Bailey, *Invisible Southerners: Ethnicity in the Civil War* (Athens: The University of Georgia Press, 2006), pp. 4, 12.

12 Cal McCarthy, *Green, Blue and Grey: The Irish in the American Civil War* (Cork: The Collins Press, 2009), pp. 10–12.

13 Adam Zamoyski, *The Polish Way* (New York: Hippocrene Books, 1987), p. 96.

14 Zamoyski, *The Polish Way*, p. 95.

15 Pawel Jasienica, *A Tale of Agony: The Commonwealth of Both Nations III* (Miami: The Institute of Polish Culture, 1992), p. 210.

16 Zamoyski, *The Polish Way*, p. 264.

Chapter 2: On the Approach to War

1 Gordon Wood, *The Idea of America: Reflections on the Birth of the United States* (New York: The Penguin Press, 2011), p. 3.

2 Ladislaus J. Siekaniec, "Poles in the U.S.: Jamestown to Appomatox," *Polish American Studies*, Vol. 17, No. 1/2 (January–June 1960), p. 8. Jerzy J. Lerski, *A Polish Chapter in Jacksonian America: The United States and the Polish Exiles of 1831* (Madison: University of Wisconsin Press, 1958), p. 97.

3 Adam Zamoyski, *The Polish Way* (New York: Hippocrene Books, 1987), p. 239.

4 Jerzy Jedlicki, *A Suburb of Europe: Nineteenth–century Polish Approaches to Western Civilization* (Budapest: CEU Press, 1988), p. 6.

5 M.B. Biskupski, *The History of Poland* (Westport: Greenwood Press, 2000), p. 12. Latin translation is mine.

6 Jan Drohojowski, *Poles In United States* (Warsaw: Krajowa Agencja Wydawnicza, 1976), p. 24. Leszek Szymanski, *Casimir Pulaski: Hero of the American Revolution* (New York: Hippocrene Books, 1979), p. 13.

7 Bogdan Grzeloński, *Poles in the United States of America, 1776–1865* (Warsaw: Interpress Publishers, 1976), pp. 202–211.

8 W.S. Kuniczak, My *Name Is Million: An Illustrated History of Poles In America* (New York: Hippocrene Books, 2000), p. 22.

9 Wawrzyniec Goslicki, *The Accomplished Senator* (Miami: The American Institute of Polish Culture, 1992), p. 52. The original work was written in Latin. This is a line–for–line reproduction of an English version, "From the Edition Printed at Venice, in the year 1568" and reproduced and printed in London in 1733.

10 Goslicki, *The Accomplished Senator*, p. 23.

11 Joseph A. Wytrwal, *America's Polish Heritage* (Detroit: Endurance Press, 1961), p. 40.

12 Zamoyski, *The Polish Way*, p. 96.

13 Ibid., p. 95.

14 Oscar Halecki, *A History of Poland* (New York: Roy Publishers, 1942), p. 193.

15 Norman Davies, *Heart of Europe: A Short History of Poland* (Oxford: Oxford University Press, 1986), p. 163.

16 Zamoyski, *The Polish Way*, p. 249.

17 John Radzilowski, *A Traveller's History of Poland* (Northampton, MA: Interlink Books, 2007), p. 133.

18 Kuniczak, *My Name Is Million,* p. 21.

19 Gary B. Nash and Graham Russell Gao Hodges, *Friends of Liberty: Thomas Jefferson, Tadeusz Kościuszko, and Agrippa Hall* (New York: Basic Books, 2008), p. 148.

20   Nash and Hodges, *Friends of Liberty*, p. 3.
21   Kuniczak, *My Name Is Million*, p. 66.
22   Nash and Hodges, *Friends of Liberty*, p. 34.
23   Neal Ascherson, *Black Sea* (New York: Hill and Wang, 1995), p. 235.
24   Robert Middlekauff, *The Glorious Cause: The American Revolution 1763–1789* (New York: Oxford University Press, 1982), p. 550.
25   Gwenda Morgan, *The Debate on the American Revolution* (Manchester: Manchester University Press, 2007), p. 19. Joseph Galloway, *Historical and Political Reflections on the Rise and Progress of the American Rebellion* (London: 1780), p. 14.
26   Kuniczak, *My Name Is Million*, p. 42.
27   Jared Sparks, *Correspondence of the American Revolution; Being Letters of Eminent Men to George Washington, from the Time of His Taking Command of the Army to the End of His Presidency*, Volume II (Boston: Little, Brown, 1853), p. 87. Letter from Count Pulaski to George Washington from Yorktown, Virginia, 19 March 1778.
28   Grzeloński, *Poles in the United States of America*, p. 75.
29   Ludwik Żychliński, *The Memoirs of Ludwik Żychliński: Reminiscences of the American Civil War, Siberia and Poland* ed. by James S. Pula (East European Monographs, Dist. Columbia University Press, 1993), pp. vii–viii.
30   Żychliński, *The Memoirs*, p. 13.
31   Żychliński, *The Memoirs*, p. 4.
32   Ibid., p. 19.
33   Drohojowski, *Poles in United States*, p. 84.
34   Żychliński, *The Memoirs*, p. 5.
35   Neal Ascherson, *The Struggles for Poland* (New York: Random House, 1987), p. 29.
36   Randall C. Jimerson, *The Private Civil War: Popular Thought During the Sectional Conflict* (Baton Rouge: Louisiana State University Press, 1988), p. 19.
37   Drohojowski, *Poles in United States*, pp. 85–86.
38   Sigmund H. Uminski, "Two Polish Confederates," *Polish American Studies*, Vol. 23, No. 2 (Jul.–Dec., 1966), p. 66. The Russian government already had confiscated Tochman's property in Poland in 1835.
39   Uminski, "Two Polish Confederates," p. 67.
40   Uminski, "Two Polish Confederates," p. 71.
41   Grzeloński, *Poles in the United States of America*, p. 227.
42   Florian Stasik, *Polish Political Émigrés in the United States of America 1831–1864* (Boulder: East European Monographs, New York: Dist. Columbia University Press, 2002), p. viii.
43   Piotr S. Wandycz, *The United States and Poland* (Cambridge: Harvard University Press, 1980), p. 81. Adam Gurowski had a son who was serving in the Russian Imperial Navy at that time.
44   Wandycz, *The United States and Poland*, p. 83.
45   Major G. Tochman, "Lecture on the social, political and literary condition of Poland, and her future prospects," *Lecture delivered before the members of the state legislatures of New York, Massachusetts, New Hampshire, Vermont, Connecticut, Virginia,*

Ohio, Indiana and Kentucky and before the members of the New Jersey state convention (Baltimore: J.D. Toy, 1844), pp. 17–18.

46   Joseph A. Wytrwal, *America's Polish Heritage*, pp. 57, 71. Grzeloński, *Poles in the United States of America*, p. 231.

47   LeRoy H. Fischer, "Lincoln's Gadfly—Adam Gurowski," *The Mississippi Valley Historical Review*, Vol. 36, No. 3 (Dec. 1949), pp. 415–434. LeRoy H. Fischer, *Lincoln's Gadfly* (Norman: University of Oklahoma Press, 1964), pp. 2, 259.

48   M.B. Biskupski, *The History of Poland*, p. 72.

49   Fischer, "Lincoln's Gadfly—Adam Gurowski," p. 418.

50   LeRoy H. Fischer, *Lincoln's Gadfly*, pp. 8–9.

51   Adam Gurowski, Diary 1863–'64–'65 (Washington, DC: W.H. & O.H. Morrison, 1866), p. 172. Diary entry from 13 April 1864. This *Diary* of 1863 is the third published and is cited as *Diary III* in subsequent footnotes.

52   Gurowski, *Diary* III, p. 173.

53   Fischer, *Lincoln's Gadfly*, p. 15.

54   Adam Gurowski, *Diary from March 4, 1861, to November 12, 1862* (Boston: Lee and Shepard, 1862), pp. 272–273. Entry from 13 September 1862. Gurowski was to publish two more diaries that were equally critical of the Lincoln administration and Union war effort. Subsequently cited as *Diary* I. Here he also differs markedly from Ludwik Żychliński's depiction of the openness of the American military and the ease of communication between officers and men.

55   Fischer, *Lincoln's Gadfly*, pp. 17–23. Gurowski, *Diary I*, p. 36.

56   Fischer, *Lincoln's Gadfly*, pp. 27–30.

57   Adam G. De Gurowski, *America and Europe* (New York: D. Appleton and Company, 1857), p. 76.

58   Gurowski, *America and Europe*, p. 77. Gordon S. Wood, *The Radicalism of the American Revolution* (New York: Vintage Books, 1993), p. 277.

59   Adam Gurowski, *Slavery in History* (New York: A.B. Burdick, 1860), pp. viii–ix.

60   Fischer, *Lincoln's Gadfly*, p. 227.

61   Fischer, *Lincoln's Gadfly*, p. 228. Gurowski, *Slavery in History*, p. 259.

62   Gurowski, *Slavery in History*, pp. 259–260.

63   Gordon S. Wood, *The Idea of America,* p. 68. Fischer, *Lincoln's Gadfly*, p. 27.

64   Craig Calhoun, "'New Social Movements' of the Early Nineteenth Century," *Social Science History*, Vol. 17, No. 3 (Autumn 1993, Duke University Press), p. 395.

65   Zamoyski, *The Polish Way*, pp. 276–277.

66   William A. Packard, "Professor Joseph Kargé, Ph.D." *Princeton College Bulletin*, Vol. V, No. 2, April 1893, p. 27.

67   Packard, "Professor Joseph Kargé," p. 20.

68   Francis C. Kajencki, *Star on Many a Battlefield: Brevet Brigadier General Joseph Kargé in the American Civil War* (Rutherford: Fairleigh Dickinson University Press, 1980), p. 22.

69   *Princeton Press*, December 31, 1892.

70   Kajencki, *Star on Many a Battlefield*, p. 23.

71   Kajencki, *Star on Many a Battlefield*, p. 26.

72 "Obituary," *New York Times*, 28 December 1892.
73 James S. Pula, *For Liberty and Justice: A Biography Of Brigadier General Włodzimierz B. Krzyżanowski, 1824–1887* (Utica, NY: Ethnic Heritage Studies Center, 2008), p. 2.
74 M.J. Duszak, "Colonel Kriz of Washington," *Polish American Studies*, Vol. 23, No. 2 (Jul.–Dec., 1966), p. 108. Eugene J. Kisluk, *Brothers from the North: The Polish Democratic Society and the European Revolutions of 1848–1849* (Boulder, Colorado: East European Monographs, 2005), p. 49. Ludwik Mieroslawski was a Polish nationalist and military leader who lead an insurrection in 1846, was sentenced to death but pardoned in the amnesties given during the Springtime of Nations in 1848. In 1860 he was chief of staff for the revolutionary forces in Sicily. Ludwik Żychliński was also under his command.
75 Pula, *For Liberty and Justice*, p. 203.
76 Stasik, *Polish Political Émigrés*, p. 54.
77 Harro Harring, *Poland Under the Dominion of Russia* (Boston, 1834), p. v. From Szymański's Introduction, "To the American Reader," in Harring's work.
78 Harring, *Poland Under the Dominion of Russia*, p. vi.
79 Tochman, "Lecture on Poland," p. 7.
80 Gurowski, *Diary* I, p. 32. From an entry of April 1862. "Count Gurowski to take a Negro Regiment," *Cleveland Morning Leader*, 17 July 1862. The small news item refers to "Count Gurowski, the celebrated *Russian* nobleman." Italics mine.
81 Gurowski, *Diary* I, p. xi.
82 Bruce Catton, *The Coming Fury* (Garden City, NY: Doubleday, 1961), p. 416.
83 Catton, *The Coming Fury*, p. 437. Gurowski, *Diary* I, p. 56.
84 David S. Heidler and Jeanne T. Heidler, eds. *Encyclopedia of the American Civil War: A Political, Social and Military History* (Santa Barbara, Denver, Oxford: ABC–CLIO, 2000), Vol. III, pp. 902–3
85 Grzeloński, *Poles In The United States of America*, p. 228.
86 Uminski, "*Two Polish Confederates*," p. 72.
87 Jefferson Davis, "Message of President Davis," *The North American Review*, Vol. 93, No. 192 (Jul. 1861), p. 217.
88 Seven states initially comprised the Confederacy. Mississippi, Florida, Alabama, Georgia and Louisiana joined South Carolina and seceded in January 1861. Texas followed 2 March 1861.
89 "Local Intelligence. Military Items," *Daily Crescent*, New Orleans, Louisiana, 6 May 1861.
90 *Daily Picayune*, New Orleans, Louisiana, 31 May 1861. The article actually cites *The Montgomery* (Alabama) *Advertiser* of 28 May 1861 in a report on Tochman's actions.
91 Edward C. Rozanski, "Civil War Poles Of Illinois," *Polish American Studies*, Vol. 23, No. 2 (1966), p. 112.
92 Rozanski, "Civil War Poles Of Illinois," p. 112.
93 *Company Muster Rolls, 24th Texas Confederate Cavalry*, National Archives, Washington, DC. Remarks written in the original Confederate Army Company

Muster rolls show that Kiołbassa joined for duty and enrolled 15 January 1862, Period:"for 3 years or war." They also confirm the duty assignment and capture in Arkansas.

94 *Regimental Description Book, 6th Regiment U.S. Colored Cavalry,* National Archives, Washington, DC. Kiołbassa's U.S. Army record lists him as a commissioned officer in the U.S. Colored Cavalry.

95 T. Lindsay Baker, *The First Polish Americans: Silesian Settlements in Texas* (College Station: Texas A&M University Press, 1979), p. 64.

96 Grzeloński, *Poles in the United States of America*, p. 152.

97 Baker, *The First Polish Americans*, p. 48.

98 Wacław Kruszka, *A History of the Poles in America to 1908: Part III; The Poles in the Eastern and Southern United States* (Washington, D.C.: The Catholic University of America Press, 1998), p. 284.

99 Grzeloński, *Poles in the United States of America*, p. 152.

100 Thomas Lindsay Baker, "The Early History of Panna Maria, Texas" (Master's thesis, Texas Tech University, 1972), p. 45.

101 Rev. Adolf Sixtus Bakanowski, *Moje Wspomnienia 1840–1863–1914* (Lwów: Nakładem XX Zmartwychwstanców, 1913), p. 296.

102 Baker, *The First Polish Americans*, p. 79.

103 Grzeloński, *Poles in the United States of America*, pp. 153–154.

104 Żychliński, *The Memoirs*, p. 52.

105 Stasik, *Polish Political Emigrés*, p. 128. Gordon S. Wood, *The Radicalism of the American Revolution*, p. 243.

106 Gurowski, *Diary I*, pp. 26–28.

107 W.H. Zawadzki, Review of *The Memoirs of Ludwik Żychliński*, ed. by James S. Pula, *The Slavonic and East European Review*, Vol. 73, No. 3 (Jul., 1995), p. 551.

108 Żychliński, *The Memoirs*, p. 65.

109 "By Telegraph from Fortress Monroe: Visit of the President," *National Republican,* Washington, DC, 11 July 1862.

110 Żychliński, *The Memoirs*, p. 66.

111 David S. and Jeanne T. Heidler, David J. Coles, eds., *Encyclopedia of the American Civil War: A Political, Social and Military History* (New York: W.W. Norton & Company, 2000), p. 635.

112 Warren W. Hassler, Jr., *Commanders of the Army of the Potomac* (Baton Rouge: Louisiana State University Press, 1962), p. 50. Gurowski, *Diary III*, p. 333. Entry of 7 September 1864. In this same passage, Gurowski mused that "the Southern animalized whites" would benefit from "the victory won by the North" since it would "be elevating them to a superior sphere transforming them from brutes into civilized beings."

113 Catton, *The Coming Fury*, p. 437.

114 LeRoy H. Fischer, *Lincoln's Gadfly*, pp. 77–82. The Peace Convention met in Washington in February 1861 in an attempt to prevent escalation to war. Southern Secessionists and Radical Republicans were opposed to its proposals.

115 "Italy—Federation," *New York Daily Tribune*, 17 November 1859.

116 Adam G. De Gurowski, *America and Europe*, pp. 61–62.

117 Gurowski, *America and Europe*, p. 170.

118 Harring, *Poland Under the Dominion of Russia*, p. xlix. From the Introduction.

Chapter 3: Allies to Adversaries

1 Sigmund H. Uminski, "Two Polish Confederates," *Polish American Studies*, Vol. 23, No. 2 (July–December, 1966), p. 65. Marian Tyrowicz, "Kasper Tochman, biographical article" translated by Peter Obst (Chicago: Polish Museum in America, 1955), pp. 1–3.

2 Bruce Allardice, *More Generals in Gray: A Companion Volume to Generals in Gray* (Baton Rouge: Louisiana State University Press, 1995), p. 222.

3 Sigmund H. Uminski, "Two Polish Confederates," p. 71.

4 Major G. Tochman, "Lecture on the social, political and literary condition of Poland, and her future prospects," *Lecture delivered before the members of the state legislatures of New York, Massachusetts, New Hampshire, Vermont, Connecticut, Virginia, Ohio, Indiana and Kentucky and before the members of the New Jersey state convention* (Baltimore: J.D. Toy, 1844), p. 9.

5 Tochman, "Lecture," p. 15.

6 "General G. Tochman," *Richmond Dispatch*, 27 September 1861.

7 *Daily Picayune*, New Orleans, 7 June 1845.

8 Bogdan Grzeloński, *Poles in the United States of America, 1776–1865* (Warsaw: Interpress Publishers, 1976), p. 220.

9 Marian Tyrowicz, "Kasper Tochman, biographical article." Tochman, from a *Letter* to Dr. Henryk Kalussowski and Count Wladyslaw Plater, 20 August 1880. "Darby" was William Darby, staff writer for the newspaper.

10 Tyrowicz, "Kasper Tochman, biographical article," p. 3.

11 Major G. Tochman, *Petition of Major G. Tochman, Attorney and Counsel of the Next of Kin and Heirs at Law of Gen. Thadeus Kościuszko*, presented to the Senate and House of Representatives of the United States Congress, December 1847, p. 1.

12 Tochman, *Petition*, p. 5.

13 Uminski, "Two Polish Confederates," pp. 67–68.

14 Tochman, *Letter*, to Joseph H. Bradley, November 1847 from *An Exposé of the Conduct of Joseph H. Bradley of Washington, DC, Counsellor "Employed by the Imperial Russian Legation," towards Major G. Tochman, of New York, Counsellor Retained by the Next of Kin and Heirs at Law of Gen. Thadeus Kosciusko, December, 1847* (Published 1848 by s.n. in Washington, D.C .), Library of Congress, p. 21.

15 Jas. W. Schaumburg, *Letter*, to Joseph H. Bradley, 5 December 1847 from *An Exposé*, p. 23.

16 Gaspard Tochman, ed., "Charter. List of Officers, and Proceedings at the special meeting, 27 June 1846" *Polish Slavonian Literary Association* (New York: 1846), p. 7. George J. Lerski, "Polish Exiles in Mid–Nineteenth Century America," *Polish American Studies*, Vol. 31, No. 2 (Autumn, 1974), p. 34.

17   Jan Drohojowski, *Poles in United States* (Warsaw: Krajowa Agencja Wydawnicza, 1976), p. 84.

18   Grzeloński, *Poles in the United States of America,* pp. 220–223.

19   Joseph A. Wytrwal, *Behold! The Polish–Americans* (Detroit: Endurance Press, 1977), p. 46.

20   André M. Fleche, *The Revolution of 1861: The American Civil War in the Age of Nationalist Conflict* (Chapel Hill: The University of North Carolina Press, 2012), p. 14.

21   Major Gaspard Tochman, *Poland, Russia and the Policy of the Latter Towards the United States* (Baltimore: John D. Toy, Printer, 1844), p. 20.

22   Tochman, *Poland, Russia,* p. 20.

23   "Major Tochman's Lecture. Polish Revolution of 1830," *The Sun,* Baltimore, Maryland, 31 January 1843 and 19 June 1843.

24   "Maj. Tochman—Poland," *Adams Sentinel,* Gettysburg (Adams County), Pennsylvania, 19 June 1843. The brief excerpt was from a *Richmond Whig* article that opposed the admission of Texas to the Union. It is an interesting coincidence that it dealt with the slavery issue and Texas relative to the Union, and its position on the page immediately followed Tochman's speech and the Gettysburg town's resolutions supporting Poland's independence.

25   Grzeloński, *Poles in the United States of America,* p. 227.

26   "Douglas Convention Staunton, Afternoon Session Second Day," *Staunton Spectator,* Staunton, Virginia, 21 August 1860.

27   Grzeloński, *Poles In The United States Of America,* p. 229.

28   Mieczyslaw Haiman, *Historja Udziału Polaków w Amerykańskiej Wojnie Domowej* (Chicago: Drukiem Dziennika Zjednoczenia, 1928), p. 124. *"Polonia,"* the Latin term for Poland, generally refers collectively to the Polish community/communities living outside of Poland.

29   G. Tochman, "Dr. Tochman's Letter to the Polish Democratic Societies in France and England, Nashville, Tenn. Dec. 26, 1861" *The Southern Literary Messenger,* Vol. 36 (Richmond: MacFarlane & Fergusson, Proprietors, 1862), p. 322.

30   Tochman, "Dr. Tochman's Letter," p. 322. Tochman stated that there were "three votes for each five 'persons bound to service' or Africans." However, he did not clarify that a slave could not individually cast a vote, nor could five slaves band together and submit three ballots.

31   G. Tochman, "Letter to the Polish Democratic Societies," p. 324. The Volume cited is listed as 34 in some sources and XXXVI in others. Italics mine.

32   G. Tochman, "Letter to the Polish Democratic Societies," and *"Letter* to his Excellency Jeff. Davis, President of the C.S.," *The Southern Literary Messenger,* Vol. 36 (Richmond: MacFarlane & Fergusson, Proprietors, 1862), pp. 325–326. Lynda Lasswell Crist and Mary Seaton Dix, eds. *The Papers of Jefferson Davis* (Baton Rouge: Louisiana State University Press, 1992), Vol. 7, p. 144.

33   Alan Lawrence Golden, "The Secession Crisis in Virginia: A Critical Study of Argument" (Ph.D. Dissertation, Ohio State University, 1990), p. 300.

34   Joseph T. Glatthaar, *Soldiering in the Army of Northern Virginia: A Statistical Portrait of the Troops Who Served under Robert E. Lee* (Chapel Hill: The University of North Carolina Press, 2011), p. 154.

35   *Daily Picayune,* New Orleans, 19 September 1861. *Official Records,* Series II, Vol. 2, p. 237. *National Republican,* Washington, DC, 9 September 1861, 25 September 1861.

36   "Gen. Tochman and the Polish Brigade," *Richmond Dispatch,* 12 September 1861.

37   Sigmund H. Uminski, "Poles and the Confederacy," *Polish American Studies,* Vol. 22, No. 2 (Jul.–Dec. 1965), p. 101. Ella Lonn, *Foreigners in the Confederacy* (Chapel Hill: The University of North Carolina Press, 1940), p. 147. Mary W. Schaller and Martin N. Schaller, eds., *Soldiering for Glory: The Civil War Letters of Colonel Frank Schaller, Twenty–Second Mississippi Infantry* (Columbia: The University of South Carolina Press, 2007), p. 1. Schaller's editors and descendants who published his letters, list him as of "French ancestry" and born in Saxony.

38   "General G. Tochman," *Richmond Dispatch,* 27 September 1861.

39   Davis, *The Papers of Jefferson Davis,* Vol. 7, p. 343.

40   "Gen. Tochman and the Polish Brigade," *Richmond Dispatch,* 12 September 1861.

41   "General G. Tochman," *Richmond Dispatch,* 27 September 1861.

42   *Richmond Dispatch,* 27 September 1861.

43   Fleche, *The Revolution of 1861,* p. 56.

44   *Daily Picayune,* New Orleans, 15 March 1863. The *Picayune* reported the situation as newsworthy since the brigade originated in New Orleans and gave attribution to the *Richmond Whig.*

45   *Case of General Tochman,* Exhibit (B.) Letter "General Tochman to Mr. Benjamin," 6 November 1863.

46   *Case of General Tochman,* Exhibit (A.) Letter "General Tochman's Letter to President Davis," 19 September 1863.

47   Davis, *The Papers of Jefferson Davis,* Vol. 9, p. 397.

48   "The Polish Question," *Staunton Spectator,* Staunton, Virginia, 21, 26 July 1863.

49   Lonn, *Foreigners in the Confederacy,* pp. 223–225.

50   *Daily Picayune,* New Orleans, 30 October 1866.

51   *Chicago Tribune,* 23 December 1880.

52   LeRoy H. Fischer, *Lincoln's Gadfly, Adam Gurowski* (Norman: University of Oklahoma Press, 1964), pp. 6–8.

53   Ward Hill Lamon, *Recollections of Abraham Lincoln, 1847–1865* (University of Nebraska Press, 1994), p. 274.

54   LeRoy H. Fischer, "Lincoln's Gadfly—Adam Gurowski," *The Mississippi Valley Historical Review,* Vol. 36, No. 3 (Dec. 1949), p. 415.

55   Fischer, "Lincoln's Gadfly," p. 416

56   Fischer, "Lincoln's Gadfly," p. 419.

57   Stephen E. Ambrose, "Lincoln and Halleck: A Study in Personal Relations," *Journal of the Illinois State Historical Society,* Vol. 52, No. 1, Lincoln Sesquicentennial (Spring 1959), pp. 223–224.

58   Bruce Catton, *The Coming Fury* (Garden City, NY: Doubleday, 1961), p. 437.

59   Fischer, *Lincoln's Gadfly,* pp. 84–86.

60   *Daily National Republican,* 13 December 1862. Advertisements for the sale of Gurowski's first diary began appearing in Washington in December. Heilprin's Bookstore at 244 Pennsylvania Avenue (near the Capitol building) sold it for $1.25.

61   Fischer, *Lincoln's Gadfly*, pp. 84–85. His dismissal was by a brief letter from the Assistant Secretary on 18 September 1862.

62   Adam Gurowski, *Diary from March 4, 1861, to November 12, 1862* (Boston: Lee and Shepard, 1862). Entry of May 1862. Cited as *Diary I* in subsequent footnotes.

63   Adam Gurowski, *Diary from November 18, 1862, to October 18, 1863* (New York: Carlton Publisher, 1864), p. 16. Entry of 22 November 1862. Cited as *Diary II* in subsequent footnotes.

64   Gurowski, *Diary II*, entry of 7 December 1862, p. 25.

65   Gurowski, *Diary II*, entry of 15 December 1862, p. 30.

66   George J. Lerski, "Polish Exiles in Mid–Nineteenth Century America," pp. 35–36.

67   Fischer, "Lincoln's Gadfly," p. 422.

68   Hans L. Trefousse, Review *Owen Lovejoy and Abraham Lincoln during the Civil War, Journal of the Abraham Lincoln Association*, Vol. 22, No. 1 (Winter 2001), p. 28.

69   Gurowski, *Diary II*, entry of 18 January 1863, p. 97.

70   *Evening Telegraph–Supplement*, Philadelphia, 17 November 1866.

71   "Obituary: Count Adam de Gurowski," *New York Times*, 6 May 1866. The "ruling powers" were the Czar and Imperial Russia.

72   Fischer, "Lincoln's Gadfly," p. 422.

73   David S. Heidler and Jeanne T. Heidler, eds. *Encyclopedia of the American Civil War: A Political, Social and Military History* (Santa Barbara, Denver, Oxford: ABC–CLIO, 2000) Vol. III, pp. 902–03. Fischer, *Lincoln's Gadfly*, passim.

74   Gurowski, *Diary II*, Author's preface to the diary.

75   Records of the U.S. Circuit Court for the Eastern District of Louisiana, New Orleans Division: Petitions, 1838–1861, National Archives, Washington, DC.

76   *New Orleans Crescent*, 20 March 1869. "Death of Colonel Szymanski," *Louisiana Democrat*, Alexandria, 26 August 1874. Harro Harring, *Poland Under the Dominion of Russia* (Boston, 1834), p. 188.

77   Florian Stasik, *Polish Political Émigrés in the United States of America 1831–1864* (Boulder: East European Monographs, New York: Dist. By Columbia University Press, 2002), p. 168.

78   *Daily Picayune*, New Orleans, 11 February 1859. *Interview*, Professor Ronald Chapman, History Department, Nunez Community College, Chalmette, Louisiana, 16 January 2014.

79   J.M Bundy, "The Last Chapter in the History of the War," in *Battles and Leaders of the Civil War*, Vol. 6, Peter Cozzens, ed. (Urbana: University of Illinois Press, 2004), p. 556. Uminski, "Poles and the Confederacy," p. 105. Lonn, *Foreigners in the Confederacy*, p. 147.

80   Edward A. Pollard, *The Lost Cause; A New Southern History of the War of the Confederates* (New York: E.B. Treat & Co., Publishers, 1866), p. 254. Arthur W. Bergeron, Jr., *Guide to Louisiana Confederate Units, 1861–1865* (Baton Rouge: Louisiana State University Press, 1989), p. 183. Lonn, *Foreigners in the Confederacy*, p. 147. Ezra J. Warner, *Generals in Gray: Lives of the Confederate Commanders* (Baton Rouge: Louisiana State University Press, 1959), p. 194.

81 John D. Winters, *The Civil War in Louisiana* (Baton Rouge: Louisiana State University Press, 1963), pp. 82–83. Case Miner, "Strategy and Tactics of Civil War Rams on the Mississippi River" (M.A. Thesis, University of Central Oklahoma, 2001), p. 31.

82 Michael D. Pierson, *The Mutiny at Fort Jackson* (Chapel Hill: The University of North Carolina Press, 2008), p.112. Winters, *The Civil War in Louisiana*, p. 95. Bergeron, *Guide*, p. 171. Powell A. Casey, *Encyclopedia of Forts, Posts, Named Camps and Other Military Installations in Louisiana, 1700–1981* (Baton Rouge: Claitor's Publishing Division, 1983), p 182.

83 John Dimitry, *Confederate Military History of Louisiana* (Pensacola, Florida: eBooks OnDisk.com, 2005), pp. 36–37.

84 Winters, *The Civil War in Louisiana*, pp. 77–79.

85 Dimitry, *Confederate Military History of Louisiana*, p. 39.

86 "The News from New–Orleans," *New York Times*, 1 May 1862.

87 Dimitry, *Confederate Military History of Louisiana*, p. 227.

88 *Official Records*, Series I, Vol. 6, p. 580.

89 Bergeron, *Guide*, p. 181.

90 Pierson, *The Mutiny at Fort Jackson*, p. 112.

91 "Report of the Commander of the Cayuga," *Evening Star*, Washington, DC, 9 May 1862. *New York Times*, 10 May 1862. *The *Star* and *Times* printed Bailey's report of his actions in the surface battle as well as the confrontation with the Chalmette Regiment with slight differences. The *Times* reported "canister at 4:00 p.m."

92 *Official Records*, Series I, Vol. 6, p. 580.

93 Winters, *The Civil War in Louisiana*, p. 95.

94 Pierson, *The Mutiny at Fort Jackson*, p. 112.

95 "Report of Capt. Bailey," *New York Times*, 11 May 1862. Italics are mine.

96 Glenn R. Conrad, ed., *A Dictionary of Louisiana Biography*, Vol. II (Lafayette: The Louisiana Historical Association, 1988), p. 777.

97 *Official Records*, Series II, Vol. 5, p. 935. From correspondence of 26 April 1863 concerning the detention of political prisoners.

98 *Official Records*, Series II, Vol. 6, p. 278.

99 *Official Records*, Series II, Vol. 6, pp. 320, 583.

100 J.T. Headley, *The Great Rebellion; A History of the Civil War in the United States*, Vol. II (Hartford: American Publishing Company, 1866), pp. 559–560. The Commissioners of Exchange had traded "acrimonious correspondence" with regard to adherence to the agreements of the cartel and, from the Union side, concerns about the treatment of captured U.S. Colored troops.

101 *Official Records*, Series II, Vol. 7, pp. 189–190. Letter from Ould to Szymański 2 June 1864.

102 *Official Records*, Series II, Vol. 7, p. 614. Letter from Ould to Szymański 18 August 1864.

103 *Official Records*, Series II, Vol. 7, pp. 922, 967. Letters from Butler to Ould of 4 October and 12 October 1864. One case to which Butler specifically referred was the use of captured U.S. Colored troops for labor.

104 *Official Records,* Series II, Vol. 7, p. 1079. Letter from Ould to Secretary of War Seddon.

105 *Daily Dispatch,* Richmond, 28 October 1864. From a reprinted letter from Robert E. Lee to Ulysses S. Grant, 19 October 1864.

106 *Daily Dispatch,* Richmond, 28 October 1864. Grant's reply to Lee's letter was written the following day, suggesting the importance both leaders attached to the matter.

107 *Official Records,* Series II, Vol. 7, p. 1059. Letter from D.G. Farragut to Colonel C.C. Dwight, 29 October 1864. Farragut was writing from Mobile Bay, Alabama, aboard the U.S. Flagship *Hartford* to Dwight in Union occupied New Orleans.

108 Headley, *The Great Rebellion,* Vol. 1, p. 91.

109 Bundy, "The Last Chapter in the History of the War," p. 553.

110 Ibid., p. 556.

111 *Shreveport Semi–Weekly News,* 6 May 1865.

112 Winters, *The Civil War in Louisiana,* p. 419. *Official Records,* Series I, Vol. 48, Part II, p. 223.

113 *Daily Picayune,* New Orleans, 29 April 1865. Bundy, "The Last Chapter in the History of the War," pp. 556–558.

114 Bundy, "The Last Chapter in the History of the War," p. 558.

115 Ibid., p. 558.

116 Ibid., p. 561.

117 Ibid., p. 560.

118 *Official Records,* Series II, Vol. 8, p. 661.

119 *Daily Picayune,* New Orleans, 15 September 1865.

120 *Louisiana Democrat,* Alexandria, 2 November 1868.

121 *Daily Picayune,* New Orleans, 16 January 1872, 15 August 1874.

122 Laura Foner, "The Free People of Color in Louisiana and St. Domingue: A Comparative Portrait of Two Three–caste Slave Societies," *Journal of Social History,* Vol. 3 No. 4, Oxford University Press (Summer 1970), p. 411. Foner's article states, "*Plaçage* was a system of extramarital unions (marriage between whites and Negroes was illegal), sometimes lasting for life, contracted between white men and colored women. The white man provided financial support for his colored *plaçée* according to an agreement contracted with the girl's parents. He could maintain his colored family on one side of town while at the same time continuing his life in white society in every respect, including if he desired, marriage with a white woman." Lisa Ze Winters, "'More Desultory and Unconnected Than Any Other'": Geography, Desire, and Freedom in Eliza Potter's *A Hairdresser's Experience in High Life,*" *American Quarterly* Vol. 61 No. 3, The Johns Hopkins University Press (September 2009), p. 456. Winters put forth a more succinct interpretation almost 40 years later, "contractual extra–marital sexual liaisons between wealthy white men and free women of color." *The Szymanski Descendants Family Tree in Mexico,* https://prezi.com/1sdons2l822k/szymanski/. Dee Dixon, "Mixed Race Left Handed Marriage—Plaçage," http://deedixon.tumblr.com/post/43375236852/mixed–race–left–handed–marriage–placage.

123 Stuart O. Landry, *History of the Boston Club* (New Orleans: Pelican Publishing Company, 1938), pp. 63, 96.

124 Landry, *History of the Boston Club*, pp. 106–109.

125 Uminski, *Two Polish Confederates*, p. 69.

126 Thomas Walter Brooks and Michael Dan Jones, *A History of the 10th Louisiana Infantry* (Gravenhurst, Ontario: Artstract Company, 1995), p. 122.

Chapter 4: Adventurers and Patriots

1 Bruce Allardice, *Confederate Colonels, A Biographical Register* (Columbia: University of Missouri Press, 2008), p. 361. Colonel Francis C. Kajencki, "The Louisiana Tiger," *Louisiana History: The Journal of the Louisiana Historical Association*, Vol. 15, No. 1 (Winter 1974), p. 51. Carl Moneyhon and Bobby Roberts, *Portraits of Conflict: A Photographic History of Louisiana in the Civil War* (University of Arkansas Press, 1990), p. 53.

2 Ludwik Żychliński, *The Memoirs of Ludwik Żychliński: Reminiscences of the American Civil War, Siberia and Poland,* ed. by James S. Pula (East European Monographs, Dist. By Columbia University Press, 1993), p. vii.

3 W.H. Zawadzki, Review of *The Memoirs of Ludwik Żychliński,* ed. by James S. Pula, *The Slavonic and East European Review,* Vol. 73, No. 3 (Jul., 1995), p. 551.

4 Pula, Introduction to *The Memoirs,* p. xviii.

5 *New York Civil War Service Records,* National Archives, Washington, DC. The *Enfans Perdu* was variably spelled in this fashion or as *Les Enfants Perdus* (see below).

6 Frederick Phisterer, *New York In The War Of The Rebellion 1861 to 1865* (Albany: Weed, Parsons and Company, 1890), p. 516. Frederick H. Dyer, *A Compendium of the War of the Rebellion* (Des Moines, Iowa: The Dyer Publishing Company, 1908), p. 1471.

7 "Departure of Les Enfants Perdus," *New York Tribune,* 21 April 1862.

8 "Military Matters," *New York Tribune,* 12 February 1862.

9 Żychliński, *The Memoirs,* p. 14.

10 "Case of Col. Felix Confort, of the 'Enfans Perdus' now imprisoned at Fortress Monroe," *New York Times,* 14 September 1862.

11 Żychliński, *The Memoirs,* p. 28.

12 Ethan S. Rafuse, *McClellan's War* (Bloomington: Indiana University Press, 2005), p. 270. Warren W. Hassler, Jr., *Commanders of the Army of the Potomac* (Baton Rouge: Louisiana State University Press, 1962), p. 79.

13 Piotr S. Wandycz, *The United States and Poland* (Cambridge, Massachusetts: Harvard University Press, 1980), p. 85.

14 Żychliński, *The Memoirs,* pp. ix–xiii. In the introduction, Pula suggests possible discrepancies between the memoirs Żychliński wrote during the war years and those compiled twenty years later. The actions described in this paper are also parallel to the citations from primary sources in this text.

15 Żychliński, *The Memoirs,* p. xi.

16 Ibid., p. 86.

17   Ibid., p. 16.

18   Ibid., p. 17.

19   Ibid., p. 65.

20   Ibid., pp. 18–19.

21   Susannah Ural Bruce, *The Harp and the Eagle: Irish–American Volunteers and the Union Army 1861–1865* (New York: New York University Press, 2002), pp. 178–180.

22   "Third Day of Mob Rule. More Murder and Destruction," *The Sun*, New York, 16 July 1863.

23   "Negro Killed and Hung Up," *The Sun*, New York, 16 July 1863.

24   Żychliński, *The Memoirs*, p. 19.

25   Shelby Foote, *The Civil War: A Narrative, Fort Sumter to Perryville* (New York: Random House, 1958, Vintage Books, 1986), p. 269. Hassler, *Commanders of the Army of the Potomac*, p. 40.

26   Frank J. Welcher, *The Union Army 1861–1865* (Bloomington: Indiana University Press, 1989), Vol. I, p. 797. Sulakowski's Louisiana troops had constructed some of the trench systems and earthworks that were deemed excellent by his fellow officers.

27   Żychliński, *The Memoirs*, p. 21.

28   "Men and Things at the Capital. The War News," *National Republican*, Washington, DC 12 April 1862.

29   Żychliński, *The Memoirs*, p. 22.

30   George B. McClellan, *McClellan's Own Story: The War for the Union, the Soldiers who Fought It, the Civilians who Directed it and His Relations to it and to Them* (New York: Charles L. Webster, 1887), pp. 142–143.

31   Żychliński, *The Memoirs*, p. 23.

32   George Stillman Hillard, *Life and Campaigns of George B. McClellan, Major General U.S. Army* (Philadelphia: J.B. Lippincott & Co. 1865), p. 63.

33   Żychliński, *The Memoirs*, p. 23.

34   "The Williamsburg Battle," *Richmond Dispatch*, 13 May 1862.

35   "Before Williamsburg," *National Republican*, Washington, DC, 13 May 1862.

36   "The Battle of Williamsburgh: How It Was Fought and Who Fought It," *New York Times*, 19 May 1862.

37   Żychliński, *The Memoirs*, p. 26.

38   Żychliński, *The Memoirs*, p. 27.

39   Phisterer, *New York In The War Of The Rebellion*, p. 516. Żychliński, *The Memoirs*, p. 24. From editor James Pula's notes on the *Memoirs* and Williamsburg battle.

40   Żychliński, *The Memoirs*, pp. 28–29. While he could give an accurate picture of daily camp life, Żychliński most likely would not have had the ability to give accurate estimates of troop strengths for the entire Army of the Potomac. Pula suggests that the reduction in force of 50,000 men was highly unlikely.

41   Żychliński, *The Memoirs*, p. 29.

42   Nils H. Randers–Pehrson, John Clagett Proctor and Mrs. Gilbert Grosvenor, "Aeronautics in the District of Columbia [with Remarks]," *Records of the Columbia Historical Society, Washington, D.C.*, Vol. 46/47 [The 38th separately bound book] 50th Anniversary Volume (1944/1945), p. 312. Patricia L. Faust, ed.,

Historical Times Illustrated Encyclopedia of the Civil War (New York: Harper & Row, 1986), p. 451.

43   "Great Battle on the Chickahominy," *New York Daily Tribune,* 2 June 1862.

44   Żychliński, *The Memoirs,* p. 28.

45   Ibid., p. 30.

46   "The Prince de Joinville on the War," *New York Times,* 15 November 1862. The *Times* published segments of de Joinville's writings and opinions of McClellan's unsuccessful Peninsula campaign.

47   Żychliński, *The Memoirs,* p. 31.

48   Ibid., pp. 64–65.

49   Ibid., pp. 31–33.

50   Ibid., p. 33.

51   Geoffrey C. Ward, *The Civil War* (New York: Alfred A. Knopf, 1990), p. 144. Mark Grimsley, *The Hard Hand of War: Union Military Policy Toward Southern Civilians, 1861–1865* (Cambridge: Cambridge University Press, 1995), p. 74.

52   Żychliński, *The Memoirs,* p. 34.

53   Ibid., p. 35.

54   "From Fortress Monroe," *National Republican,* Washington, DC, 25 July 1862. General Dix later was in charge of the suppression of the New York draft riots the following year.

55   Żychliński, *The Memoirs,* p. 35.

56   Ibid., p. 35.

57   Ibid., p. 37.

58   Ibid., p. 84.

59   Ibid., p. 40.

60   Harry Williams, "The Attack Upon West Point During the Civil War," *The Mississippi Valley Historical Review,* Vol. 25, No. 4 (Mar., 1939), pp. 492–493.

61   Ezra J. Warner, *Generals in Blue: Lives of the Union Commanders* (Baton Rouge: Louisiana State University Press, 1964), p. xx. Ezra J. Warner, *Generals in Gray, Lives of the Confederate Commanders* (Baton Rouge and London: Louisiana State University Press, 1959), p. xx.

62   Żychliński, *The Memoirs,* pp. 45–47.

63   Ibid., p. 48.

64   Ibid., pp. 49–50.

65   Ibid., p. 40.

66   Ibid., pp. 44–45.

67   Napier Bartlett, *Military Record of Louisiana,* Part II (Baton Rouge: Louisiana State University Press, 1964), p. 43.

68   Lawrence Lee Hewitt and Arthur W. Bergeron, Jr., eds., *Louisianans in the Civil War* (Columbia and London: University of Missouri Press, 2002), p. 122.

69   Bruce S. Allardice, *Confederate Colonels: A Biographical Register* (Columbia and London: University of Missouri Press, 2008), p. 361. Ella Lonn, *Foreigners in the Confederacy* (Chapel Hill: University of North Carolina Press, 1940), p. 101. Sulakowski's enforcement of discipline is detailed below in the text.

70   *Houma Ceres,* Houma, Louisiana, 19 July 1855. *Daily Picayune,* New Orleans, 20 June 1873.

71   Bartlett, *Military Record of Louisiana,* p. 45.

72   Lonn, *Foreigners in the Confederacy,* p. 101.

73   "The Riot at Grand Junction," *Memphis Appeal,* 4 August 1861. *Nashville Patriot,* 7 August 1861.

74   *Nashville Patriot,* 7 August 1861.

75   Terry L. Jones, "Wharf–Rats, Cutthroats and Thieves: The Louisiana Tigers, 1861–1862," *Louisiana History: The Journal of the Louisiana Historical Association,* Vol. 27, No. 2 (Spring 1986), p. 153.

76   Jones, "Wharf–Rats, Cutthroats and Thieves," p. 154.

77   *Nashville Patriot,* 7 August 1861. From an account of an eyewitness at the event on the 3rd of August provided to the newspaper.

78   *Nashville Patriot,* 7 August 1861. Kajencki, "The Louisiana Tiger," pp. 49–51. Bartlett, *Military Record of Louisiana,* p. 46.

79   Lonn, *Foreigners in the Confederacy,* p.101.

80   Arthur W. Bergeron, Jr., *Guide to Louisiana Confederate Units, 1861–1865* (Baton Rouge: Louisiana State University Press, 1989), pp. 107–108. Terry L. Jones, *Lee's Tigers: The Louisiana Infantry in the Army of Northern Virginia* (Baton Rouge: Louisiana State University Press, 1987), p. 7.

81   William C. Oates, *The War Between the Union and the Confederacy and Its Lost Opportunities with a History of the 15th Alabama Regiment and the Forty–eight Battles in Which It Was Engaged* (New York and Washington: The Neale Publishing Company, 1905), *pp. 75–76.*

82   F.B. Farinholt, *Confederate Veteran,* Volume V (Nashville: S.A. Cunningham Publisher, 1897), p. 467. Farinholt was writing years later about his experiences in the Army of Northern Virginia. He was correct about Sulakowski having military experience in Europe, but not at the Siege of Sebastopol. That siege took place in 1854–1855, when Sulakowski was already living in America.

83   "Disgraceful Conduct of Part of the 14th Louisiana Regiment at Petersburg, Va.," *Daily Picayune,* New Orleans, 20 September 1861.

84   *Official Records,* Series I, Vol. 11, Part I, p. 318. George B. McClellan, "The Peninsular Campaign," in R.U. Johnson and C.C. Buel, eds. *Battles and Leaders of the Civil War,* Vol. 2 (New York: Castle, 1884–1888), p. 169.

85   Bartlett, *Military Record of Louisiana,* pp. 44–47.

86   Warner, *Generals in Gray,* p. 55. Jones, *Lee's Tigers,* p. 43. Kajencki, "The Louisiana Tiger," p. 54.

87   Bruce Allardice, *Confederate Colonels,* p. 361. Bergeron, *Guide,* p. 106. Jones, "Wharf Rats," p. 164. Bartlett, *Military Record of Louisiana,* p. 47.

88   Bartlett, *Military Record of Louisiana,* pp. 46–47.

89   Jones, *Lee's Tigers,* p. 43.

90   Schaller, eds., *Soldiering for Glory,* pp. 50–54. From a letter written 3 September 1861. Schaller still had been in New Orleans when the riot occurred. He arrived

with the 2nd regiment en route to Virginia and viewed the wreckage the first wave of Louisiana troops had caused.

91 Bruce Allardice, *Confederate Colonels*, p. 361. Sulakowski possibly denounced the war to avoid arrest by the occupying Federal authorities under General Benjamin Butler.

92 Arthur W. Bergeron, Jr., ed., *The Civil War in Louisiana* (Lafayette: Center for Louisiana Studies, University of Louisiana at Lafayette, 2002), p. 131.

93 Kajencki, *The Louisiana Tiger,* pp. 54–55. *Official Records,* Series I, Vol. 26, Part II, p. 65.

94 "Gen. Magruder," *Dallas Herald,* 29 November 1862.

95 Paul D. Casdorph, *Prince John Magruder: His Life and Campaigns* (New York: John Wiley & Sons, Inc., 1996), pp. 226–234, 238.

96 Casdorph, *Prince John Magruder,* pp. 243–250. *Dallas Herald,* 11 March 1863.

97 Bogdan Grzeloński, *Poles in the United States of America, 1776–1865* (Warsaw: Interpress Publishers, 1976), p. 171. Casdorph, *Prince John Magruder,* p. 251.

98 *Official Records,* Series I, Vol. 26, Part II, pp. 189–190.

99 Casdorph, *Prince John Magruder,* p. 251. Warner, *Generals in Gray,* pp. 53–54. Born near Cork, Ireland, Cleburne had been in the British Army before he emigrated to America in 1849. He was a successful lawyer before the war and became colonel of the 15th Arkansas regiment in 1861. He led troops in battle at Shiloh, Perryville (Kentucky), Murfreesboro (Stone's River) and Chattanooga before meeting his end in the Confederate defeat at Franklin, Tennessee, on 30 November 1864.

100 Allardice, *Confederate Colonels,* p. 361.

101 *Official Records,* Series I, Vol. 26, Part II, pp. 449–450.

102 *Official Records,* Series I, Vol. 26, Part II, p. 450. R. Curtis Tyler, "Santiago Vidaurri and the Confederacy," *The Americas,* Vol. 26, No. 1 (Jul., 1969), p. 66.

103 *Official Records,* Series 1, Vol. 53, Supplement, pp. 986–987. "Cortina" is Juan N. Cortina. He was working with Federal military authorities who were supplying him with arms. Secretary of State William H. Seward suspected General Herron, the Union commander at Brownsville, of being "in connivance" with Cortina in the trade of illegal arms and contraband (Correspondence of 28 May 1864, *Official Records,* Series I, Vol. 53, Supplement, pp. 594–595).

104 *Official Records,* Series 1, Vol. 53, Supplement, p. 987.

105 Lonn, *Foreigners in the Confederacy,* pp. 225–226. Major Bninicki's name is listed in various sources also as "Buynicki" (very unlikely spelling for a Polish surname), or even Bukaty.

106 Lonn, *Foreigners in the Confederacy,* pp. 225–228. Richard N. Current, ed., *Encyclopedia of the Confederacy* (New York: Simon & Schuster, 1993), p. 981. McCrae had been a Mississippi governor and congressman and was chief financial agent for the Confederacy in Europe. He later monetarily supported Jefferson Davis in his defense against treason charges in 1867. That same year he helped form a colony of ex–Confederates in British Honduras, where he died in 1877.

107 "Wanted Polish Soldiers. A Curious Story of the War of the Rebellion," *The Sun,* New York, 29 December 1889.

108 "Arrival of the Grand Duke," *Daily Picayune,* New Orleans, 13 February 1872. *Semi-Weekly Louisianian,* New Orleans, 15 February 1872. Kajencki, "The Louisiana Tiger", p. 57. Lonn, *Foreigners in the Confederacy,* p. 145.

109 "Died. Col. Valery Sulakowski," *Daily Picayune,* New Orleans, 20 June 1873. Kajencki, "The Louisiana Tiger," pp. 57–58.

110 "A Heroic Act. A Single Man Combats and Subdues a Hundred," *Lafayette Advertiser,* Lafayette, Louisiana, 28 June 1873.

Chapter 5: The Model New American Officers

1 Francis C. Kajencki, *Star on Many a Battlefield: Brevet Brigadier General Joseph Kargé in the American Civil War* (Rutherford: Fairleigh Dickinson University Press, 1980), p.13.

2 Ezra J. Warner, *Generals in Blue: Lives of the Union Commanders* (Baton Rouge: Louisiana State University Press, 1964), pp. 273–274.

3 *Regimental Index Card, 58th New York Infantry,* National Archives, Washington, DC.

4 Francis B. Heitman, *Historical Register and Dictionary of the United States Army* (Washington: Government Printing Office, 1903), p. 1900. Abbreviations in the original register entry are spelled out for clarity.

5 Ezra J. Warner, *Generals in Blue: Lives of the Union Commanders,* pp. 273–274.

6 James S. Pula, *For Liberty and Justice: A Biography of Brigadier General Włodzimierz B. Krzyżanowski, 1824–1887* (Utica, NY: Ethnic Heritage Studies Center, 2008), p. 2. The concept of "crusader" is inherent in Pula's research. He dedicates his doctoral thesis to "the men of Krzyżanowski's brigade, the anonymous heroes of the anti–slavery crusade."

7 Gen. Włodzimierz Krzyżanowski, *Wspomnienia z pobytu w Ameryce Gen. Włodzimierza Krzyżanowskiego Podczas Wojny, 1861–1864* (Chicago: Polish Museum of America, 1963). The English title is: *Memoirs of Gen. Wladimir Krzyżanowski from a Stay in America During the War, 1861–1864.* In subsequent references the original Polish version is cited as *Wspomnienia.*

8 Pula, *For Liberty and Justice,* pp. 198–199. However, the Radical Republicans were frequently at odds with Lincoln and his conciliatory positions toward the South.

9 Murray M. Horowitz, "Ethnicity and Command: The Civil War Experience," *Military Affairs,* Vol. 42, No. 4 (Dec., 1978), p. 187.

10 M.J. Duszak, "Colonel Kriz of Washington," *Polish American Studies,* Vol. 23, No. 2 (Jul.–Dec., 1966), p.109.

11 M.J. Duszak, "Colonel Kriz of Washington," pp. 108–109.

12 Pula, *For Liberty And Justice,* p. 189. "Letter to Mary Milroy from R.H. Milroy," Papers, 17 November 1864, *General Robert H. Milroy Collection,* Jasper County, Indiana Library.

13 *Company B, District of Columbia Militia Documents,* National Archives.

14 Pula, *For Liberty and Justice,* p. 21.

15 Ibid., p. 23.

16 Ibid., p. 33.

17 Frederick Phisterer, *New York In The War Of The Rebellion 1861 to 1865* (Albany: Weed, Parsons and Company, 1890), p. 418.

18 Pula, *For Liberty and Justice,* p. 34.

19 Phisterer, *New York In The War Of The Rebellion,* p. 418.

20 Frederick H. Dyer, *A Compendium of the War of the Rebellion* (Des Moines, Iowa: The Dyer Publishing Company, 1908), p. 1426.

21 Pula, *For Liberty And Justice,* p. 35.

22 Ella Lonn, *Foreigners In The Union Army and Navy* (Baton Rouge: Louisiana State University Press, 1951), pp. 199–200.

23 Pula, *For Liberty and Justice,* p. 37. Peter Cozzens, *Shenandoah 1862* (Chapel Hill: The University of North Carolina Press, 2008), p. 229. William J. Miller, "Such Men as Shields, Banks and Frémont: Federal Command in Western Virginia, March–June 1862," in *The Shenandoah Valley Campaign of 1862,* Gary W. Gallagher, ed. (The University of North Carolina Press, 2003), p. 59.

24 Pula, *For Liberty and Justice,* p. 37.

25 Miller, "Such Men," p. 68.

26 James S. Pula, "Krzyżanowski's Civil War Brigade," *Polish American Studies,* Vol. 28, No. 2 (Autumn, 1971), p. 24. Jonathan M. Berkey, "In the Very Midst of the War Track: The Valley's Civilians and the Shenandoah Campaign," in *The Shenandoah Valley Campaign of 1862,* Gary W. Gallagher, ed. (Chapel Hill: University of North Carolina Press, 2003), p. 89.

27 Robert K. Krick, *Conquering the Valley: Stonewall Jackson at Port Republic* (New York: William Morrow and Company, 1996), pp. 16–17.

28 *Official Records of the Union and Confederate Armies,* Series I, Vol. 12 (Washington: Government Printing Office, 1885), p. 783.

29 Krick, *Conquering the Valley,* p. 197.

30 *Official Records,* pp. 672–673.

31 Duszak, "Colonel Kriz of Washington," p. 108. Pula, *For Liberty And Justice,* p. 41. An artist's rendering by Arthur Szyk depicts Krzyżanowski leading his men at Cross Keys with a saber in hand rather than a bayonet. Major General Richard S. Ewell was one of Jackson's subordinates in the Confederate command.

32 *Official Records,* Series I, Vol. 15, p. 42.

33 Krick, *Conquering the Valley,* p. 204.

34 Krick, *Conquering the Valley,* pp. 197–198.

35 *Official Records,* Series I, Vol. 12, pp. 672–673.

36 Pula, *For Liberty and Justice,* p. 45–47. Pula, as Krzyżanowski's biographer, challenges Robert K. Krick's criticism and categorizes it as one made by a "Southern apologist" who endeavors to "belittle the competence of yet another Union officer" while heaping "adulation" on the Confederate commanders.

37 Krick, *Conquering the Valley,* pp. 202–207. Krick cited Pula's 1978 published work, *For Liberty and Justice: The Life and Times of Wladimir Krzyżanowski.* The biography of Krzyżanowski referenced here is Pula's updated Second Edition published in 2008.

38   William F. Fox, *Regimental Losses in the American Civil War, 1861–1865* (Albany Publishing Company, 1889), p. 562.

39   Pula, *For Liberty and Justice*, p. 45.

40   J.T. Headley, *The Great Rebellion; A History of the Civil War in the United States*,

41   Vol. 1 (Hartford: American Publishing Company, 1866), p. 472.

42   James F. Huntington, "Operations in the Shenandoah Valley," in *Papers of the Campaigns in Virginia 1861–1862*, Vol. I, ed. Theodore F. Dwight, Military Historical Society of Massachusetts (Boston: Houghton and Mifflin, 1895), pp. 330–337.

43   Pula, *For Liberty and Justice*, p. 38.

44   Pula, *For Liberty and Justice*, p. 45.

45   Dyer, *A Compendium of the War of the Rebellion*, p. 1426. Phisterer, *New York in the War of the Rebellion*, p. 418.

46   Pula, "Krzyzanowski's Civil War Brigade," p. 29.

47   Pula, *For Liberty and Justice*, p. 49.

48   John J. Hennessy, *Return to Bull Run: The Campaign and Battle of Second Manassas* (New York: Simon & Schuster, 1993), p. 23. Shelby Foote, *The Civil War: A Narrative, Fort Sumter to Perryville* (New York: Random House, 1958, Vintage Books, 1986), pp. 620–621.

49   Hennessy, *Return to Bull Run*, p. 205.

50   *Official Records*, Series I, Vol. 12, p. 312.

51   Pula, *For Liberty and Justice*, p. 64.

52   J.F.J. Caldwell, *The history of a brigade of South Carolinians, known first as "Gregg's" and subsequently as "McGowan's brigade"* (Philadelphia: King and Baird, 1886), p. 34.

53   Pula, *For Liberty and Justice*, p. 64. Edward J. McCrady, *Gregg's Brigade of South Carolina in the Second Battle of Manassas* (Richmond: W.E. Jones, 1885), pp. 22–24. Caldwell, *McGowan's Brigade*, p. 34.

54   Caldwell, *McGowan's Brigade*, p. 36

55   Hennessy, *Return to Bull Run*, p. 405. *Official Records*, Series I, Vol. 12, p. 312.

56   *Official Records*, Series I, Vol. 12, p. 313.

57   Ibid., p. 313.

58   Geoffrey C. Ward, *The Civil War* (New York: Alfred A. Knopf, 1990), pp. 146–147.

59   Foote, *The Civil War: A Narrative*, Vol. I, p. 642.

60   Pula, *For Liberty and Justice*, p. 73.

61   *Official Records*, Series I, Vol. 21, p. 936.

62   Pula, *For Liberty And Justice*, p. 81.

63   Letter from Carl Schurz to President Abraham Lincoln, 28 October 1862, *Officers Papers*, National Archives.

64   Carl Schurz, *The Reminiscences of Carl Schurz*, Vol. II (New York: McClure Co., 1907), p. 407.

65   Pula, *For Liberty and Justice*, p. 91.

66   "The Battles on the Rappahannock, Hooker's Position," *New York Times*, 5 May 1863.

67   Ernest B. Furgurson, *Chancellorsville 1863* (New York: Alfred A. Knopf, 1992), p. 62. Pula, *For Liberty and Justice*, pp. 95–97.

68 Carl Schurz, *Reminiscences*, p. 403.
69 Pula, *For Liberty and Justice*, p. 97.
70 Ward, *The Civil War*, pp. 201–202. Furgurson, *Chancellorsville 1863*, p. 18.
71 Letter from Abraham Lincoln to Joseph Hooker, from Walter H. Hebert, *Fighting Joe Hooker* (Lincoln: University of Nebraska Press, 1944), p. 13.
72 Pula, *For Liberty and Justice*, p. 99.
73 *Official Records*, Series I, Vol. 25, Part I, p. 171. General Orders No. 47, issued by Hooker from his headquarters near Falmouth, Virginia, on 30 April 1863, claimed a "succession of splendid achievements." His General Orders No. 49 of 6 May contain his false statements that he captured 5,000 prisoners and put "*hors de combat* 18,000 of his chosen troops." Hebert, *Fighting Joe Hooker*, p. 196.
74 Headley, *The Great Rebellion*, Vol. I, p. 186.
75 Furgurson, *Chancellorsville 1863*, p. 90.
76 Schurz, *Reminiscences*, p. 405.
77 Furgurson, *Chancellorsville 1863*, p. 160.
78 *Official Records*, Series I, Vol. 25, Part I, pp. 660–661.
79 *Official Records*, Series I, Vol. 25, pp. 666–668. Pula, *For Liberty And Justice*, p. 279.
80 *Official Records*, Series I, Vol. 25, p. 668. Pula, *For Liberty and Justice*, p. 279.
81 Schurz, *Reminiscences*, pp. 424–425.
82 Schurz, *Reminiscences*, p. 428.
83 Furgurson, p. 166. Pula, *For Liberty and Justice*, pp. 100–101.
84 *Official Records*, Series I, Vol. 25, Part II, *Correspondence*, pp. 421–422.
85 Christian Keller, *Chancellorsville and the Germans: Nativism, Ethnicity and Civil War Memory* (New York: Fordham University Press, 2010), p. 1.
86 "Bloody Battle and Glorious Victory," *Richmond Examiner*, 7 May 1863. *Staunton Spectator*, Staunton, Virginia, 12 May 1863.
87 "Hooker's Battles," *Daily National Republican*, Washington, DC, 6 May 1863.
88 "Latest From Hooker's Army. Has Changed His Base," *Daily National Republican*, Washington, DC, 7 May 1863.
89 "The Army of the Potomac," *New York Times*, 5 May 1863, p. 8. This is a continuation of an article begun on p. 1. "Devin" refers to General Charles Devens, Jr. who was not an ethnic German. He was a Harvard graduate from Boston, entered the army from the Massachusetts militia, and was later appointed Attorney General of the United States by President Rutherford B. Hayes.
90 Pula, *For Liberty and Justice*, p.109.
91 Krzyżanowski, *Wspomnienia*, p. 77. The adjective *tchórzowski* means "cowardly" and is especially demeaning in that it is rooted in the Polish word for polecat or possibly by extension to the American skunk. My translation and interpretation.
92 *Official Records*, Series I, Vol. 25, p. 658.
93 Krzyżanowski, *Wspomnienia*, p. 78.
94 *Official Records*, Series I, Vol. 25, pp. 658–659.
95 Schurz, *Reminiscences*, pp. 438–440.
96 Pula, *For Liberty and Justice*, p. 111.

97   *Official Records,* Series I, Vol. 25, Part I, p. 629.

98   Warren W. Hassler, Jr. *Commanders of the Army of the Potomac* (Baton Rouge: Louisiana State University Press, 1962), pp. 149–150. Hooker greatly exaggerated the number of captured Confederate prisoners and the casualties he inflicted (he said 5,000 and 18,000 respectively)—both were false. The actual number captured was less than 2,000 and the total casualty figure for the Southern side was 12,463 including the 1708 missing.

99   *Report of the Joint Committee on the Conduct of the War* (Washington: Government Printing Office, 1865), p. 30.

100 *Report of the Joint Committee on the Conduct of the War* (Washington: Government Printing Office, 1865), p. 127.

101 Theodore Ayrault Dodge, *The Campaign of Chancellorsville* (Boston: Ticknor, 1881), pp. 2–3.

102 Pula, *For Liberty and Justice,* p. 113.

103 Krzyżanowski, *Wspomnienia,* p. 77. "*Zimną krew*" literally translates as "with cold blood" and the expression "*zachować zimną krew*" is to "keep cool," as in behavior or demeanor.

104 Ward, *The Civil War,* p. 215.

105 Oliver Otis Howard, *The Autobiography of Oliver Otis Howard,* Vol. I (New York: The Baker & Taylor Company, 1907), pp. 386, 390. Pula, *For Liberty and Justice,* p. 115.

106 Pula, *For Liberty and Justice,* p. 119.

107 Headley, *The Great Rebellion,* Vol. I, pp. 197–198.

108 Harry Willcox Pfanz, *Gettysburg: The First Day* (University of North Carolina Press, 2001), p. 141. Pula, *For Liberty and Justice,* p. 122. That part of Pennsylvania had a significant German population and the local townspeople showed special appreciation for the regiments of the Eleventh Corps.

109 Pula, *For Liberty and Justice,* p. 122.

110 Fairfax Downey, *The Guns at Gettysburg* (New York: Collier Books, 1962), p. 48.

111 Edwin C. Bearss with J. Parker Hills, *Receding Tide: Vicksburg and Gettysburg, The Campaigns That Changed the Civil War* (Washington: National Geographic Society, 2006), p. 318.

112 Pfanz, *Gettysburg: The First Day,* p. 238.

113 Pula, *For Liberty and Justice,* p. 129.

114 Krzyżanowski, *Wspomnienia,* p. 79.

115 Pula, *For Liberty and Justice,* p. 127.

116 Pfanz, *Gettysburg: The First Day,* p. 238.

117 Schurz, *Reminiscences,* Vol. III, p. 9.

118 Bearss and Hills, *Receding Tide,* p. 319.

119 Pula, *For Liberty and Justice,* pp. 132–134.

120 Pula, "Krzyżanowski's Civil War Brigade," p. 48.

121 "The Great Battles," *New York Times,* 4 July 1863.

122 Pula, *For Liberty and Justice,* p. 136.

123 Schurz, *Reminiscences,* Vol. III, p. 26. Krzyżanowski wrote in his memoirs that he himself gave the orders for the bayonet charge.

124 Merl E. Reed and J. Warren, eds., "The Gettysburg Campaign—A Louisiana Lieutenant's Eyewitness Account," *Pennsylvania History,* Vol. 30, No. 2 (April, 1963), p. 189. The letter is from Lieutenant J. Warren Jackson, to his wounded brother, R. Stark Jackson. Both were from Cheneyville, Louisiana, in Rapides Parish.

125 "The Rebel Invasion," *Cleveland Morning Leader,* Cleveland, Ohio, 4 July 1863. Pula, *For Liberty and Justice,* p. 139.

126 *Official Records,* Series I, Vol. 27, Part I, pp. 742–743.

127 "The Fight at Gettysburg," *Evening Star,* Washington, DC 3 July 1863.

128 Bearss and Hills, *Receding Tide,* pp. 363–364.

129 Pula, *For Liberty and Justice,* p. 141. George R. Stewart, *Pickett's Charge: A Microhistory of the Final Attack at Gettysburg, July 3, 1863* (Boston: Houghton Mifflin Company, 1959), pp. 173–174.

130 Reed and Warren, "The Gettysburg Campaign," p. 188.

131 Pula, *For Liberty and Justice,* p. 141. Schurz, *Reminiscences,* Vol. III, pp. 34–36.

132 Pula, *For Liberty and Justice,* pp. 142–144.

133 Charles G. Stevenson, "A Search and a Reappraisal," *Polish American Studies,* Vol. 23, No. 2 (Jul.–Dec., 1966), pp. 107–108.

134 "Details of Wednesday's Battle," *New York Times,* 6 July 1863. The *Times* reported "the conduct of the corps partially redeemed the reputation lost at Chancellorsville, though … there was great confusion and a great many stragglers were lost."

135 "The Battle at Gettysburg," *Raftsman's Journal,* Clearfield, Pennsylvania, 15 July 1863. Excerpt from an article labeled as an "eyewitness account."

136 "The New Fourth of July," *Raftsman's Journal,* Clearfield, Pennsylvania, 15 July 1863. A separate opinion article, though not specified as such, that took a fiercely pro–Union tone.

137 Samuel Penniman Bates, *Martial Deeds of Pennsylvania* (Philadelphia: T.H. Davis & Company, 1876), p. 635. Coincidently with the transfer of the Eleventh Corps, Longstreet also had been transferred after Gettysburg to a new command in the western theatre of operations.

138 Pula, *For Liberty and Justice,* pp. 148–149. Frederick Phisterer, *Statistical Record of the Armies of the United States,* Vol. 13 (New York: Charles Scribner's Sons, 1883), p. 283. *Letter,* from General Oliver O. Howard 28 December 1863, National Archives. The *Statistical Record* lists Krzyżanowski as "Waldemir."

139 Steven E. Woodworth and Charles D. Grear, eds., *The Chattanooga Campaign* (Carbondale: Southern Illinois University Press, 2012), p. 1. Pula, *For Liberty and Justice,* p. 153.

140 Pula, *For Liberty and Justice,* p.155.

141 Schurz, *Reminiscences,* Vol. III, pp. 59–60. Howard, *Autobiography,* Vol. 1, p. 464. Pula, *For Liberty and Justice,* pp. 156–157.

142 Schurz, *Reminiscences,* Vol. III, p. 56.

143 Stewart Bennett, "Lookout Mountain Frowned Down Upon Us," in *The Chattanooga Campaign,* Steven E. Woodworth and Charles D. Grear, eds. (Carbondale: Southern Illinois University Press, 2012), p. 40. Schurz, *Reminiscences,* Vol. III, p. 65.

144 *Official Records,* Series I, Vol. 31, Part III, p. 4. Schurz, *Reminiscences,* Vol. III, p. 65.

145 Krzyżanowski, *Wspomnienia*, p. 80.

146 Krzyżanowski, *Wspomnienia*, pp. 81–82. Pula, *For Liberty and Justice*, pp. 163–164.

147 "Return and Reception of the Fifty-eighth and Sixty-eighth Regiments," *New York Times*, 27 January 1864.

148 Krzyżanowski, *Wspomnienia*, p. 84. Pula, *For Liberty and Justice*, p. 167.

149 Bennett, "Lookout Mountain," pp. 47–48. *Official Records*, Series I, Vol. 31, Part I, p. 184. Pula, *For Liberty and Justice*, p. 183.

150 *Official Records*, Series I, Vol. 31, Part I, pp. 208–211. Pula, *For Liberty and Justice*, p. 183–184. Pula states that the court wished to escape the "potential wrath of a superior officer" and "chose to avoid any real decision by placing the blame for a failure which it admitted did not exist on the one person who was not present to defend himself."

151 *Official Records*, Series I, Vol. 52, Part I, p. 537. Howard's correspondence of 29 March 1864.

152 *Official Records*, Series I, Vol. 32, Part I, p. 32. *Official Records*, Series I, Vol. 31, Part I, p. 73, correspondence from C.A. Dana to Secretary of War, E.M. Stanton, 29 October 1863. Pula, *For Liberty and Justice*, pp. 185–186.

153 Pula, *For Liberty and Justice*, pp. 188–192.

154 "Letter to R.H. Milroy from W. Krzyżanowski," written at Stevenson, Alabama, 20 March 1865, *Milroy Collection*, Jasper County Public Library.

155 "Milroy Papers," I, 394, Jasper County, Indiana Library.

156 "Milroy Papers," I, 394, Jasper County, Indiana Library. Pula, *For Liberty and Justice*, pp. 192, 195. John H. Eicher and David J. Eicher, *Civil War High Commands* (Stanford: Stanford University Press, 2001), p. 337.

157 Krzyżanowski, *Wspomnienia*, p. 96.

158 Pula, *For Liberty and Justice*, p. 193, 199.

159 Pula, *For Liberty and Justice*, p. 198.

160 Pula, *For Liberty and Justice*, p. 201.

161 Krzyżanowski, *Wspomnienia*, p. 104.

162 Lonn, *Foreigners in the Confederacy* (Chapel Hill: University of North Carolina Press, 1940), p. 1. Pula, *For Liberty and Justice*, p. 203. Krzyżanowski, *Wspomnienia*, p. 45.

163 Pula, *For Liberty and Justice*, pp. 208–210.

164 Krzyżanowski, *Wspomnienia*, p. 104.

165 Pula, *For Liberty and Justice*, p. 262–265. Duszak, "Colonel Kriz of Washington," p. 110.

166 Teofil Lachowicz, *Polish Freedom Fighters on American Soil: Polish Veterans in America from the Revolutionary War to 1939* (Minneapolis: Hillcrest Two Harbors Press, 2011), p. 43.

167 Francis C. Kajencki, *Star on Many a Battlefield: Brevet Brigadier General Joseph Kargé in the American Civil War* (Rutherford: Fairleigh Dickinson University Press, 1980), p.11.

168 *Princeton Press*, 31 December 1892.

169 Kajencki, *Star on Many a Battlefield*, p. 23.

170 John O. Raum, *The History of New Jersey: From Its Earliest Settlements to the Present* (Philadelphia: John E. Potter and Company, 1877), p. 172.

171 Kajencki, *Star on Many a Battlefield*, p. 19.

172 Mark M. Boatner, III, *The Civil War Dictionary* (New York: David McKay Co., 1959), p. 448. While it lists Kargé's country of origin as Germany, the *Dictionary* gives Poland as "Waldimir" Krzyzanowski's birthplace.

173 Kajencki, *Star on Many a Battlefield*, p. 13.

174 New Jersey Historical Society, *Proceedings of the New Jersey Historical Society*. Vol. 81, Oct. 1963.

175 Kajencki, *Star on Many a Battlefield*, p. 29.

176 Kajencki, *Star on Many a Battlefield*, pp. 29–32.

177 Henry R. Pyne, *The History of the First New Jersey Cavalry* (Trenton: J.A. Beecher, 1871), p. 22. Henry Pyne was chaplain of the regiment.

178 Fairfax Downey, *Clash of Cavalry: The Battle of Brandy Station, June 9, 1863* (New York: David McKay, Co., Inc., 1959), p. 30.

179 "A Camp Festival. Feast in Commemoration of the Polish Revolution of 1830 in Gen. Blenker's Division—Col. Krzyzanowski Presides," *New York Times,* 5 December 1861.

180 Kajencki, *Star on Many a Battlefield*, pp. 35–38.

181 Pyne, *The History of the First New Jersey Cavalry*, p. 24. Wyndham, like Ludwik Żychliński, had fought in Italy under Garibaldi prior to coming to the United States.

182 Colin R. Ballard, *The Military Genius of Abraham Lincoln* (New York: The World Publishing Company, 1952), pp. 75–76.

183 "Military Nominations and Confirmations," *New York Tribune,* 29 April 1862. Pyne, *First New Jersey Cavalry*, pp. 38–41.

184 Pyne, *First New Jersey Cavalry*, p. 43.

185 Ezra J. Warner, *Generals in Gray: Lives of the Confederate Commanders* (Baton Rouge: Louisiana State University Press, 1959), p. 14. Ashby was born at "Rose Bank" in Fauquier County, Virginia. Pyne wrote that they had passed Ashby's home in their approach to Front Royal.

186 Kajencki, *Star on Many a Battlefield*, p. 47.

187 Pyne, *First New Jersey Cavalry*, p. 49.

188 *Official Records*, Series I, Vol. 12, Part I, p. 678.

189 *Official Records*, Series I, Vol. 12, Part I, p. 679.

190 Kajencki, *Star on Many a Battlefield*, p. 49.

191 "Overtaking the Enemy. Independent Advance of Col. Wyndham. A Successful Ambuscade," *New York Times,* 14 June 1862. The account is from two separate articles. Charles H. Webb was the *New York Times* correspondent who provided an eyewitness account.

192 Francis F. Wayland and Albert Tracy, "Frémont's Pursuit of Jackson in the Shenandoah Valley: The Journal of Colonel Albert Tracy, March–July 1862," *The Virginia Magazine of History and Biography*, Vol. 70, No. 2 (Apr., 1962), p. 192. *Official Records*, Series I, Vol. 12, Part I, p. 679–680. Pyne, *First New Jersey Cavalry*, p. 56.

193 John Esten Cooke, *The Wearing of the Gray: Being Personal Portraits, Scenes and Adventures from the War* (New York: E.B. Treat & Co., 1867), p. 66. Krick, *Conquering The Valley*, p. 26. Cooke also had described Wyndham as a "military dandy."

194 Pyne, *History of the First New Jersey Cavalry*, p. 55.

195 "From Gen. Fremont's Army," *New York Tribune*, 12 June 1862.

196 *Official Records*, Series I, Vol. 12, Part I, p. 18. Foote, *The Civil War*, p. 459.

197 Kajencki, *Star on Many a Battlefield*, pp. 66–72. *New Brunswick Times*, New Jersey, 27 February 1862.

198 Pyne, *History of the First New Jersey Cavalry*, pp. 82–83.

199 Kajencki, *Star on Many a Battlefield*, pp. 73–74.

200 Pyne, *History of the First New Jersey Cavalry*, p. 94.

201 Kajencki, *Star on Many a Battlefield*, p. 77.

202 "The War in Virginia. Brilliant Cavalry Charges," *New-York Daily Tribune*, 26 August 1862. At about this time, Kargé's countryman, "Acting Brigadier" (according to the Tribune's account) Krzyżanowski, had his brigade engaged in skirmishes with Confederate pickets along the Rappahannock River between Brandy Station and Culpeper, Virginia. This was the beginning of the first phase of the Second Manassas Campaign.

203 Pyne, *History of the First New Jersey Cavalry*, p. 97.

204 *Official Records*, Series I, Vol. 12, Part II, p. 90.

205 Kajencki, *Star on Many a Battlefield*, pp. 81–82.

206 Kajencki, *Star on Many a Battlefield*, p. 85.

207 *Official Records*, Series I, Vol. 19, Part II, p. 8.

208 *Official Records*, Series I, Vol. 19, Part II, p. 8. "The Situation," *National Republican*, Washington, DC, 1 October 1862. Patricia L. Faust, ed., *Historical Times Illustrated Encyclopedia of the Civil War* (New York: Harper & Row, 1986), p. 558. Terms of parole dictated that prisoners were not to take up arms until they were exchanged for an enemy soldier of equal rank. The rules stated that parole should take place within ten days of capture.

209 Kajencki, *Star on Many a Battlefield*, pp. 86–87.

210 Pyne, *History of the First New Jersey Cavalry*, pp. 124–125. Kajencki, *Star on Many a Battlefield*, p. 88.

211 *Official Records*, Series 1, Vol. 21, pp. 28–29. Kargé's report to Bayard of 4 December 1862 from Brooke's Station, Virginia.

212 Kajencki, *Star on Many a Battlefield*, p. 94.

213 *Official Records*, Series 1, Vol. 12, Part II, p. 91.

214 Kajencki, *Star on Many a Battlefield*, pp. 97–108. Raum, *The History of New Jersey*, Vol. 2, p. 435.

215 Kajencki, *Star on Many a Battlefield*, pp. 110–112. George E. Waring, Jr. was well known for his work as a sanitation engineer. He supervised the drainage and construction of Central Park in New York before the war and the development of the Memphis sewer system afterwards.

216 Andrew Nelson Lytle, *Bedford Forrest and His Critter Company* (Nashville: J.S. Sanders & Company, 1931), p. 244.

217 Lytle, *Bedford Forrest,* p. 247. Kajencki, *Star on Many a Battlefield,* pp. 115–116.

218 Kajencki, *Star on Many a Battlefield,* p. 116.

219 John F. Marszalek, *Sherman: A Soldier's Passion For Order* (New York: The Free Press, 1993), p. 250.

220 William T. Sherman, *Memoirs of General William T. Sherman* (New York: Da Capo Press, 1984), p. 394.

221 Charles F. Ritter and John L. Wakelyn, eds., *Leaders of the American Civil War: A Biographical and Historiographical Dictionary* (Westport, CT: Greenwood Press, 1998), p. 372.

222 George E. Waring, *Whip and Spur* (Boston: J.R. Osgood and Company, 1875), p. 109.

223 *Official Records,* Series 1, Vol. 32, Part I, p. 283.

224 "Gen. Sherman's Movements," *New York Times,* 2 March 1864.

225 Waring, *Whip and Spur,* p. 115.

226 Sherman, *Memoirs,* p. 395.

227 *Official Records,* Series I, Vol. 32, Part III, pp. 288–318. Sherman wrote to his immediate superior, Lieutenant General U. S. Grant, about Hurlbut's lack of "boldness."

228 Kajencki, *Star on Many a Battlefield,* pp. 140–142. *Official Records,* Series I, Vol. 32, Part III, p. 566.

229 *Official Records,* Series I, Vol. 32, Part III, p. 623. This particular reference was in a letter written by Brigadier General James R. Chalmers, Forrest's First Division Cavalry commander. He was reporting on the capture of Fort Pillow in this report of 20 April and in an addendum 7 May 1864. The battle at the Fort was controversial because of the "massacre" of black Union soldiers who had surrendered. Some Confederates maintained that the Union soldiers had resumed fighting after feigning surrender. Chalmers stated that "the enemy made no attempt to surrender, no white flag was elevated nor was the U.S. flag lowered until pulled down by our men."

230 Kajencki, *Star on Many a Battlefield,* p. 144.

231 Benjamin Franklin Cooling, *To the Battles of Franklin and Nashville and Beyond: Stabilization and Reconstruction in Tennessee and Kentucky, 1864–1865* (Knoxville: The University of Tennessee Press, 2011) p. 155.

232 *Official Records,* Series I, Vol. 32, Part I, p. 699. The account is from Sturgis' report to Headquarters in Memphis, 12 May 1864.

233 *Official Records,* Series I, Vol. 32, Part I, p. 702. From the report of Major P. Jones Yorke, Second New Jersey Cavalry, 11 May 1864.

234 *New York Times,* 8 May 1864.

235 *Official Records,* Series I, Vol. 39, Part I, p. 87. Stewart Bennett, *The Battle of Brice's Crossroads* (Charleston, SC: The History Press, 2012), p. 32.

236 Stewart Bennett, *The Battle of Brice's Crossroads,* pp. 32–33. *Chicago Daily Tribune,* 6 February 1882. From the account of Fred W. Snell.

237 *Official Records,* Series I, Vol. 39, Part I, p. 91.

238 *Official Records,* Series I, Vol. 39, Part I, p. 91. Dr. Lonnie E. Maness, "Strategic Victories or Tactical Defeats? Nathan Bedford Forrest at Brice's Crossroads,

Harrisburg, and the Memphis Raid," *Journal of Confederate History*, Vol. 1, No. 1 (Summer 1988), pp. 179–180.

239 *Official Records*, Series I, Vol. 39, Part I, p. 87.

240 *Official Records*, Series I, Vol. 39, Part I, p. 88.

241 "Details of Sturgis' Expedition and Disaster," *Indiana Herald*, Bloomington, Indiana, 22 June 1864. This is Kargé's Second New Jersey Cavalry which in official reports numbers 400 men.

242 Lytle, *Bedford Forrest and His Critter Company*, p. 293.

243 *Indiana Herald*, Bloomington, Indiana, 22 June 1864.

244 *Official Records*, Series I, Vol. 39, Part I, p. 152. Sturgis' official written report gives the strength of Kargé's detail at 400 as opposed to the *Indiana Herald* report of 300.

245 "War and Wire. Further Facts about the Celebrated Sturgis Expedition," *Chicago Daily Tribune*, 6 March 1882.

246 *Official Records*, Series I, Vol. 39, Part I, p. 225. In an addendum to the report made on 28 June 1864 the official casualty count was listed at 492 on page 231 of the *Official Records*.

247 *Official Records*, Series I, Vol. 39, Part I, p. 96. From Sturgis' report to Sherman in turn submitted by Sherman to Adjutant–General, Washington, DC, from the field near Atlanta, 24 August 1864.

248 Kajencki, *Star on Many a Battlefield*, pp. 166–168.

249 *Official Records*, Series I, Vol. 39, Part I, p. 387.

250 Kajencki, *Star on Many a Battlefield*, pp. 182–183. *Official Records*, Series I, Vol. 39, Part I, p. 395.

251 Edwin C. Bearss, "Grierson's Winter Raid on the Mobile and Ohio Railroad," *Military Affairs*, Volume 24, No. 1 (Spring 1960), pp. 21–22. Bearss incorrectly refers to Kargé as "a native of Germany," which was not a political entity at the time. Kargé referred to and identified himself as a Pole who had emigrated from Prussia and had served in the Prussian army.

252 Michael B. Ballard, *The Civil War in Mississippi: Major Campaigns and Battles* (Oxford: University Press of Mississippi, 2011), p. 267.

253 "Cavalry Charge on a Stockade," *New York Times*, 13 January 1865. Ballard, *The Civil War in Mississippi: Major Campaigns and Battles*, p. 270.

254 *The Daily Picayune*, New Orleans, 20 January 1865. Though occupied by Federal forces since late April 1862, the paper continued to print pro-Southern reports and stated that the damage was not so severe considering the Union troops were operating "in a clear field."

255 Kajencki, *Star on Many a Battlefield*, pp. 211–215. Kargé's *Service Records*, National Archives.

256 Bruce J. Dinges and Shirley A. Leckie, eds., *A Just and Righteous Cause: Benjamin H. Grierson's Civil War Memoir* (Carbondale: Southern Illinois University, 2008), p. 341.

257 "Funeral of Gen. Kargé," *New York Times*, 18 December 1892. *Princeton Press*, 31 December 1892.

258 Inscription from Kargé's gravestone.

Chapter 6: Undying Grey and Dyed Blue

1 T. Lindsay Baker, *The First Polish Americans: Silesian Settlements in Texas* (College Station:Texas A&M University Press, 1979), pp. 21–22.

2 "Correspondence from Upper Silesia," *Czas*, Kraków, 9 October 1855. My translation from the original edition of the Kraków daily newspaper. There was considerably more freedom of the press in Austrian held Poland. Polish language journals had much greater flexibility than their counterparts across the border in Prussian dominated Upper Silesia.

3 Baker, *The First Polish Americans*, p. 19.

4 Baker, *The First Polish Americans*, pp. 9–10.

5 Edward J. Dworaczyk, *The First Polish Colonies of America in Texas: Containing Also the General History of the Polish People in Texas* (San Antonio:The Naylor Company, 1936), p. 2.

6 Baker, *The First Polish Americans*, p. 8. Maria Starczewska, "The Historical Geography of the Oldest Polish Settlement in America," *The Polish Review*,Vol. 12, No. 2 (Spring 1967), p. 17.

7 "Items of German News," *New York Times*, 18 September 1854. Baker, *The First Polish Americans*, pp. 12–15.

8 Andrzej Brozek, "The Roots of Polish Migration to Texas," *Polish American Studies*, Vol. 30, No. 1 (Spring 1973), p. 22.

9 Dworaczyk, *The First Polish Colonies of America in Texas*, p. 97. Brozek, "The Roots of Polish Migration to Texas," p. 23. Baker, *The First Polish Americans*, pp. 15–16.

10 *Gwiazdka Cieszyńska*, Cieszyn, 26 July 1856.

11 *Czas*, Kraków, 22 May 1856.

12 Baker, *The First Polish Americans*, p. 23–25.

13 Ron Tyler, ed. *The New Handbook of Texas*, Vol. 5 (Austin:The Texas State Historical Association, 1996), p. 44.

14 Starczewska, "The Historical Geography of the Oldest Polish Settlement in America," pp. 23–26.

15 "News From Texas," *Daily Picayune*, New Orleans, 15 March 1856. *New York Times*, 24 March 1856.

16 Dworaczyk, *The First Polish Colonies of America in Texas*, p. 27. Lonn, *Foreigners in the Confederacy* (Chapel Hill: The University of North Carolina Press, 1940), p. 128. Joseph Kyrisk's name appears sometimes as "Kyrish" or "Kyricz."

17 Baker, *The First Polish Americans*, pp. 69–70. Robert Plocheck, "Polish Texans," *Texas Almanac, 2004–2005* (Dallas:Texas State Historical Society, 2005).

18 *Company Muster Roll, 24th Texas Cavalry*, 29 March 1862, National Archives, Washington, D.C. Compiled Service Records of Confederate Soldiers Who Served in Organizations from the State of Texas, National Archives, Washington, DC. Dworaczyk, *The First Polish Colonies of America in Texas*, p. 27.

19 *Official Records*, Series I, Vol. 17, Part I, p. 705. Shelby Foote, *The Civil War: A Narrative, Fredericksburg to Meridian* (New York: Random House, 1958, Vintage Books, 1986), pp. 134–135. Foote's estimate of the Confederate troops

is probably accurate although General Churchill wrote that he had "3,000 effectives."

20 *Official Records,* Series I, Vol. 17, Part I, p. 705.

21 *Official Records,* Series I, Vol. 13, p. 770. From a report 29 October 1862 from Colonel R.A. Cameron, 34th Indiana Volunteers to Brigadier General Hovey, Commanding U.S. Forces, Helena, Arkansas. Baker, *The First Polish Americans,* p. 70.

22 *Official Records,* Series I, Vol. 17, Part I, pp. 780–781.

23 *Official Records,* Series I, Vol. 17, Part I, p. 781.

24 *Official Records,* Series I, Vol. 17, Part I, p. 781.

25 Richard N. Current, ed., *Encyclopedia of the Confederacy* (New York: Simon & Schuster, 1993), p. 311.

26 *Official Records,* Series I, Vol. 17, Part I, pp. 784–785. Wilke's Regiment is not to be confused with Wilke's Texas Light Artillery, in which there were also many Texas Poles.

27 L.V. Caraway, "The Battle of Arkansas Post," *Confederate Veteran,* Vol. 14 (March 1906), p. 128. Caraway was writing from his home in Granbury, Texas. The town was named after Confederate General Hiram B. Granbury, for whom later the Brigade and the 24th Regiment were also named.

28 Caraway, "The Battle of Arkansas Post," p. 128.

29 Baker, *The First Polish Americans,* p. 71–72. Helen Busyn, "Peter Kiołbassa: Maker of Polish America," *Polish American Studies,* Vol. 8, No. 3/4 (July–December 1951), p. 69. Dworaczyk, *The First Polish Colonies of America in Texas,* p. 98. Dworaczyk has Kiołbassa captured at Little Rock, which, as seen in McClernand's report, is a considerable distance upriver from Fort Hindman/Arkansas Post. He also has him joining the Union army in Arkansas. Kiołbassa remained a prisoner in Union hands until his internment at Camp Butler, Illinois.

30 *Official Records,* Series II, Vol. 5, p. 240. R.O. Ould, Confederate exchange agent, letter of protest to Lieutenant Colonel W.H. Ludlow, Agent of Exchange for the U.S. Army.

31 *Official Records,* Series II, Vol. 5, p. 240.

32 Baker, *The First Polish Americans,* p. 72.

33 Baker, *The First Polish Americans,* p. 76. Sister Mary Patricia Jurczynska, S.S.J. "A Study of the Participation of the Poles in the American Civil War" (Master of Arts Thesis, St. John College, 1949), p. 111. "Texas Death Certificates 1890–1976," *Texas State Board of Health* (Texas State Library).

34 Edmund L. Kowalczyk, "Jottings from the Polish American Past," *Polish American Studies,* Vol. 11, No. 1/2 (January–June, 1954), p. 38. Edward C. Rozanski, "Civil War Poles of Illinois," *Polish American Studies,* Vol. 23, No. 2 (July–December, 1966), p. 113. Busyn, "Peter Kiołbassa: Maker of Polish America," p. 69. Baker, *The First Polish Americans,* p. 72. *Organization Index to Pension Files of Veterans Who Served Between 1861 and 1900,* National Archives. Shortly after Peter joined the Illinois Cavalry, another Kiołbassa, Ignatz (Ignacy or Ignatius), joined the regiment after his release and formally changing of allegiances at Camp Butler. He was of no relation to Peter Kiołbassa and

was originally from a different family of the same name in Silesia. Rozanski and Kowalczyk both incorrectly refer to Peter and Ignatz Kiołbassa as brothers.

35   Helen Busyn, "The Political Career of Peter Kiołbassa," *Polish American Studies,* Vol. 7, No. 1/2 (January–June 1950), p. 8.

36   Robert B. Leach, "The Role of the Union Cavalry during the Atlanta Campaign," (Master's Thesis, Army Command and General Staff College, Fort Leavenworth, Kansas: 1994), p. 86.

37   Henry Stone, "Repelling Hood's Invasion of Tennessee," in R.U. Johnson and C.C. Buel, eds., *Battles and Leaders of the Civil War* (New York: Castle, 1884–1888), p. 443. The situation facing the 16th and 14th Illinois in this action was related in 1887 by Major Henry C. Connelly of the 14th Illinois Cavalry.

38   *Company Muster Rolls, 6th Cavalry, U.S.C.T.,* January–March 1865, National Archives, Washington, DC.

39   Helen Busyn, "The Political Career of Peter Kiołbassa," p. 9.

40   Dworaczyk, *The First Polish Colonies of America in Texas,* p. 29.

41   Busyn, "The Political Career of Peter Kiołbassa," pp. 10–11.

42   Busyn, "The Political Career of Peter Kiołbassa," p. 12.

43   *Chicago Eagle,* 14 June 1902. From an advertisement, "Peter Kiołbassa, Notary Public and Real Estate Conveyancer."

44   Busyn, "The Political Career of Peter Kiołbassa," p. 13. Arthur W. Thurner, "Polish Americans in Chicago Politics, 1890–1930," *Polish American Studies,* Vol. 28, No. 1 (Spring 1971), p. 23.

45   Victor R. Greene, "For God and Country: The Origins of Slavic Catholic Self-Consciousness in America," *Church History,* Vol. 35, No. 4 (Cambridge University Press, December 1966), p. 449.

46   Arthur W. Thurner, "Polish Americans in Chicago Politics, 1890–1930," p. 21. Busyn, "The Political Career of Peter Kiołbassa," p. 17.

47   Thurner, "Polish Americans in Chicago Politics," p. 36. Busyn, "The Political Career of Peter Kiołbassa," p. 16.

48   "Caring for the Pension Funds," *Daily Inter Ocean,* Chicago, 17 May 1891. "He Refuses to Obey," *Chicago Daily Tribune,* 23 December 1891. "Cregier Democrats Unable to Select a Campaign Committee," *Chicago Daily Tribune,* 28 March 1891.

49   "Poles Repudiate Kiołbassa," *Chicago Daily Tribune,* 23 October 1892.

50   "The Polish Americans Protest Strongly Against the Passage of the Immigration Restriction Bill," *Chicago Eagle,* 12 February 1898. Kiołbassa penned the appeals as Honorary President of the Polish Union.

51   "They Appeal to Congress," *Chicago Eagle,* 12 February 1898. "Applications Filed," *Daily Inter Ocean,* Chicago, 25 March 1893. As Chicago city treasurer, Kiołbassa met with various officials in Washington on the treaty with Russia and immigration issues.

52   Alfred Theodore Andreas, *History of Chicago: From the Earliest Period to the Present Time,* Vol. 3, *From the Fire of 1871 until 1885* (Chicago: The A.T. Andreas Company, Publishers, 1886), p. 564.

53   *Chicago Daily Tribune,* 24 June 1905.

54 Sigmund H. Uminski, "Poles and the Confederacy," *Polish American Studies,* Vol. 22, No. 2 (Jul.–Dec., 1965), p. 75.

55 Edward Pinkowski, *Pills, Pen & Politics: The Story of General Leon Jastremski, 1843– 1907* (Wilmington, Delaware: Captain Stanislaw Mlotkowski Memorial Brigade Society, 1974), pp. 25–29. "Interesting Career of Civil War Veteran and Journalist," *Lafayette Advertiser,* Lafayette, Louisiana, 22 November 1907.

56 *Lafayette Advertiser,* Lafayette, Louisiana, 22 November 1907.

57 Arthur W. Bergeron, Jr., *Guide to Louisiana Confederate Units, 1861–1865* (Baton Rouge: Louisiana State University Press, 1989), p. 96. Pinkowski, *Pills, Pen & Politics,* p. 37.

58 Leon Jastremski, *Letter, September 1861,* from *Leon Jastremski Family Papers,* Louisiana State University.

59 Col. Francis C. Kajencki, "The Louisiana Tiger," *Louisiana History: The Journal of the Louisiana Historical Association,* Vol. 15, No. 1 (Winter 1974), p. 52.

60 Fred Ober, "The Campaign of the Peninsula," in *Reminiscences,* Civil War Papers, 10 September 1872, Louisiana Historical Association Collection, Tulane University.

61 Charles I. Batchelor, *Letter to Albert Batchelor, 10 October 1861,* Albert A. Batchelor Papers, Louisiana State University.

62 Terry L. Jones, *Lee's Tigers: The Louisiana Infantry in the Army of Northern Virginia* (Baton Rouge: Louisiana State University Press, 1987), pp. 23–24.

63 Jones, *Lee's Tigers,* pp. 30–31.

64 Jones, *Lee's Tigers,* p. 61. *Official Records,* Series I, Vol. 11, Part I, pp. 450, 568. Shelby Foote, *The Civil War, Fort Sumter to Perryville,* p. 411.

65 Bergeron, *Guide,* p. 97. Pinkowski places Jastremski in the fighting at Savage Station on 29 June but Bergeron has the Tenth Louisiana's next action after Williamsburg at Malvern Hill on 1 July 1862.

66 "The Battle of the 25th of June," *Daily Dispatch,* Richmond, 5 July 1862. Italics are in the original article.

67 Cornelius M. Buckley, ed. and translator, *A Frenchman, A Chaplain, a Rebel: The War Letters of Pere Louis–Hippolyte Gache, S.J.* (Chicago: Loyola University Press, 1981), p. 43. Lonn, *Foreigners in the Confederacy,* pp. 105–106.

68 Robert Stiles, *Four Years Under Marse Robert* (New York: The Neale Publishing Company, 1903), pp. 80–81.

69 Col. R.G. Lowe, "The Dreux Battalion," *Confederate Veteran,* Volume V (Nashville: S.A. Cunningham Publisher, 1897), p. 55.

70 Jones, *Lee's Tigers,* p. 107.

71 *Shreveport Semi–Weekly News,* Louisiana, 8 August 1862. From a letter written by Captain Alex Bowman of the Caddo Rifles on 1 July 1862.

72 Douglas Southall Freeman, *Lee* (New York: Charles Scribner's Sons, 1961), p. 216. Jones, *Lee's Tigers,* p. 107.

73 *Official Records,* Series I, Vol. 11, Part II, p. 806. Wright had "not more than 3,000 men" opposing 8,000 Federal troops whose operations "were conducted by General McClellan in person."

74 *Official Records,* Series I, Vol. XI, Part II, p. 672, from the report of General J. Bankhead Magruder to General Robert E. Lee on the Battle of Malvern Hill. R.A. Brock, ed., *Southern Historical Society Papers,* XXXVIII (Richmond: Southern Historical Society, 1910), p. 211. Pinkowski, *Pills, Pen & Politics,* pp. 39–41. Jones, *Lee's Tigers,* pp. 108–109.

75 *Official Records,* Series I, Vol. 11, Part II, pp. 724–725, from the report of Brigadier General Paul J. Semmes on Malvern Hill. Bergeron, *Guide,* p. 97.

76 Uminski, "Two Polish Confederates," p. 76. Pinkowski, *Pills, Pen & Politics,* p. 41.

77 Pinkowski, *Pills, Pen & Politics,* p. 41.

78 Jones, *Lee's Tigers,* p. 112. Italics mine. Joseph W.A. Whitehorne, *The Second Battle of Manassas* (Washington: Center of Military History, 1990), p. 26. Whitehorne's Order of Battle lists the 10th Louisiana in Stafford's Brigade of Jackson's Division (Brig. Gen. William E. Starke vice William Taliaferro) of the Left Wing (Maj. Gen. Thomas J. Jackson). Other Orders of Battle list Starke's Brigade as the Fourth Brigade in the Division.

79 Jones, Lee's Tigers, p. 118.

80 *Official Records,* Series I, Vol. 12, Part II, p. 658.

81 *Official Records,* Series I, Vol. 12, Part II, pp. 668–669.

82 *Official Records,* Series I, Vol. 12, Part II, p. 669. John H. Worsham, *One of Jackson's Foot Cavalry* (New York: The Neal Publishing Company, 1912), p. 132.

83 Hennessy, *Return to Bull Run,* p. 357.

84 William C. Oates, *The War Between the Union and the Confederacy and Its Lost Opportunities with a History of the 15th Alabama Regiment and the Forty-eight Battles in Which It Was Engaged* (New York and Washington: The Neale Publishing Company, 1905), p. 145.

85 Jones, *Lee's Tigers,* pp. 124–125.

86 Pinkowski, *Pills, Pen & Politics,* pp. 41–42. Jones, *Lee's Tigers,* pp. 117–118. Foote, *The Civil War,* Vol. I, p. 619.

87 Freeman, *Lee,* p. 247. Jones, *Lee's Tigers,* p. 127. Pinkowski, *Pills, Pen & Politics,* p. 42.

88 *Official Records,* Series I, Vol. 19, Part I, p. 951.

89 Bergeron, *Guide,* p. 97. Pinkowski, *Pills, Pen & Politics,* p. 43.

90 "Later From The South. The Terrific Fight at Sharpsburg, Maryland," *The Evening Star,* Washington, DC, 27 September 1862. The *Star* noted that this account came from "A Southern Account of the Battle of Antietam."

91 Jones, *Lee's Tigers,* p. 133. Pinkowski, *Pills, Pen & Politics,* p. 43.

92 "Our Losses in the late Battles at Manassas and in Maryland," *Staunton Spectator,* Staunton, Virginia, 7 October 1862.

93 "By Coale & Barr. The News," *Abingdon Virginian,* 3 October 1862.

94 Pinkowski, *Pills, Pen & Politics,* p. 43–44. Jones, *Lee's Tigers,* p. 144.

95 Carl Schurz, *The Reminiscences of Carl Schurz, Volume Two, 1852–1863* (New York: McClure Co., 1907), p. 428.

96 Oliver O. Howard, "The Eleventh Corps at Chancellorsville," in R.U. Johnson and C.C. Buel, eds. *Battles and Leaders of the Civil War,* Vol. III (New York: Castle, 1884–1888), p. 191.

97   "Interesting Career of Civil War Veteran and Journalist," *Lafayette Advertiser,* Lafayette, Louisiana, 22 November 1907. Ezra J. Warner, *Generals in Gray: Lives of the Confederate Commanders* (Baton Rouge and London: Louisiana State University Press, 1959), p. 224. Jones, *Lee's Tigers,* pp. 146–148.

98   *Official Records,* Series I, Vol. 27, Part II, pp. 512–514. Bergeron, *Guide,* p. 97.

99   "From Virginia," *Opelousas Courier,* Opelousas, Louisiana, 26 September 1863.

100 John Mitchell Vanderslice, *Gettysburg: Where and How the Regiments Fought, and the Troops They Encountered* (Philadelphia: J.B. Lippincott & Company, 1897), p. 145.

101 Pinkowski, *Pills, Pen & Politics,* pp. 45–46. Jones, *Lee's Tigers,* pp. 170–177.

102 Pinkowski, *Pills, Pen & Politics,* p. 46.

103 "Avis," *Opelousas Courier,* Opelousas, Louisiana, 25 July 1863. Jones, *Lee's Tigers,* p. 180.

104 Bergeron, *Guide,* p. 97.

105 James M. Gillispie, *Andersonvilles of the North* (Denton: University of North Texas Press, 2008), pp. 190–191.

106 Pinkowski, *Pills, Pen & Politics,* pp. 53–58.

107 *Letter* from Leon Jastremski to John Jastremski, 19 July 1864, Jastremski Family Papers, Louisiana State University.

108 Isaac W.K. Handy, *United States Bonds; or Duress by Federal Authority: A Journal of Current Events During and Imprisonment of Fifteen Months at Fort Delaware* (Baltimore: Turnbull Brothers, 1874), p. 251.

109 Jurczynska, "A Study of the Participation of the Poles in the American Civil War," p. 42. Kenneth W. Noe, *Perryville* (Lexington: The University Press of Kentucky, 2001), p. 97. Ezra J. Warner, *Generals in Blue: Lives of the Union Commanders* (Baton Rouge: Louisiana State University Press, 1964), pp. 424–25. Charles Allan Baretski, "General Albin Francis Schoepf —A Preliminary View," *Polish American Studies,* Vol. 23, No. 2 (Jul.–Dec., 1966), p. 93.

110 Uminski, "Two Polish Confederates," p. 76. Pinkowski, *Pills, Pen & Politics,* p. 60. "From Fortress Monroe: Attempt to Rescue The Rebel Prisoners Put Under Fire," *National Republican,* Washington, DC, 29 August 1864. The Captain and First Mate, "implicated in an attempt to liberate" the prisoners, "were tried for the lives before a court–martial." Pinkowski refers to the steamer transport ship as the *Crescent,* whereas the ship is sometimes listed as the *Crescent City* (named after New Orleans) in some editions of the newspaper.

111 J. Ogden Murray, *The Immortal Six Hundred: A Story of Cruelty to Confederate Prisoners of War* (Winchester: The Eddy Press Corporation, 1905), p. 10.

112 Pinkowski, *Pills, Pen & Politics,* p. 62.

113 General Clement A. Evans, ed. *Confederate Military History,* Vol. X (Atlanta: Confederate Publishing Company, 1899), p. 456.

114 Mauriel Phillips Joslyn, *Immortal Captives: The Story of 600 Confederate Officers and the United States Prisoner of War Policy* (Shippensburg, Pennsylvania: White Mane Publishing Company, 1996), pp. 99–100, 112.

115 Pinkowski, *Pills, Pen & Politics,* p. 68. "From Port Royal," *National Republican,* Washington, DC, 6 September 1864.

116 *Official Records*, Series I, Vol. 47, Part II, pp. 412–413. Gillmore wrote this dispatch to Halleck from Hilton Head Island, South Carolina, on 13 February 1863.

117 *Official Records*, Series I, Vol. 47, Part II, pp. 697–698.

118 Murray, *The Immortal Six Hundred*, pp. 223–225. Joslyn, *Immortal Captives*, pp. 245–246.

119 Murray, *The Immortal Six Hundred*, p. 226. From correspondence from Jastremski to Murray of 26 December 1904. Murray cites Jastremski's surname as "Jestremeska" in his text.

120 Pinkowski, *Pills, Pen & Politics*, pp. 79–80.

121 Joslyn, *Immortal Captives*, p. 270.

122 Thomas Walter Brooks and Michael Dan Jones, *A History of the 10th Louisiana Infantry* (Gravenhurst, Ontario: Artstract Company, 1995), p. 122.

123 Pinkowski, *Pills, Pen & Politics*, p. 80.

124 Joslyn, *Immortal Captives*, p. 270.

125 *Lafayette Advertiser*, Lafayette, Louisiana, 22 November 1907. Joslyn, *Immortal Captives*, p. 270.

126 Pinkowski, *Pills, Pen & Politics*, pp. 84–87.

127 *Lafayette Advertiser*, Lafayette, Louisiana, 22 November 1907. Pinkowski, *Pills, Pen & Politics*, p. 87.

128 "Belligerent Negroes," *Advocate*, Baton Rouge, 24 June 1876. *Daily Picayune*, New Orleans, 26 June 1876.

129 Pinkowski, *Pills, Pen & Politics*, pp. 88–89. The Knights of the White Camelia (spelled as such with one "l") were a Southern reaction to Reconstruction. Their membership in Louisiana consisted of former Confederate officers, professionals, businessmen and educated members of society. They were most effective in the late 1860's in their efforts to control and intimidate black and Republican voters. By 1870 they had largely disbanded.

130 Pinkowski, *Pills, Pen & Politics*, p. 90. Joslyn, *Immortal Captives*, p. 270. Uminski, "Two Polish Confederates," p. 78. "About Louisiana Capitolian," *Chronicling America, Historic American Newspapers*, Library of Congress, http://www.chroniclingamerica.loc.gov. lccn/sn88064592.

131 "The Democratic State Central Committee," *Louisiana Capitolian*, Baton Rouge, 30 August 1879.

132 Pinkowski, *Pills, Pen & Politics*, p. 100.

133 United Confederate Veterans, *Minutes of the United Confederate Veterans* (Atlanta: Constitution Book and Job Office, 1891), p. 5.

134 Herman Hattaway, "The United Confederate Veterans in Louisiana," *Louisiana History: The Journal of the Louisiana Historical Association*, Vol. 16, No. 1 (Winter 1975), p. 9. Uminski, "Two Polish Confederates," p. 78.

135 Leon Jastremski, *Confederate Veteran* (Nashville, Tennessee: S.A. Cunningham, September, 1904), Vol. XII, p. 425.

136 "Death of Gen. Jastremski Casts Gloom Over State," *Weekly Iberian*, New Iberia, Louisiana, 30 November 1907. *State-Times*, Baton Rouge, 28 May 1974. Joslyn,

Immortal Captives, p. 270. Uminski, "Two Polish Confederates," p. 81. Pinkowski, *Pills, Pen & Politics*, pp. 120–121.

Chapter 7: Reweaving an Uneasy Fabric

1   Ernest Duvergier de Hauranne, *A Frenchman in Lincoln's America (Huit Mois en Amérique: Lettres et Notes de Voyage, 1864–1865),* Volume One, translated and edited by Ralph H. Bowen (Chicago: R.R. Donnelley & Sons Company, 1974), p. xlvii.

2   See above, pp. 126,136, and Żychliński, *The Memoirs,* p. 64.

3   LeRoy H. Fischer, *Lincoln's Gadfly* (Norman: University of Oklahoma Press, 1964), p. 264.

4   See pp. 276–277 for Kiołbassa, p. 73 for Tochman.

5   Timothy Mason Roberts, *Distant Revolutions: 1848 and the Challenge to American Exceptionalism* (Charlottesville: University of Virginia Press, 2009), p. 60. Roberts especially cites a speech by newspaper editor and politician, John W. Forney.

ACKNOWLEDGEMENTS

I would like to thank Marina G. Kelley, whose support and assistance were invaluable. She also proved to be a tireless proofreader.

I also express my gratitude to the following: Edie Ambrose a colleague and superb Louisiana historian at Southeastern Louisiana University; my brother and sister Brian and Paula Bielski who have always listened to my stories with interest; Philip Blood who planted the early concept in my head while we were in Poland; the late Bob Bushaway a British historian who enjoyed good discussion of the American Civil war; Tom and Carolyn Crosby for enabling my return to the academic world; Peter Gray at Birmingham; my adviser for the final stages of doctoral work at Birmingham, Jonathan Gumz; Parker Hills, a friend and colleague, whose on-site Civil War battlefield presentations make the war come alive; Hal Jespersen for his superb maps; my friend and colleague Yakir Katz for his unwavering support on many levels; Harry Laver, friend, historian and colleague whose advice and help were invaluable; my friend Peter Little; James Pula for the copy of the original Polish Krzyżanowski *Memoirs*; Carole Sargent at Georgetown for her advice on publishing; Terri Sercovich for her excellent work preparing the photos; Gary Sheffield who launched my doctoral research and advised me brilliantly; my always upbeat and encouraging editor, Steve Smith and the professional team at Casemate; Michael Snape my insightful and congenial reader of my doctoral thesis; Tulane University and Library in New Orleans; Civil War historian Susannah Ural; Carrie Williamson for her support and marketing assistance; Dave Zabecki who wrote the Foreword and originally recommended and got me started at the University of Birmingham.

BIBLIOGRAPHY

Newspapers

Adams Sentinel, Gettysburg (Adams County), Pennsylvania
Advocate, Baton Rouge, Louisiana
Chicago Daily Tribune
Chicago Eagle
Cleveland Morning Leader
Czas (The Times), Kraków, Poland
Daily Crescent, New Orleans
Daily Dispatch, Richmond, Virginia
Daily Inter Ocean, Chicago
Daily National Republican, Washington
Daily Picayune, New Orleans
Dallas Herald
Evening Star, Washington
Evening Telegraph, Philadelphia
Galveston Daily News, Texas
Gwiazdka Cieszyńska (Cieszyn Star), Cieszyn, Poland
Houma Ceres, Houma, Louisiana
Indiana Herald
Lafayette Advertiser, Lafayette, Louisiana
Louisiana Capitolian, Baton Rouge, Louisiana
Louisiana Democrat, Alexandria, Louisiana
Memphis Appeal

Nashville Patriot
National Republican, Washington
New York Daily Tribune
New Brunswick Times, New Jersey
New York Times
Opelousas Courier, Opelousas, Louisiana
Princeton Press
Raftsman's Journal, Clearfield, Pennsylvania
Richmond Dispatch
Richmond Examiner
State-Times, Baton Rouge
Staunton Spectator, Virginia
The Sun, Baltimore, Maryland
The Sun, New York
Washington Post
Washington Star

Primary Sources

Manuscript Collections

Fauquier County (Virginia) Civil War Centennial Committee
Gettysburg Battlefield Memorial Commission, Gettysburg, Pennsylvania
Jasper County Indiana Library, *General Robert H. Milroy Collection.*
Louisiana State University, *Albert A. Batchelor Papers*
Louisiana State University, *Leon Jastremski Family Papers*
Louisiana State University, *The Papers of Jefferson Davis*
National Archives, Washington, D.C.
New Jersey Historical Society, *Proceedings of the New Jersey Historical Society*
Southern Historical Society, *Southern Historical Society Papers,* Richmond, Virginia
Texas State Board of Health
Tulane University, Army of Northern Virginia Papers
Tulane University, Louisiana Historical Association Collection

Published Primary Sources

Bakanowski, Rev. Adolf Sixtus. *Moje Wspomnienia 1840–1863–1914.* Lwów: Nakładem XX Zmartwychwstanców, 1913.

Bartlett, Napier. *Military Record of Louisiana.* Baton Rouge: Louisiana State University Press, 1964.

Batchelor, Charles I. *Letter to Albert Batchelor, 10 October 1861,* Albert A. Batchelor Papers, Louisiana State University.

Bates, Samuel Penniman. *Martial Deeds of Pennsylvania.* Philadelphia: T.H. Davis & Company, 1876.

Brock, R.A., ed. *Southern Historical Society Papers,* XXXVIII. Richmond: Southern Historical Society, 1910.

Buckley, Cornelius M., ed. and translator, *A Frenchman, A Chaplain, a Rebel: The War Letters of Pere Louis-Hippolyte Gache, S.J.* Chicago: Loyola University Press, 1981.

Bundy, J.M. "The Last Chapter in the History of the War," in *Battles and Leaders of the Civil War,* Cozzens, Peter, ed. Urbana: University of Illinois Press, 2004.

Caldwell, J.F.J. *The history of a brigade of South Carolinians, known first as "Gregg's" and subsequently as "McGowan's brigade."* Philadelphia: King and Baird, 1886.

Cooke, John Esten. *The Wearing of the Gray: Being Personal Portraits, Scenes and Adventures from the War.* New York: E.B. Treat & Co., 1867.

Crist, Lynda Lasswell and Dix, Mary Seaton, eds. *The Papers of Jefferson Davis.* Baton Rouge: Louisiana State University Press, 1992.

Davis, Jefferson. "Message of President Davis." *The North American Review,* Vol. 93, No. 192, 1861.

Ditterline, Theodore. *Sketch of the Battles of Gettysburg, July 1,2, and 3d, 1863.* C.A. Alvord Electrotype and Printer, 1863.

Dix, John Adams. *The Memoirs of John Adams Dix, Compiled by his son, Morgan Dix.* New York: Harper & Brothers, 1883.

Dodge, Theodore Ayrault. *The Campaign of Chancellorsville.* Boston: Ticknor, 1881.

Evans, General Clement A., ed. *Confederate Military History,* Vol. X. Atlanta: Confederate Publishing Company, 1899.

Farinholt, F.B. *Confederate Veteran,* Volume V. Nashville: S.A. Cunningham Publisher, 1897.

Fauquier County Civil War Centennial Committee. *The Years of Anguish 1861–1865.*

Gurowski, Adam G. De. *America and Europe.* New York: D. Appleton and Company, 1857.

Gurowski, Adam. *Diary from March 4, 1861, to November 12, 1862.* Boston: Lee and Shepard, 1862.

Gurowski, Adam. *Diary from November 18, 1862, to October 18, 1863*. New York: Carlton Publisher, 1864.

Gurowski, Adam. *Diary 1863–'64–'65*. Washington, DC: W.H. & O.H. Morrison, 1866.

Gurowski, Adam. *Slavery in History*. New York: A.B. Burdick, 1860.

Handy, Isaac W.K. *United States Bonds; or Duress by Federal Authority: A Journal of Current Events During and Imprisonment of Fifteen Months at Fort Delaware*. Baltimore: Turnbull Brothers, 1874.

Harring, Harro. *Poland Under the Dominion of Russia*. Boston, 1834.

Hassler, Warren W., Jr. *Commanders of the Army of the Potomac*. Baton Rouge: Louisiana State University Press, 1962.

Hauranne, Ernest Duvergier de. *A Frenchman in Lincoln's America. Huit Mois en Amérique: Lettres et Notes de Voyage, 1864–1865* translated and edited by Ralph H. Bowen. Chicago: R.R. Donnelley & Sons Company, 1974.

Headley, J.T. *The Great Rebellion; A History of the Civil War in the United States*, Vols. I & II. Hartford: American Publishing Company, 1866.

Howard, Oliver Otis. *The Autobiography of Oliver Otis Howard*, Vol. 1. New York: The Baker & Taylor Company, 1907.

Howard, Oliver O. "The Eleventh Corps at Chancellorsville," in R.U. Johnson and C.C. Buel, eds. *Battles and Leaders of the Civil War*, Vol. III. New York: Castle, 1884–1888.

Johnson, R.U. and Buel, C.C., eds. *Battles and Leaders of the Civil War*. New York: Castle, 1884–1888.

Krzyżanowski, Włodzimierz. *Wspomnienia z pobytu w Ameryce Gen. Włodzimierza Krzyżanowskiego podczas wojny, 1861–1864*. Chicago: Polish Museum of America, 1963.

McClellan, George B. *McClellan's Own Story: The War for the Union, the Soldiers who Fought It, the Civilians who Directed it and His Relations to it and to Them*. New York: Charles L. Webster, 1887.

Miller, Robert H. "The Letters of Lieutenant Robert H. Miller to His Family, 1861–1862," Conner, Forrest P., ed. *Virginia Magazine of History and Biography*, LXX. 1962.

Murray, J. Ogden. *The Immortal Six Hundred: A Story of Cruelty to Confederate Prisoners of War*. Winchester: The Eddy Press Corporation, 1905.

Oates, William C. *The War Between the Union and the Confederacy and Its Lost Opportunities with a History of the 15th Alabama Regiment and the Forty-eight Battles in Which It Was Engaged*. New York and Washington: The Neale Publishing Company, 1905.

Ober, Fred. "The Campaign of the Peninsula," in *Reminiscences*, Civil War Papers, 10 September 1872, Louisiana Historical Association Collection, Tulane University.

Official Records of the Union and Confederate Armies. Washington: Government Printing Office, 1885.

Pyne, Henry R. *The History of the First New Jersey Cavalry.* Trenton: J.A. Beecher, 1871.

Reed, Merl E. and Warren, J. eds. "The Gettysburg Campaign—A Louisiana Lieutenant's Eyewitness Account," *Pennsylvania History,* Vol. 30, No. 2. April, 1963.

Report of the Joint Committee on the Conduct of the War. Washington: Government Printing Office, 1865.

Roemer, Jacob. *Reminiscences of the War of the Rebellion, 1861–1865.* Flushing, NY: Pub. By the estate of Jacob Roemer, 1897.

Schaller, Mary W. and Schaller, Martin N., eds. *Soldiering for Glory: The Civil War Letters of Colonel Frank Schaller, Twenty-Second Mississippi Infantry.* Columbia: The University of South Carolina Press, 2007.

Schurz, Carl. *The Reminiscences of Carl Schurz.* New York: McClure Co., 1907.

Sherman, William T. *Personal Memoirs.* New York: Charles L. Webster & Co., 1891.

Sherman, William Tecumseh. *Memoirs of General William T. Sherman by Himself: In 2 Vols.* New York: D. Appleton & Co., 1875.

Sherman, William T. *Memoirs of General William T. Sherman.* New York: Da Capo Press, 1984.

Sparks, Jared. *Correspondence of the American Revolution; Being Letters of Eminent Men to George Washington, from the Time of His Taking Command of the Army to the End of His Presidency,* Volume II. Boston: Little, Brown, 1853.

Stiles, Robert. *Four Years Under Marse Robert.* New York: The Neale Publishing Company, 1903.

Stone, Henry. "Repelling Hood's Invasion of Tennessee," in Johnson, R.U. and Buel, C.C., eds. *Battles and Leaders of the Civil War.* New York: Castle, 1884–1888.

Tochman, Gaspard, ed. "Charter. List of Officers, and Proceedings at the special meeting, 27 June 1846," *Polish Slavonian Literary Association.* New York: 1846.

Tochman, Major G. "Lecture on the social, political and literary condition of Poland, and her future prospects," *Lecture delivered before the members of the state legislatures of New York, Massachusetts, New Hampshire, Vermont, Connecticut, Virginia, Ohio, Indiana and Kentucky and before the members of the New Jersey state convention.* Baltimore: J.D. Toy, 1844.

Tochman, G. *An Exposé of the Conduct of Joseph H. Bradley of Washington, DC, Counsellor" employed by the Imperial Russian Legation": Towards Major G. Tochman, of New York, Counsellor Retained by the Next of Kin and Heirs at Law of Gen. Thadeus Kosciusko, December, 1847.* Washington: s.n. 1848.

Tochman, G. *Petition of Major G. Tochman, attorney and counsel of the next of kin and heirs at law of Gen. Thadeus Kosciusko.* Washington, D.C.: s.n., December, 1847.

Tochman, Major Gaspard. *Poland, Russia and the Policy of the Latter Towards the United States.* Baltimore: John D. Toy, Printer, 1844.

Waring, George E. *Whip and Spur.* Boston: J.R. Osgood and Company, 1875.

Żychliński, Ludwik. *The Memoirs of Ludwik Żychliński: Reminiscences of the American Civil War, Siberia and Poland* ed. by James S. Pula. East European Monographs, Dist. By Columbia University Press, 1993.

Secondary Sources

Allardice, Bruce. *Confederate Colonels, A Biographical Register.* Columbia: University of Missouri Press, 2008.

Allardice, Bruce. *More Generals in Gray: A Companion Volume to Generals in Gray.* Baton Rouge: Louisiana State University Press, 1995.

Ambrose, Stephen E. *Halleck: Lincoln's Chief of Staff.* Baton Rouge: Louisiana State University Press, 1962.

Ambrose, Stephen E. "Lincoln and Halleck: A Study in Personal Relations," *Journal of the Illinois State Historical Society,* Vol. 52, No. 1, Lincoln Sesquicentennial. Spring, 1959.

Andreas, Alfred Theodore. *History of Chicago: From the Earliest Period to the Present Time,* Vol. 3, *From the Fire of 1871 until 1885.* Chicago: The A.T. Andreas Company Publishers, 1886.

Ardrea, M. "The Societies of St. Stanislaus Kostka Parish, Chicago," *Polish American Studies,* Vol. 9, No. 1/2. January–June 1952.

Ascherson, Neal. *Black Sea.* New York: Hill and Wang, 1995.

Ascherson, Neal. *The Struggles for Poland.* New York: Random House, 1987.

Bailey, Anne J. *Invisible Southerners: Ethnicity in the Civil War.* Athens: The University of Georgia Press, 2006.

Baker, T. Lindsay. *The First Polish Americans: Silesian Settlements in Texas.* College Station: Texas A&M University Press, 1979.

Baker, Thomas Lindsay. "The Early History of Panna Maria, Texas". Master's thesis, Texas Tech University, 1972.

Ballard, Colin R. *The Military Genius of Abraham Lincoln.* New York: The World Publishing Company, 1952.

Ballard, Michael B. *The Civil War in Mississippi: Major Campaigns and Battles.* Oxford: University Press of Mississippi, 2011.

Baretski, Charles Allan. "General Albin Francis Schoepf—A Preliminary View," *Polish American Studies,* Vol. 23, No. 2. Jul.–Dec., 1966.

Beale, Howard K. "On Rewriting Reconstruction History," *The American Historical Review,* Vol. 45, No. 4. Jul., 1940.

Bearss, Edwin C. with Hills, J. Parker. *Receding Tide: Vicksburg and Gettysburg, The Campaigns That Changed the Civil War*. Washington: National Geographic Society, 2006.

Bearss, Edwin C. *Forrest at Brice's Cross Roads and in north Mississippi in 1864*. Press of Morningside Bookshop, 1979.

Bearss, Edwin C. "Grierson's Winter Raid on the Mobile and Ohio Railroad," *Military Affairs*, Volume 24, No. 1. Spring, 1960.

Bearss, Edwin C. *Protecting Sherman's Lifeline: The Battles of Brice's Crossroads and Tupelo, 1864*. Washington: Office of Publications, National Park Service, 1971.

Bennett, Stewart. *The Battle of Brice's Crossroads*. Charleston, SC: The History Press, 2012.

Bennett, Stewart. "Lookout Mountain Frowned Down Upon Us," in *The Chattanooga Campaign*, Woodworth, Steven E. and Grear, Charles D., eds. Carbondale: Southern Illinois University Press, 2012.

Bergeron, Arthur W., Jr., ed. *The Civil War in Louisiana*. Lafayette: Center for Louisiana Studies, University of Louisiana at Lafayette, 2002.

Bergeron, Arthur W., Jr. *Guide to Louisiana Confederate Units, 1861–1865*. Baton Rouge: Louisiana State University Press, 1989.

Berkey, Jonathan M. "In the Very Midst of the War Track: The Valley's Civilians and the Shenandoah Campaign," in *The Shenandoah Valley Campaign of 1862*, Gary W. Gallagher, ed. Chapel Hill: University of North Carolina Press, 2003.

Biskupski, M.B. *The History of Poland*. Westport: Greenwood Press, 2000.

Biskupski, M.B. and Pula, James S. *Polish Democratic Thought from the Renaissance to the Great Emigration: Essays and Documents*. East European Monographs: Columbia University Press, 1990.

Boatner, Mark M. III. *The Civil War Dictionary*. New York: David McKay Co., 1959.

Boyer, Paul S., ed. *The Oxford Companion to United States History*. Oxford: Oxford University Press, 2000.

Brooks, Thomas Walter and Jones, Michael Dan. *A History of the 10th Louisiana Infantry*. Gravenhurst, Ontario: Artstract Company, 1995.

Brozek, Andrzej. "The Roots of Polish Migration to Texas," *Polish American Studies*, Vol. 30, No. 1. Spring 1973.

Bruce, Susannah Ural. "The Harp and the Eagle: The Impact of Civil War Military Service in the Union Army on the Irish in America". Doctoral Dissertation, Kansas State University, 2002.

Burlingame, Michael. *Abraham Lincoln, A Life*. Baltimore: The Johns Hopkins University Press, 2008.

Burton, William L. *Melting Pot Soldiers: The Unions Ethnic Regiments*. New York, Fordham University Press, 1998.

Busyn, Helen. "Peter Kiołbassa: Maker of Polish America," *Polish American Studies,* Vol. 8, No. 3/4. July–December 1951.

Busyn, Helen. "The Political Career of Peter Kiołbassa," *Polish American Studies,* Vol. 7, No. 1/2. January–June 1950.

Calhoun, Craig. "'New Social Movements' of the Early Nineteenth Century" *Social Science History,* Vol. 17, No. 3. Duke University Press: Autumn 1993.

Caraway, L.V. "The Battle of Arkansas Post," *Confederate Veteran,* Vol. 14. March 1906.

Casey, Powell A. Encyclopedia of Forts, Posts, Named Camps and Other Military Installations in Louisiana, 1700–1981. Baton Rouge: Claitor's Publishing Division, 1983.

Casdorph, Paul D. *Prince John Magruder: His Life and Campaigns.* New York: John Wiley & Sons, Inc., 1996.

Catton, Bruce. *The Coming Fury.* Garden City, NY: Doubleday, 1961.

Cole, Arthur C. "President Lincoln and the Illinois Radical Republicans," *The Mississippi Valley Historical Review,* Vol. 4, No. 4. Mar., 1918.

Conrad, Glenn R., ed. *A Dictionary of Louisiana Biography,* Vol. II. Lafayette: The Louisiana Historical Association, 1988.

Cooling, Benjamin Franklin. *To the Battles of Franklin and Nashville and Beyond: Stabilization and Reconstruction in Tennessee and Kentucky, 1864–1865.* Knoxville: The University of Tennessee Press, 2011.

Coulter, E. Merton. *The Confederate States of America, 1861–1865.* Baton Rouge: Louisiana State University Press, 1950.

Cozzens, Peter. *Shenandoah 1862.* Chapel Hill: The University of North Carolina Press, 2008.

Current, Richard N., ed. *Encyclopedia of the Confederacy.* New York: Simon & Schuster, 1993.

Dauphine, James G. "The Knights of the White Camelia and the Election of 1868: Louisiana's White Terrorists; A Benighting Legacy," *Louisiana History: The Journal of the Louisiana Historical Association,* Vol. 30, No. 2. Spring, 1989.

Davies, Norman. *God's Playground.* New York: Columbia University Press, 1982.

Davies, Norman. *Heart of Europe: A Short History of Poland.* Oxford: Oxford University Press, 1986.

Dimitry, John. *Confederate Military History of Louisiana.* Pensacola, Florida: eBooksOnDisk.com, 2005.

Dinges, Bruce J. and Leckie, Shirley A., eds. *A Just and Righteous Cause: Benjamin H. Grierson's Civil War Memoir.* Carbondale: Southern Illinois University, 2008.

Downey, Fairfax. *Clash of Cavalry: The Battle of Brandy Station, June 9, 1863.* New York: David McKay, Co., Inc., 1959.

Downey, Fairfax. *The Guns at Gettysburg.* New York: Collier Books, 1962.

Drohojowski, Jan. *Poles in United States.* Warsaw: Krajowa Agencja Wydawnicza, 1976.

Duszak, M.J. "Colonel Kriz of Washington," *Polish American Studies*, Vol. 23, No. 2. Jul.–Dec., 1966.

Dworaczyk, Edward J. *The First Polish Colonies of America in Texas: Containing Also the General History of the Polish People in Texas.* San Antonio: The Naylor Company, 1936.

Dyer, Frederick H. *A Compendium of the War of the Rebellion.* New York: T. Yoseloff, 1959.

Eicher, John H. and David J. *Civil War High Commands.* Stanford: Stanford University Press, 2001.

Engle, Stephen D. 'Yankee Dutchmen' in Ural, Susannah J., ed., *Civil War Citizens: Race, Ethnicity, and Identity in America's Bloodiest Conflict.* New York and London: New York University Press, 2010.

Faust, Patricia L., ed. *Historical Times Illustrated Encyclopedia of the Civil War.* New York: Harper & Row, 1986.

Fischer, LeRoy H. *Lincoln's Gadfly, Adam Gurowski.* Norman: University of Oklahoma Press, 1964.

Fischer, LeRoy H. "Lincoln's Gadfly—Adam Gurowski," *The Mississippi Valley Historical Review,* Vol. 36, No. 3. Dec. 1949.

Fitzharris, Joseph C. "Field Officer Courts and U.S. Civil War Military Justice," *The Journal of Military History,* Vol. 68, No. 1. Jan., 2004.

Fleche, André M. *Revolution of 1861: The American Civil War in the Age of Nationalist Conflict.* Chapel Hill: The University of North Carolina Press, 2012.

Fleche, André M. "The Revolution of 1861: The Legacy of the European Revolutions of 1848 and the American Civil War,". Ph.D. Dissertation, University of Virginia, 2006.

Foner, Laura. "The Free People of Color in Louisiana and St. Domingue: A Comparative Portrait of Two Three-caste Slave Societies" *Journal of Social History* Vol. 3 No. 4. Oxford University Press (1970): 406–30.

Foote, Shelby. *The Civil War: A Narrative,* three volumes. New York: Random House, 1958, Vintage Books, 1986.

Foster, B.T. *Dress rehearsal for Hard War: William T. Sherman and the Meridian Expedition.* Meridian: Mississippi State University, 2003.

Fox, William F. *Regimental Losses in the American Civil War, 1861–1865.* Albany Publishing Company, 1889.

Freeman, Douglas Southall. *Lee.* New York: Charles Scribner's Sons, 1961.

Furgurson, Ernest B. *Chancellorsville 1863.* New York: Alfred A. Knopf, 1992.

Gallagher, Gary W. *The Union War.* Cambridge, Massachusetts: Harvard University Press, 2011.

Gallagher, Gary W. *The Confederate War.* Cambridge, Massachusetts: Harvard University Press, 1997.

Galloway, Joseph. *Historical and Political Reflections on the Rise and Progress of the American Rebellion.* London: 1780.

Gillispie, James M. *Andersonvilles of the North.* Denton: University of North Texas Press, 2008.

Glatthaar, Joseph T. *Soldiering in the Army of Northern Virginia: A Statistical Portrait of the Troops Who Served under Robert E. Lee.* Chapel Hill: The University of North Carolina Press, 2011.

Golden, Alan Lawrence. "The Secession Crisis in Virginia: A Critical Study of Argument". Ph.D. Dissertation, Ohio State University, 1990.

Goslicki, Wawrzyniec. *The Accomplished Senator.* Miami: The American Institute of Polish Culture, 1992.

Greene, Victor R. "For God and Country: The Origins of Slavic Catholic Self-Consciousness in America," *Church History,* Vol. 35, No. 4. Cambridge University Press, December 1966.

Grimsley, Mark. *The Hard Hand of War: Union Military Policy Toward Southern Civilians, 1861–1865.* Cambridge: Cambridge University Press, 1995.

Grzeloński, Bogdan. *Poles in the United States of America, 1776–1865.* Warsaw: Interpress Publishers, 1976.

Haiman, Mieczyslaw. *Historja Udziału Polaków w Amerykańskiej Wojnie Domowej* (Chicago: Drukiem Dziennika Zjednoczenia, 1928.

Halecki, Oscar. *A History of Poland.* New York: Roy Publishers, 1942.

Hassler, Warren W., Jr. *Commanders of the Army of the Potomac.* Baton Rouge: Louisiana State University Press, 1962.

Hattaway, Herman. "The United Confederate Veterans in Louisiana," *Louisiana History: The Journal of the Louisiana Historical Association,* Vol. 16, No. 1. Winter 1975.

Hebert, Walter H. *Fighting Joe Hooker.* Lincoln: University of Nebraska Press, 1944.

Heidler, David S. and Heidler, Jeanne T., eds. *Encyclopedia of the American Civil War: A Political, Social and Military History.* New York: W.W. Norton & Company, 2000 and Santa Barbara, Denver, Oxford: ABC-CLIO, 2000.

Heitman, Francis B. *Historical Register and Dictionary of the United States Army.* Washington: Government Printing Office, 1903.

Hendrick, Burton J. *Statesmen of the Lost Cause: Jefferson Davis and His Cabinet.* New York: Literary Guild of America, Inc., 1939.

Hennessy, John J. *Return to Bull Run: The Campaign and Battle of Second Manassas.* New York: Simon & Schuster, 1993.

Henry, Robert Selph. "As General Forrest Used to Say," *The Sewanee Review* Vol. 52, No. 2. Spring, 1944.

Henry, Robert Selph. *First with the most Forrest.* Indianapolis: Bobbs-Merrill, 1944.

Henry, Robert Selph. *The Story of the Confederacy.* Indianapolis: Bobbs-Merrill, 1931.

Hewitt, Lawrence Lee and Bergeron, Arthur W., Jr. *Louisianians in the Civil War.* Columbia and London: University of Missouri Press, 2002.

Hillard, George Stillman. *Life and Campaigns of George B. McClellan, Major General U.S. Army.* Philadelphia: J.B. Lippincott & Co. 1865.

Hoffman, Daniel G. "Historic Truth and Ballad Truth: Two Versions of the Capture of New Orleans," *The Journal of American Folklore,* Vol. 65, No. 257, July–September, 1952.

Horowitz, Murray M. "Ethnicity and Command: The Civil War Experience," *Military Affairs,* Vol. 42, No. 4. Dec. 1978.

Huntington, James F. "Operations in the Shenandoah Valley," in *Papers of the Campaigns in Virginia 1861–1862,* Vol. I, Dwight, Theodore F., ed. Military Historical Society of Massachusetts. Boston: Houghton and Mifflin, 1895.

Jasienica, Pawel. *A Tale of Agony: The Commonwealth of Both Nations III.* Miami: The Institute of Polish Culture, 1992.

Jedlicki, Jerzy. *A Suburb of Europe: Nineteenth-century Polish Approaches to Western Civilization.* Budapest: CEU Press, 1988.

Jimerson, Randall C. *The Private Civil War: Popular Thought During the Sectional Conflict.* Baton Rouge: Louisiana State University Press, 1988.

Jones, Terry L. *Lee's Tigers: The Louisiana Infantry in the Army of Northern Virginia.* Baton Rouge: Louisiana State University Press, 1987.

Jones, Terry L. "Wharf-Rats, Cutthroats and Thieves: The Louisiana Tigers, 1861–1862," *Louisiana History: The Journal of the Louisiana Historical Association,* Vol. 27, No. 2. Spring, 1986.

Joslyn, Mauriel Phillips. *The Immortal Captives: The Story of 600 Confederate Officers and the United States Prisoner of War Policy.* Shippensburg, Pennsylvania: White Mane Publishing Company, 1996.

Jurczynska, Sister Mary Patricia, S.S.J. "A Study of the Participation of the Poles in the American Civil War". Master of Arts Thesis, St. John College, 1949.

Kajencki, Colonel Francis C. "The Louisiana Tiger," *Louisiana History: The Journal of the Louisiana Historical Association,* Vol. 15, No. 1. Winter, 1974.

Kajencki, Francis C. *Star on Many a Battlefield: Brevet Brigadier General Joseph Kargé in the American Civil War.* Rutherford: Fairleigh Dickinson University Press, 1980.

Kantowicz, Edward R. Review of *American Immigrant Leaders, 1800–1910: Marginality and Identity* by Greene, Victor R., *American Journal of Sociology,* Vol. 94, No. 2. September 1988.

Keller, Christian. *Chancellorsville and the Germans: Nativism, Ethnicity and Civil War Memory.* New York: Fordham University Press, 2010.

Kisluk, Eugene J. *Brothers from the North: The Polish Democratic Society and the European Revolutions of 1848–1849.* Boulder: East European Monographs, 2005.

Kowalczyk, Edmund L. "Jottings from the Polish American Past," *Polish American Studies,* Vol. 11, No. 1/2. January–June, 1954.

Krick, Robert K. *Conquering the Valley: Stonewall Jackson at Port Republic.* New York: William Morrow and Company, 1996.

Kruszka, Wacław. *A History of the Poles in America to 1908: Poles in the Eastern and Southern States.* Vol. 3. Washington: The Catholic University of America Press, 1998.

Kuniczak, W.S. *My Name is Million: An Illustrated History of Poles in America.* New York: Hippocrene Books, 2000.

Lachowicz, Teofil. *Polish Freedom Fighters on American Soil: Polish Veterans in America from the Revolutionary War to 1939.* Minneapolis: Hillcrest Two Harbors Press, 2011.

Lamartine, Alphonse de. *Histoire de la Révolution de 1848,* Vol. 1. Brussels: Kiessling et Comp., 1849

Lamon, Ward Hill. *Recollections of Abraham Lincoln, 1847–1865.* University of Nebraska Press, 1994.

Landry, Stuart O. *History of the Boston Club.* New Orleans: Pelican Publishing Company, 1938.

Lang, James O. "Gloom Envelops New Orleans: April 24 to May 2, 1862," *Louisiana History: The Journal of the Louisiana Historical Association,* Vol. 1, No. 4. Autumn, 1960.

Leach, Robert B. "The Role of the Union Cavalry during the Atlanta Campaign,". Master's Thesis, Army Command and General Staff College, Fort Leavenworth, Kansas: 1994.

Lerski, George J. "Polish Exiles in Mid-Nineteenth Century America," *Polish American Studies, Vol. 31, No. 2.* Autumn, 1974.

Lerski, Jerzy J. *A Polish Chapter in Jacksonian America: The United States and the Polish Exiles of 1831.* Madison: University of Wisconsin Press, 1958.

Linderman, Gerald. *Embattled Courage: The Combat Experience in the American Civil War.* New York: Simon & Schuster, 2008.

Longacre, Edward G. *Jersey Cavaliers: A History of the First New Jersey Volunteer Cavalry, 1861–1865.* Hightstown, NJ: Longstreet House, 1992.

Lonn, Ella. *Desertion During the Civil War.* Gloucester: Peter Smith, 1966, Lincoln: University of Nebraska Press, 1998.

Lonn, Ella. *Foreigners In The Union Army and Navy.* Baton Rouge: Louisiana State University Press, 1951.

Lonn, Ella. *Foreigners in the Confederacy*. Chapel Hill: The University of North Carolina Press, 1940.

Lytle, Andrew Nelson. *Bedford Forrest and His Critter Company*. Nashville: J.S. Sanders & Company, 1931.

Maness, Dr. Lonnie E. "Strategic Victories or Tactical Defeats? Nathan Bedford Forrest at Brice's Crossroads, Harrisburg, and the Memphis Raid," *Journal of Confederate History*, Vol. 1, No. 1. Summer 1988.

Marszalek, John F. *Sherman: A Soldier's Passion For Order*. New York: The Free Press, 1993.

McCarthy, Cal. *Green, Blue and Grey: The Irish in the American Civil War*. Cork: The Collins Press, 2009.

McCrady, Edward J. *Gregg's Brigade of South Carolina in the Second Battle of Manassas*. Richmond: W.E. Jones, 1885.

McPherson, James M. *Battle Cry of Freedom*. New York: Oxford University Press, 1988.

McPherson, James M. *For Cause and Comrades: Why Men Fought in the Civil War*. New York: Oxford University Press, 1997.

McWhiney, Grady and Jamieson, Perry D. *Attack and Die: Civil War Military Tactics and the Southern Heritage*. Tuscaloosa: The University of Alabama Press, 1982.

Mehrländer, Andrea. *The Germans of Charleston, Richmond and New Orleans During the Civil War Period, 1850–1870*. Berlin/New York: Walter de Gruyter & Co., 2011.

Middlekauff, Robert. *The Glorious Cause: The American Revolution 1763–1789*. New York: Oxford University Press, 1982.

Miller, William J. "Such Men as Shields, Banks and Frémont: Federal Command in Western Virginia, March–June 1862," in *The Shenandoah Valley Campaign of 1862,* Gary W. Gallagher, ed. The University of North Carolina Press, 2003.

Miner, Case. "Strategy and Tactics of Civil War Rams on the Mississippi River." Master's thesis, University of Central Oklahoma, 2001.

Mingus, Scott L. *The Louisiana Tigers in the Gettysburg Campaign, June–July 1863*. Baton Rouge: Louisiana State University Press, 2009.

Moneyhon, Carl and Roberts, Bobby. *Portraits of Conflict: A Photographic History of Louisiana in the Civil War*. University of Arkansas Press, 1990.

Morgan, Gwenda. *The Debate on the American Revolution*. Manchester: Manchester University Press, 2007.

Nash, Gary B. and Hodges, Graham Russell Gao. *Friends of Liberty: Thomas Jefferson, Tadeusz Kościuszko, and Agrippa Hall*. New York: Basic Books, 2008.

National Archives, Washington, DC.

New Jersey Historical Society. *Proceedings of the New Jersey Historical Society*, Vol. 81, Oct. 1963.

Noe, Kenneth W. *Perryville*. Lexington: The University Press of Kentucky, 2001.

Packard, William A. *Joseph Karge: A Memorial Sketch*. New York: Anson D. F Randolph and Co., 1893.

Packard, William A. "Professor Joseph Kargé, Ph.D.," *Princeton College Bulletin*, Vol. V, No. 2. April 1893.

Pfanz, Harry Willcox. *Gettysburg: The First Day*. University of North Carolina Press, 2001.

Phisterer, Frederick. *New York In The War Of The Rebellion 1861 to 1865*. Albany: Weed, Parsons and Company, 1890.

Phisterer, Frederick. *Statistical Record of the Armies of the United States*, Vol. 13. New York: Charles Scribner's Sons, 1883.

Pennsylvania at Gettysburg, Report of the Gettysburg Battlefield Memorial Commission. Harrisburg: W. Stanley Ray, 1914.

Pierson, Michael D. *The Mutiny at Fort Jackson*. Chapel Hill: The University of North Carolina Press, 2008.

Pinkowski, Edward. *Pills, Pen & Politics: The Story of General Leon Jastremski, 1843–1907*. Wilmington, Delaware: Captain Stanislaw Mlotkowski Memorial Brigade Society, 1974.

Plocheck, Robert. "Polish Texans," *Texas Almanac, 2004–2005*. Dallas: Texas State Historical Society, 2005.

Pollard, Edward A. *The Lost Cause; A New Southern History of the War of the Confederates*. New York: E.B. Treat & Co., Publishers, 1866.

Pula, James S. "Krzyżanowski's Civil War Brigade," *Polish American Studies*, Vol. 28, No. 2. Autumn, 1971.

Pula, James S. "Polish-American Catholicism: A Case Study in Cultural Determinism," *U.S. Catholic Historian*, Vol. 27, No. 3. Summer 2009.

Pula, James S. *For Liberty And Justice: A Biography Of Brigadier General Włodzimierz B. Krzyżanowski, 1824–1887*. Utica, NY: Ethnic Heritage Studies Center, 2008.

Pula, James S. *The History of a German-Polish Civil War Brigade*. San Francisco: R&E Research, 1976.

Pula, J.S. "Na Polu Chwały: The Life and Times of Włodzimierz Krzyżanowski: Polish Immigrant, Civil War General, Federal Agent". Doctoral Dissertation: Purdue University, 1972.

Rafuse, Ethan S. *McClellan's War*. Bloomington: Indiana University Press, 2005.

Raum, John, O. *The History of New Jersey: From Its Earliest Settlements to the Present*. Philadelphia: John E. Potter and Company, 1877.

Randers-Pehrson, Nils H., Proctor, John Clagett and Grosvenor, Mrs. Gilbert. "Aeronautics in the District of Columbia [with Remarks]." *Records of the*

Columbia Historical Society, Washington, D.C., Vol. 46/47 [The 38th separately bound book] 50th Anniversary Volume. 1944/1945.

Radzilowski, John A. *A Traveller's History of Poland*. Northhampton, MA: Interlink Books, 2007.

Ritter, Charles F. and Wakelyn, John L., eds. *Leaders of the American Civil War: A Biographical and Historiographical Dictionary*. Westport, CT: Greenwood Press, 1998.

Roberts, Timothy Mason. *Distant Revolutions: 1848 and the Challenge to American Exceptionalism*. Charlottesville: University of Virginia Press, 2009.

Robertson, James I., Jr. *Soldiers Blue and Gray*. Columbia: University of South Carolina Press, 1988.

Robertson, James I. *Tenting Tonight: The Soldier's Life*. Alexandria, VA: Time-Life Books, 1984.

Rozanski, Edward C. "Civil War Poles Of Illinois," *Polish American Studies*, Vol. 23, No. 2. 1966.

Ryan, Charlton. "From Fact to Myth: The Story of Panna Maria," *Polish American Studies*, Vol. 49, No. 1. Spring 1992.

Siekaniec, Ladislaus J. "Poles in the U.S.: Jamestown to Appomatox," *Polish American Studies*, Vol. 17, No. 1/2. January–June 1960.

Sifakis, Stewart. *Compendium of the Confederate Armies*. New York: Facts on File, 1992.

Spruill, Matt III and Matt IV. *Summer Lightning: A Guide to the Second Battle of Manassas*. Knoxville: The University of Tennessee Press, 2013.

Starczewska, Maria. "The Historical Geography of the Oldest Polish Settlement in America," *The Polish Review*, Vol. 12, No. 2. Spring, 1967.

Stasik, Florian. *Polish Political Émigrés in the United States of America 1831–1864*. Boulder: East European Monographs, New York: Dist. By Columbia University Press, 2002.

Stevenson, Charles G. "A Search and a Reappraisal," *Polish American Studies*, Vol. 23, No. 2. Jul.–Dec., 1966.

Stewart, George R. *Pickett's Charge, A Microhistory of the Final Attack at Gettysburg, July 3, 1863*. Boston: Houghton Mifflin Company, 1959.

Stryker, William S., ed. *Official Register of the Officers and Men of New Jersey in the Civil War, 1861–1865*. Trenton: John L. Murphy, 1876.

Szymanski, Leszek. *Casimir Pulaski: Hero of the American Revolution*. New York: Hippocrene Books, 1979.

Taylor, Joe Gray. "New Orleans and Reconstruction," *Louisiana History: The Journal of the Louisiana Historical Association*, Vol. 9, No. 3. Summer, 1968.

Temple, Brian. *The Union Prison at Fort Delaware: A Perfect Hell on Earth*. Jefferson, NC: McFarland & Co., 2003.

Thurner, Arthur W. "Polish Americans in Chicago Politics, 1890–1930," *Polish American Studies,* Vol. 28, No. 1. Spring, 1971.

Trefousse, Hans L. Review of *Owen Lovejoy and Abraham Lincoln during the Civil War, Journal of the Abraham Lincoln Association,* Vol. 22, No. 1. Winter, 2001.

Tyler, R. Curtis. "Santiago Vidaurri and the Confederacy," *The Americas,* Vol. 26, No. 1. Jul., 1969.

Tyler, Ron, ed., *The New Handbook of Texas,* Vol. 5. Austin: The Texas State Historical Association, 1996.

Tyrowicz, Marian. "Kasper Tochman, biographical article" translated by Peter Obst. Chicago: Polish Museum in America, 1955.

Uminski, Sigmund H. "Poles and the Confederacy," *Polish American Studies,* Vol. 22, No. 2. Jul.–Dec., 1965.

Uminski, Sigmund H. "Two Polish Confederates," *Polish American Studies,* Vol. 23, No. 2. Jul.–Dec., 1966.

Ural, Susannah J. ed. *Civil War Citizens: Race, Ethnicity, and Identity in America's Bloodiest Conflict.* New York and London: New York University Press, 2010.

Vanderslice, John Mitchell. *Gettysburg: Where and how the Regiments Fought, and the Troops They Encountered.* Philadelphia: J.B. Lippincott & Company, 1897.

Waldo, Arthur L. *The True Heroes of Jamestown.* Miami: American Institute of Polish Culture, 1977.

Wandycz, Piotr S. *The United States and Poland.* Cambridge, Massachusetts: Harvard University Press, 1980.

Ward, Geoffrey C. *The Civil War.* New York: Alfred A. Knopf, 1990.

Warner, Ezra J. *Generals in Blue: Lives of the Union Commanders.* Baton Rouge: Louisiana State University Press, 1964.

Warner, Ezra J. *Generals in Gray: Lives of the Confederate Commanders.* Baton Rouge and London: Louisiana State University Press, 1959.

Wayland, Francis F. and Tracy, Albert. "Frémont's Pursuit of Jackson in the Shenandoah Valley: The Journal of Colonel Albert Tracy, March–July 1862," *The Virginia Magazine of History and Biography,* Vol. 70, No. 2. Apr., 1962.

Weland, Gerald. *O.O. Howard, Union General.* Jefferson, North Carolina: McFarland & Company, Inc. Publishers, 1995.

Welcher, Frank J. *The Union Army 1861–1865.* Bloomington: Indiana University Press, 1989.

Whitehorne, Joseph W.A. *The Second Battle of Manassas.* Washington: Center of Military History, 1990.

Wieczerzak, Joseph W. *A Polish Chapter in Civil War America: The Effect of the January Insurrection on American Opinion and Diplomacy.* New York: Twayne Publishers, Inc., 1967.

Williams, Harry. "The Attack Upon West Point During the Civil War," *The Mississippi Valley Historical Review*, Vol. 25, No. 4. March, 1939.

Winters, John D. *The Civil War in Louisiana*. Baton Rouge: Louisiana State University Press, 1963.

Winters, Lisa Ze. "'More Desultory and Unconnected Than Any Other': Geography, Desire, and Freedom in Eliza Potter's 'A Hairdresser's Experience in High Life'". *American Quarterly*, Vol. 61 No. 3. The Johns Hopkins University Press (September 2009): 455–475.

Wood, Gordon S. *The American Revolution*. New York: The Modern Library, 2002.

Wood, Gordon S. *The Idea of America: Reflections on the Birth of the United States*. New York: The Penguin Press, 2011.

Wood, Gordon S. *The Radicalism of the American Revolution*. New York: Vintage Books, 1993.

Woodworth, Steven E. and Grear, Charles D., eds. *The Chattanooga Campaign*. Carbondale: Southern Illinois University Press, 2012.

Wytrwal, Joseph A. *America's Polish Heritage*. Detroit: Endurance Press, 1961.

Wytrwal, Joseph A. *Behold! The Polish-Americans*. Detroit: Endurance Press, 1977.

Zamoyski, Adam. *The Polish Way*. New York: Hippocrene Books, 1987.

Zawadzki, W.H. Review of *The Memoirs of Ludwik Żychliński*, ed. by Pula, James S. *The Slavonic and East European Review*, Vol. 73, No. 3. Jul., 1995.

INDEX